The Regulation of Internet Pornography

The regulation of pornography has always been a contentious issue, which has sparked wide-ranging debates surrounding the acceptability and place of pornography in society. The use of the internet to distribute and access pornography has magnified this debate and has presented a number of challenges for the law in terms of effective and proportionate regulation. Following unsuccessful attempts by states to transpose traditional laws to cyberspace, a new and radical regulatory framework eventually evolved for regulating internet pornography. In this process, the focus of the law has changed from merely controlling the publication and distribution of obscene material to a model that aims to deter private consumption of illegal content. In addition, various self- and co-regulatory initiatives have been introduced with the involvement of non-state actors, imposing a certain degree of *de facto* liability on intermediaries, all of which raise interesting issues.

This book examines the relevant regulatory responses to internet pornography, with particular reference to the UK, but also drawing comparisons with other countries where relevant. It argues that the internet has fundamentally, and in many ways irreversibly, changed the regulation of pornography. Classifying internet pornography into three broad categories – child pornography, extreme pornography, and adult pornography – the book provides an in-depth analysis of the legal issues involved in regulating internet pornography, and argues that the notions of obscenity and indecency on their own will not provide an adequate basis for regulating online pornography. The book identifies the legitimising factors that will lend credibility and normative force to the law in order to successfully regulate pornography in cyberspace. It is the only comprehensive text that rigorously addresses the regulation of internet pornography as a whole, and offers valuable insights that will appeal to academics, students, policy makers, and those working in the areas of broader internet governance and online child protection.

Abhilash Nair is Senior Lecturer in Internet Law at Aston University, Birmingham. He has published widely in the area of internet pornography, and has advised various international and national bodies on regulating illegal content, content-related cybercrime and online child safety laws. He is a member of the UK Council for Child Internet Safety (UKCCIS) Evidence Working group, and Editor-in-Chief of the *European Journal of Law and Technology*.

Routledge Research in Information Technology and E-Commerce Law

Titles in this series include:

Law of Electronic Commercial Transactions
Contemporary Issues in the EU, US and China
Faye Fangfei Wang

Online Dispute Resolution for Consumers in the European Union
Pablo Cortés

The Current State of Domain Name Regulation
Domain Names as Second Class Citizens in a Mark-dominated World
Konstantinos Komaitis

International Internet Law
Joanna Kulesza

The Domain Name Registration System
Liberalisation, Consumer Protection and Growth
Jenny Ng

Law of Electronic Commercial Transactions, 2nd Edition
Contemporary Issues in the EU, US and China
Faye Fangfei Wang

Cyberthreats and the Decline of the Nation-State
Susan W. Brenner

Balancing Privacy and Free Speech
Unwanted Attention in the Age of Social Media
Mark Tunick

Social Networks as the New Frontier of Terrorism
#Terror
Laura Scaife

'This book tackles some of society's most troubling problems as they manifest themselves in the digital age. It offers much needed clarification and a reasoned assessment of the key risks associated with internet pornography – to children and the wider public, and to freedom of expression and other fundamental rights. For those concerned with child protection especially, this book explains what you need to know. For those interested in the evolution of internet governance, it provides a thought-provoking case study.'

Professor Sonia Livingstone OBE
Department of Media and Communications,
London School of Economics and Political Science.

'One in three of all human internet users on the planet is a child. In parts of the developing world this rises to closer to one in two while in higher income countries it is generally around one in five. Thus, whatever else we might imagine, hope or want the internet to be, unquestionably it is a medium for children just as much as it is a medium for any other identifiable constituency. Yet historically and still today many policymakers start form the generally unstated assumption that internet users are adults and to the extent that there are any challenges surrounding young people's use of the technology it is a second order problem, essentially a trivial or detailed concern that should be dealt with by "someone else", probably parents, schools or the police. Definitely not themselves.

Free speech and freedom of artistic expression are concepts of fundamental importance in every liberal democracy but so is the imperative to shield children from experiences which are likely to harm their development as they make their way towards adulthood. The tension is therefore clear. How do we reconcile and balance the rights of those who have an undisputed entitlement to access legal pornographic material with those of children who, according to many laws and much research, need to be protected from it?

Hitherto, apparently legal pornography has been freely accessible on the internet on a scale and of a nature never seen before. Should we be indifferent towards this development, believing no harm will come of it or not caring whether it does or not? How should we view and respond to the growing number of attempts being made to replicate in the online world regimes which approximate to those which have commonly been adopted in the physical world which seek to curb children's ability to view pornography? These questions are being debated on every continent and the protagonists will be eternally grateful to Abhilash Nair for this timely, thoughtful, comprehensive and impeccably researched book'

John Carr OBE
Secretary, Children's Charities' Coalition on Internet Safety
Visiting Senior Fellow, London School of Economics and Political Science

The Regulation of Internet Pornography

Issues and Challenges

Abhilash Nair

Routledge
Taylor & Francis Group
LONDON AND NEW YORK

First published 2019
by Routledge
2 Park Square, Milton Park, Abingdon, Oxon OX14 4RN

and by Routledge
52 Vanderbilt Avenue, New York, NY 10017, USA

First issued in paperback 2020

Routledge is an imprint of the Taylor & Francis Group, an informa business

British Library Cataloguing-in-Publication Data
A catalogue record for this book is available from the British Library

Library of Congress Cataloging-in-Publication Data
Names: Nair, Abhilash, author.
Title: The regulation of internet pornography issues and challenges / Abhilash Nair.
Description: Abingdon, Oxon ; New York, NY : Routledge, 2019. | Series: Routledge research in IT and e-commerce law | Includes index.
Identifiers: LCCN 2018029466 | ISBN 9780415745772 (hbk)
Subjects: LCSH: Internet pornography–Law and legislation.
Classification: LCC K5293 .N35 2019 | DDC 344.05/4702854678--dc23
LC record available at https://lccn.loc.gov/2018029466

ISBN 13: 978-0-367-58349-1 (pbk)
ISBN 13: 978-0-415-74577-2 (hbk)

Typeset in Galliard
by Integra Software Services Pvt. Ltd.

To my loving parents

Contents

Acknowledgements

There are many people I need to thank in writing this monograph. The idea and encouragement for producing this book stemmed from conversations five years ago with Dr Ken Russell, editor of the *International Review of Law, Computers and Technology*. I would like to thank Ken for all his help and support.

I am grateful to my employer, Aston University, and in particular Aston Law School, who have been extremely supportive in enabling me to find the time to complete this work. I am also grateful to my previous employer, University of Strathclyde, for their support.

I am indebted to Professor Sonia Livingstone OBE of the London School of Economics for the many stimulating chats we have had on children's rights in the online environment, and also for her valuable comments on a draft of this book. I am also very grateful to John Carr OBE, Secretary, Children's Charities' Coalition on Internet Safety, for his comments on the draft. Special thanks are due to Dr Subhajit Basu, of the University of Leeds, who read many earlier drafts of the book and offered constructive comments, sometimes at short notice and often at the cost of his time with his wife (who still remains friends with me). Thanks are also due to Dr James Griffin of Exeter University and Sam Burton of Sheffield Hallam University for the time and trouble they have taken to read draft chapters from the book and offer helpful comments.

The research and thinking underpinning this book has been influenced by many colleagues outside academia, who do important work in the areas of internet governance and child protection. I have had many opportunities to work closely with them as part of my research and engagement activities outside the university. They have provided me with valuable insights, which enabled me to put the law in context in terms of the 'real world' realities. This no doubt provoked my thinking, which has been invaluable for this project. I am particularly grateful to, and in no particular order, Jutta Croll of Zentrum für Kinderschutz im Internet, Marie-laure Lemineur of ECPAT International, Susie Hargreaves OBE of the Internet Watch Foundation, Vidya Reddy of Tulir, Chennai, colleagues at INHOPE, and members of the UKCCIS Evidence Working Group.

I am also grateful to the editorial team at Routledge for all their support and patience throughout the time that I have taken to complete this monograph – Katie

Carpenter, Mark Sapwell, Olivia Manley, Brianna Ascher, Siobhan Poole and Nicola Sharpe – and also to the anonymous reviewers who offered very helpful comments. Thanks are also due to the production team and Liz Dittner for all their help.

Finally, this book would not have been possible without the love and support of my family and friends. I could not possibly express in words my gratitude to my parents for all their unconditional love and support. Thanks are also due to my sister, whose commitment and selflessness towards her work has inspired me and many others. I am privileged to have wonderful friends, and owe special thanks to Bronwen and Chris who have been tremendously supportive throughout. Anu – your patience would put a saint to shame and I am forever grateful for your kindness and understanding, without which this book would not have happened. I love you very much.

1 Introduction

Internet pornography – issues and challenges

Pornography is not the creation of the internet – it predates all forms of existing modern media and can be traced back to ancient times. The controversy surrounding its acceptability and place in society, and the debates on how to regulate pornography, also pre-date the internet by a long way. The ways in which pornography is created, stored and distributed have evolved with technological advances over time – starting with the traditional print media, mostly in the form of books and top-shelf magazines, followed by VHS cassettes, and a few years later CD-ROMs, DVDs and BlueRays. All of these had a common characteristic: content was stored and distributed on a physical medium. For states, this meant that controlling the publication and distribution of pornography within their geographical boundaries was realistic and, in theory, possible. The arrival of the internet and the World Wide Web in the 1990s fundamentally changed the distribution and access models of pornography. Pornography transcends geographical boundaries, nation states and cultures, raising newer challenges for regulation. The traditional regulatory models for pornography that were designed on the basis of physical boundaries suddenly started looking dated and ineffective.

The volume of pornography available through the internet is also unprecedented. [1] Pornography rapidly became so popular and widespread on the internet that at one point 'the internet' became synonymous with pornography: concerns about the internet becoming an increasingly growing repository of pornography even led to moral panic in the 1990s. Whilst many of these early apprehensions turned out to be exaggerated, it remains the case that a vast amount of pornographic content is available on the internet and it remains a thriving industry. The nature of internet pornography, in turn, is so varied that, arguably, it caters to all

1 For example, Pornhub's statistics for the year 2017 reveal that 595,482 hours of pornography was uploaded in the year, with a cumulative data transfer of 3,732 petabytes which, in their own words, is the equivalent data to 'fill the memory of every iPhone currently used in the world'. This information pertains just to Pornhub, only one of the many large porn sites in the world. See https://www.pornhub.com/insights/2017-year-in-review, accessed 5 July 2018.

possible tastes and preferences, ranging from soft erotica to abhorrent content such as images of child sexual abuse, bestiality, sexual violence and exploitation.

The way pornography is accessed on the internet has also evolved with time. Early pornographic material included images and video that could be downloaded onto one's computer. Cam-girl sites such as Jennicam.com also started emerging in the 1990s.[2] Streaming videos that do not require active downloading were not common then, largely because the internet was mainly accessed through dial-up modems at relatively low speeds compared to the modern-day superfast broadband. The anonymity and relative ease of accessing content from the comfort of one's home, as opposed to physically obtaining it from a 'real person' in a traditional brick and mortar outlet, has practically rendered pornography a lot more accessible to more people than before. Whilst this gives the impression that the consumption of pornography has become a lot more 'private' because of the internet, it will be clear after reading this book that it is not necessarily the case in light of the various legislative and regulatory initiatives that impose liability on end users for certain categories of pornography.

It is not the purpose of this book to revisit the rights and wrongs of pornography *per se*. There is a wealth of existing literature and debates surrounding pornography and its regulation from various perspectives well before the internet even became a popular medium of information and communication.[3] It is not my intention to re-state or re-examine those arguments. Instead, the book specifically focuses on the issues and challenges raised by pornography published and accessed through the internet, and examines how the internet has necessitated a fundamental change in the traditional modalities of regulation. The focus therefore is very much on the law and regulation of pornography from the perspective of the internet and related digital technologies. The book explores a number of questions in this context – how effective has transposing traditional regulatory principles to cyberspace been in the context of pornography? What are the key regulatory and legal changes brought about by the internet? How different are these to traditional models of regulation of pornography? Are such changes simply a part of the process of the law adapting to technology – as happened with the emergence of other forms of technology prior to the internet – or do the changes constitute a fundamental, irreversible step change in the way we now approach the regulation of pornography? The following sub-questions also arose in the process of examining these issues: do all types of internet pornography merit the same regulatory response? Have legal responses resulted

2 See David S Wall, *Cybercrime: The Transformation of Crime in the Internet Age* (Polity 2007) 105.

3 See for example Andrea Dworkin, *Pornography: Men Possessing Women* (Women's Press 1981); Catherine MacKinnon, 'Pornography as Defamation and Discrimination' (1991) *B.U.L Rev.* 71 793–815; Catherine Itzin, *Pornography: Women, Violence and Civil Liberties* (OUP 1992); Susanne Kappeler, *The Pornography of Representation* (Polity Press 1986); Susan M Easton, *The problem of pornography: regulation and the right to free speech* (Routledge 1994); Joel Feinberg, *The Moral Limits of the Criminal Law, Volume 4, Harmless Wrongdoing* (OUP 1988).

in over-regulation – with implications for individual freedoms? These are complex questions, and, as will be seen from the book, the answer will vary depending on the category of pornography which is the subject of regulation. In order to answer these research questions, I classify internet pornography into three broad categories: child pornography, extreme pornography and adult pornography, and each of these categories is examined in three separate parts in the book.

First to be examined is child pornography, perhaps more appropriately called child sexual exploitation material, which is almost universally regarded as abhorrent and illegal.[4] I further classify child pornography into three sub-sets: real, pseudo and virtual child pornography for the purpose of our analysis, as explained in Chapter 2. It is obvious that the discussion on child pornography regulation will take up significant space in this book owing to its general nature of illegality across jurisdictions and the seriousness of the underlying offence. The general recognition that child abuse images represent actual harm to children and also that states have a compelling interest in protecting children have resulted in robust legislative measures in many, if not all, countries. There are, however, wide variations in the way different countries regulate child sexual exploitation material, especially in relation to pseudo and virtual child pornography that do not involve physical abuse of children in their creation. It is also the case, at the time of writing, that some countries do not have adequate laws to specifically address child pornography. The lack of international harmony obviously poses challenges to effectively combating child pornography on the borderless internet. Countries with stronger resolve and political will to address the problem had to think of new and rather innovative ways of combating online child pornography, resulting in significant changes to the regulatory landscape in terms of both substantive law and enforcement strategies.

Using UK law as the platform but also referring to other jurisdictions where appropriate, the book examines how child pornography laws have evolved over the last four decades due to the internet and related digital technologies.[5] As will be seen from Chapter 3, the law has come a long way from its earlier position of treating child pornography as mere 'obscene material' to a more robust and fit-for-purpose tool that recognises the harm inherent in producing child pornography. New offences were introduced specifically criminalising the production, distribution and possession of child pornography, the various justifications and challenges of which are analysed in Chapters 3 and 4. In this process, the focus of the law has shifted steadily away from just targeting the publication and distribution of content to imposing criminal liability on end-users. This has occurred in

4 Referring to images that depict the sexual abuse and exploitation of children as 'child pornography' is controversial for a number of reasons. This is explained in more detail in Chapter 2.

5 Reference to UK law in the book pertains primarily to the law of England and Wales, although the corresponding laws within the areas discussed in the book are broadly similar in principle in Scotland and Northern Ireland, but with some exceptions.

two ways: first, through judicial interpretation of the 'making' offence whereby downloading from the internet is treated essentially as producing child pornography,[6] and second, by introducing specific simple possession offences for child pornography.

Criminalising the simple possession of child pornography is one of the significant changes in regulatory strategy necessitated by the internet. Simple possession offences do not require further intention to distribute or share the material – the mere fact of intentional possession for private consumption would suffice. In doing so, the law has essentially criminalised conduct that is carried out in private. In light of the inherent intrusive nature of simple possession offences, it is pertinent to carefully examine its relevance and proportionality in the context of online child pornography. There are a number of issues worth considering in this context. In true common law tradition, legislation in the UK does not define 'possession' and it was left to the courts to interpret its meaning. As will be seen from the discussion in Chapter 3, this turned out to be a less than straightforward concept to define. For example, should someone who accessed an image on the internet without actively downloading it to a hard disk be considered as in possession of child pornography, merely because the computer will have automatically downloaded a copy into its cache? Is criminalising simple possession justified for pseudo images where no physical harm was caused to a child during its creation? What about fictitious and computer-generated child pornography that do not depict real persons? The rationale, proportionality as well as efficacy of simple possession offences for each category of child pornography – real, pseudo and virtual – are examined in detail in the book. I argue that each of these categories of child pornography raises a fairly distinct set of issues, which lawmakers need to recognise in order to formulate appropriate legal responses and a broader regulatory strategy.

Criminalising fictitious child pornography, referred to in this book as 'virtual pornography', raises a slightly different set of issues and is therefore examined separately in Chapter 4. There are strong arguments for and against criminalising simple possession of virtual pornography. Admittedly, it took me a while to be convinced, but having weighed all the pros and cons I am of the view that criminalising the possession of virtual child pornography can be justified on the basis of a reasoned risk of harm to children. I will set out the reasoning behind my argument in some detail in Chapter 4, but at this stage it would suffice to say that the legitimacy for criminalising virtual pornography stems from a credible *risk of harm* to children as opposed to *actual* evidence of harm, which has traditionally provided the legal basis for regulation in other areas, for example adult pornography (albeit not in the context of proscribing private consumption).

6 This is the consequence of a landmark case in the UK, *R v Bowden* [2000] QB 88. Other jurisdictions, e.g. Canada and the United States, have specific access offences, as discussed in Chapter 3.

Any discussion of child pornography would be incomplete without considering the issue of self-generated pornography created by children. Law has been slow to catch up with what has apparently become normative behaviour among teenagers, and in the pursuit of child protection it has had the effect of victimising the very people the law is seeking to protect. This is an unintended consequence of the law: current child pornography laws were drafted before internet enabled mobile devices and smartphones became so prevalent. I argue that the law needs to be responsive to changing norms in cyberspace and realities of life, and the laws that were created to protect children should not be used as a tool to incarcerate them for actions that stem from the immaturity and naivety attributed to children that formed the foundation for strict child protection laws in the first place.

Legislation is only part of the solution for combating child pornography on the internet. Correctly identifying and removing the content from the internet is the bigger and more important task, which is probably the victims' most immediate concern. This is not to say that tracking down the perpetrators is not a priority, but this is not something that can be achieved by legislation alone, and usually follows the step of locating the content. Enforcement of child pornography laws requires the cooperation of actors outside traditional law enforcement agencies, something which states recognised soon enough. The regulatory landscape accordingly underwent a significant change, paving the way for non-state actors entering the regulatory framework. For example, in the UK the Internet Watch Foundation was established in 1996 with the support of internet service providers and funding from the European Commission to act as an independent hotline to receive reports of child pornography from the public, assess, and take down illegal content with the cooperation of internet service providers and law enforcement authorities both nationally and internationally. From a UK perspective this model has worked remarkably well: at the time of its inception in 1996, 18 per cent of all child abuse images in the world were hosted in the UK, a figure which now stands at less than 0.1 per cent.[7] In spite of such success stories, the involvement of non-state actors with powers to judge and effectively block content has attracted criticism. Such models rely on Code, i.e. the architecture of the internet, to regulate. In Chapter 5, I analyse the legal, policy and practical considerations stemming from self and co-regulatory models for child pornography. As should be clear by the end of that chapter, the broader regulatory framework for child pornography has undergone a fundamental and irreversible change in order to respond to the challenges raised by the internet and digital technologies. In this process, greater liability and accountability have been imposed on intermediaries, in addition to the end users of content, as noted above. The traditional immunity that certain intermediaries enjoyed for illegal content is no longer sacred: whilst the hard law has not changed substantially in

7 Internet Watch Foundation, Annual Report 2016, p 13, available at https://www.iwf.org.uk/report/2016-annual-report, accessed 5 July 2018.

relation to intermediary liability as yet, the *de facto* position reveals that intermediaries have significant responsibility in combating online child pornography, and increasingly have had to take on the role of enforcers of the law. Whilst this is outwardly seen as 'voluntary participation', in reality this can be attributed to threats of legislation for non-compliance which may adversely affect the protection that intermediaries currently enjoy. I argue that, in the future, intermediaries will assume greater liability for illegal content as well as lawful adult pornography, as demonstrated in Chapters 5 and 7.

The second category of pornography examined in the book comes under a relatively new classification from a legal perspective referred to as 'extreme pornography'. This does not involve children, but represents the more extreme forms of adult pornography, for example 'snuff' videos and other depiction of violence in a sexual context, bestiality, necrophilia and an array of other acts that many would find abhorrent and offensive. In 2008 the UK introduced a fairly robust law that criminalises the simple possession of extreme pornography.[8] This was a significant change for the regulation of pornography: traditional regulation of adult pornography, extreme or not, focused on controlling the production and distribution of obscene material. Apart from instances where possession was with the intention of further distribution, the law did not criminalise private consumption of any form of adult pornography. The criminalisation of the possession of extreme pornography raises a number of issues and now forms part of the wider debates on internet pornography. I examine these issues in light of the purported harm the law seeks to prevent, as well as the desirability of morality-based legislation and its implications for individual freedoms. Whilst it is not disputed that the violent and degrading treatment of women, or of any human being regardless of gender, should have no place in a civilised society, it is questionable whether the law actually addresses any of these fundamental issues it seeks to remedy. My central argument is that the law focuses on the wrong targets, i.e., end-user individuals, and does not really address the actual harm or the crime it seeks to root out. Extreme pornography law as it currently stands offers a classic example of bad law-making in cyberspace: a law that does not achieve its intended objective, is unenforceable, moralistic and has the potential for abuse and oppression. Such laws also fall foul of some of the traditional and well-recognised principles of criminal law, which I demonstrate by referring to the Millian harm principle and Feinberg's offence theory, as well as drawing from the debates of Hart and Dworkin. I argue in this chapter that the law should return its focus to the point of supply rather than its current focus on criminalising consumption.

The third category of pornography, examined in Chapter 7, comprises all other forms of adult pornography, and is perhaps the most complex from a regulatory perspective. Adult pornography is perceived by societies in different ways around the globe and its regulation consequently varies substantially internationally.

8 Criminal Justice and Immigration Act 2008, s 63.

Some countries have traditionally been intolerant of pornography *per se*, and have responded with a complete prohibition on its production, distribution and consumption within their geographical boundaries. Most Western countries, however, have generally held more liberal attitudes towards lawful adult pornography. This does not mean that adult pornography was not regulated; traditionally state controls over the publication and distribution of pornography that would be classed as 'obscene' have existed for a long time. However, obscenity laws did not tend to target the private consumption, with the exception of child pornography and, more recently, extreme pornography. The traditional regulatory model that focused on the publisher and distributor generally worked well for the offline world with clear geographical boundaries, as states could enforce the law with relative ease over individuals based within their respective jurisdictions. Physical importation of goods could also, in theory, be policed and many countries have traditionally had laws that regulate the importation of pornographic and obscene materials.[9] As the internet transformed the distribution and access models of pornography with the disappearance of physical boundaries in cyberspace, states came to realise that the traditional regulatory model focusing on controlling publication and distribution was no longer an effective way of policing adult pornography.

For those countries that traditionally had a total ban on pornography within their physical boundaries, the threat from the internet was obvious – people could simply access material from the privacy of their homes, bypassing the need for physical importation that carried risk of prosecution if caught. State response to this also was fairly predictable – access to pornography on the internet was simply blocked, which largely worked for the average individual, but not for those with the technical knowledge to bypass the filters using VPN or other proxies. The real challenge was for the countries that had more liberal views on pornography and with 'medium' levels of existing regulation, for example where the private consumption was legal and the regulation focused largely on the publication and distribution of obscene material. Imposing a complete ban on adult pornography would not be a desirable solution for such countries as that would amount to censorship and in most cases would be deemed unconstitutional. At the same time, transposing the traditional offline model of controlling the distribution and publication of obscene adult pornography to cyberspace proved to be problematic, especially if the publisher is based abroad. Developments in the United States, home to a sizeable pornography industry, had particularly strong implications for other countries that followed the regulatory model of controlling the publication and distribution of obscene material. In internet terms, it meant that effective regulation would depend on how the US regulates its adult pornography industry in light of the vast volume of pornographic content originating in the US.

9 E.g., s 42 of the Customs Consolidation Act 1876 prohibited the importation of obscene materials into the United Kingdom.

Concerns that the internet is becoming a repository of inappropriate content which children can easily access led to a moral panic in the United States in the 1990s, resulting in calls for regulatory measures. There were also opposing arguments and calls for leaving the internet free and unregulated, mainly from free speech and civil libertarian groups such as the American Civil Liberties Union. The Government responded with two unsuccessful attempts at legislation that sought to regulate adult pornography on the internet by requiring content providers to prevent minors accessing content that was 'harmful' to them – initially with the Communications Decency Act 1996 and later with the Child Online Protection Act 1998; the relevant provisions of both were held by the courts to be unconstitutional.[10] The implication of the ruling was that adult internet pornography has been largely left unregulated in the United States – which practically also affected the rest of the world. Whilst other countries could use their national laws to regulate pornography produced and distributed within their geographical boundaries, it did not solve the problem of their citizens being able to freely access content originating from abroad. As noted earlier, requiring local internet service providers to block *all* pornography would probably offer a solution for this – something which a number of countries with traditionally strict laws actually did – but for the more liberal societies, where the private consumption of pornography is permissible, this would not be an option without risking the criticism, and possible judicial challenges, on the basis of excessive censorship.

So what options do other states have in order to regain their right to exercise control over adult pornography? The book analyses the complexities of regulating adult pornography by examining the relevant legislative initiatives and poses a number of questions in the process. Is it simplistic to state that 'what is illegal offline should be illegal online' in the context of adult pornography? Should traditional legal principles that apply to offline pornography be transposed to cyberspace at all, or does the internet call for an entirely different regulatory strategy, including liability imposed on actors who have traditionally enjoyed immunity? How, if at all, has the regulatory landscape changed for adult pornography? These are rather vexed questions which do not always have easy answers, given the constantly evolving cultural and normative considerations in cyberspace that shape behaviour and attitudes towards pornography and speech generally. What is clear, however, is that the regulation of adult pornography is also undergoing a radical change, albeit this has been much slower than other specific types of illegal content such as child pornography and adult extreme pornography. As readers will see from the discussion in the book, states will continue in their efforts to regain their long lost control over the distribution of adult pornography on the internet. Twenty years after the first legislative attempt in the United States to regulate adult pornography on the internet, the United Kingdom has taken legislative action aimed at regulating websites that are based

10 These are discussed in considerable detail in Chapter 7.

abroad which, *inter alia*, requires websites to institute mandatory age verification before targeting consumers in the UK.[11] The mechanics and finer aspects of how the new law would work in practice are too early to judge, but what is clear is that the notion that the internet is an unregulatable space in relation to adult pornography is unlikely to last very long. Any laws that control adult pornography need to be consistent with the prevailing norms and standards of the relevant cyberspace communities. Laws that purport to simply uphold the moralistic perception of the rulers over the ruled are not likely to succeed, and therefore a regulatory framework premised purely on the notions of obscenity and indecency will inevitably fail. I argue that the sole legitimising factor that might lend normative force to the regulation of adult pornography is the prevention of children's access to adult content. For this purpose, current content-focused regulation will need to give way to access-focused regulatory models, as I explain in Chapter 7.

Relatively new forms of 'pornography' such as self-generated images and the non-consensual disclosure of private images (commonly referred to as 'revenge pornography') have been the subject of discussion and regulation in a number of jurisdictions and raise important legal issues. These are examined only briefly in the book; as I point out in Chapter 7, these themes sit on the periphery of our core discussion. 'Revenge-pornography' and other forms of online sexual abuse such as 'up-skirting', sextortion, etc. are primarily a form of offending that go beyond the scope of content offences. These categories of material are not produced primarily for the purpose of sexual arousal; instead they are intended to cause distress or harassment, or to blackmail and take financial or other advantage of the victims. Therefore, the appropriate remedy does not lie within pornography laws and it merits legal responses that are proportionate to the nature and seriousness of these offences.

Law-making in cyberspace is a tricky affair. We have come a long way from the early predictions of cyber libertarians that the internet will not be subject to laws of the physical world.[12] In terms of content regulation, the internet has become heavily regulated in relation to child pornography, at least from the perspective of substantive law. There are laws that prohibit extreme pornography, and new forms of control are now being rolled out for adult pornography. We can also see a progressively increasing reliance on Code to regulate content on the internet with unprecedented involvement of private actors that now permeate the regulatory framework. What does this mean for the law and fundamental rights?

My main argument, which I undertake by examining the three broad categories of pornography, is that the internet has fundamentally and in many ways

11 Digital Economy Act 2017, discussed in Chapter 7.

12 See e.g. David R Johnson and David Post, 'Law and Borders – the Rise of Law in Cyberspace', (1996) 48(5) *Stanford Law Review* 1367–1402; John Perry Barlow, 'A Declaration of the Independence of Cyberspace', Davos 1996, available at https://www.eff.org/cyberspace-independence, accessed 5 July 2018.

irreversibly changed the regulation of pornography. States have attempted to apply traditional laws to cyberspace without a lot of success, and despite earlier predictions that internet specific legislation is unnecessary[13] a new and radical regulatory framework has developed. This has had the effect that the traditional focus of the law on the publisher and distributor of content has now shifted to end-users, and to a considerable extent also to intermediaries. In terms of child pornography, the prevention of harm or a reasoned risk of harm to children renders the current legal framework legitimate and proportionate. I argue that the relative success of the regulation of child pornography would not offer a legitimate precedent for regulating extreme pornography. As for adult pornography, I argue that preventing children's access to adult content will provide the sole basis for regulating adult pornography, and the delicate balance between limiting children's access to adult content and the right of adults to consume lawful pornography can be achieved only by access-focused regulation rather than content-focused regulation.

13 For example, the UK Parliament set up a Home Affairs Committee to evaluate existing legislative provisions and to make recommendations for change. The Committee recommended that there was no need for *sui generis* legislation for addressing internet pornography, and instead put forth a number of recommendations for amending existing legislation. Consequently, various existing legislation was amended to factor in the recommendations.

PART I

2 Online child pornography

Preliminary considerations

The abuse of children by adults for the purpose of sexual gratification is a serious crime which merits a robust response. Recording the sexual abuse of children and making it available on the internet further aggravates the suffering caused to the child by documenting the abuse in a public space for others to see. Therefore, in this sense, making images of child abuse available for others to view is perhaps as heinous as the underlying physical abuse that a child has been subjected to in the first place. There is international recognition of the need to protect children from all forms of sexual exploitation, which is evident from the provisions of the United Nations Convention on the Rights of the Child (UNCRC), one of the most popular international human rights instruments in the world.[1] The Convention specifically requires Signatory States to take appropriate measures to 'prevent the exploitative use of children in pornographic performances and materials'.[2]

Portraying children in a sexually explicit context would be deemed inherently indecent by most civilised societies. In addition to the indecency of the images, child pornography raises unique issues from a child protection and safety perspective that renders it not just a content-related offence, but one that provokes a greater compelling interest on the part of the state to protect children from physical abuse and exploitation. As the creation of child pornography generally involves the physical abuse of an actual child, it should also be seen as a 'contact offence' resulting in the physical sexual exploitation of a real child. This is not necessarily the case with respect to pseudo or virtual child pornography, where no real children are physically abused for the production of the material (although there is some evidence that such images could be used in the grooming process to abuse children, and therefore causes indirect harm), but in all other cases child

1 United Nations Convention on the Rights of the Child, 1989, Art 34. The Convention is the most widely ratified international human rights treaty in history. As at January 2018, all UN Member States except for the Unites States have ratified the Convention.

2 Art 34(c). See also the Optional Protocol to the Convention on the Rights of the Child on the sale of children, child prostitution and child pornography 2000, which provides details on the measures necessary to implement the relevant provisions of the Convention.

pornography goes beyond the indecency or inappropriateness of the image on the screen and depicts the actual physical abuse or exploitation of a child. Regulatory response to child pornography therefore ought to be robust, which is reflected in the law in a number of jurisdictions as criminal sanctions include lengthy prison sentences.[3]

It is pertinent at the outset to clarify the terminology used in this book in relation to 'child pornography'. Whilst 'child pornography' is a term used widely in legislative texts (including the UNCRC 1989) to refer to sexually explicit images of children, there is also some criticism surrounding the appropriateness of the use of 'pornography' in this context. For instance, the Internet Watch Foundation is of the view that the use of the terms 'child pornography', 'kiddie porn', etc. act to legitimise images that are not 'pornography', but permanent records of the sexual exploitation of children and should therefore be more accurately referred to as 'child sexual abuse images'.[4] There is also significant academic criticism on the use of 'pornography' to describe material depicting children in a sexualised context. For example, Taylor and Quayle[5] highlight the offensiveness of associating 'child' with the term 'pornography' which is linked to erotica and therefore inappropriate in relation to the depiction of child sexual abuse.[6] Gillespie, while acknowledging the inappropriateness of the term 'pornography' to describe such material, also points out the difficulties in finding a suitable alternative term – for example, not all graphic representation will involve the actual abuse of a child, in which case it would be inaccurate to refer such images as 'child abuse images'. He argues that 'child exploitation material' might be a broader term as it would encompass a wider range of situations underpinning the imagery where, for instance, a child's face is morphed to an adult's body – the child does not suffer any physical abuse but nevertheless is subject to 'exploitation'.[7] But then, referring to all child pornography as 'child sexual exploitation material' does not do justice to material that is produced as result of physical abuse of children and is therefore problematic as an umbrella term. It is the case that our current understanding of the word 'child pornography' encompasses a wide range of sexual representation of children, which may or may not include actual physical abuse of a child. References to 'child pornography' in this book, therefore, is only made with the intention that it more accurately resonates with the existing legislation both nationally in many jurisdictions and internationally rather than attempting to recognise such images as

3 For example, in the UK, the maximum sentence for production of child pornography is ten years in prison and or a fine (s 6(2), Protection of Children Act 1978).

4 See https://www.iwf.org.uk/about-iwf/remit-vision-and-mission, accessed 5 July 2018.

5 See Max Taylor and Ethel Quayle, *Child Pornography: An Internet Crime* (Brunner-Routledge 2003).

6 See Alisdair A Gillespie, *Child Pornography: Law and Policy* (Routledge 2011) 1; Susan SM Edwards, 'Prosecuting "child pornography": Possession and taking of Indecent Photographs of Children' (2000) 22 *Journal of Social Welfare and Family Law* 2000, 1–21, 1.

7 Gillespie, ibid.

pornographic in any way, and it is fully acknowledged that it is not an accurate description in a literary sense.[8] The terms 'child abuse images/imagery', 'child sexual abuse material' and 'child sexual exploitation material' are used interchangeably in the book, unless specifically stated otherwise. References to 'images' include both still and moving images.

The second clarification to be made in terms of terminology is in relation to 'real', 'pseudo' and 'virtual' child pornography used in this book. References to 'real' child pornography include material that is produced as a result of actual physical abuse of a child. The term 'virtual child pornography' has often been used collectively and interchangeably to include pseudo photographs in some jurisdictions. For example, in the US virtual child pornography can include wholly computer-generated pornography, as well as pornography produced by morphing images of children, and images portraying adults who look like underage persons.[9] For the purposes of this book, however, the reference to 'virtual pornography' primarily includes non-photographic images of children such as computer-generated images, cartoons, drawings etc., and does not include real or pseudo photographs.[10] This is in line with the legislative approach in the UK.[11] Pseudo images are essentially photograph-based: for example, images that are produced by blending or morphing, such as superimposing the face of a child onto the body of an adult to give the overall impression of a child. Pseudo-photographs could also include images of young adults digitally modified or altered to portray the impression of an underage person. Pseudo child pornography is treated with more or less the same seriousness as real child pornography in the UK and, like real child pornography, it is an offence to produce, distribute or possess such

8 ECPAT International, a non-governmental organisation that campaigns against the sexual exploitation and trafficking of children, initiated an Interagency Working Group (IWG) with a remit to address the absence of common terminology to accurately describe the sexual exploitation and abuse of children. The IWG comprises a number of partners including the UN Special Rapporteur on the Sale of Children, Child Prostitution and Child Pornography, the Special Representative to the UN Secretary General on Violence against Children, UNICEF, ITU, INTERPOL, etc. The IWG released a 'Terminology Guidelines for the Protection of Children from Sexual Exploitation and Sexual Abuse' on the 14 June 2016 with a view to clarifying and harmonising key terms and definitions relating the sexual exploitation and abuse of children. See http://luxembourgguidelines.org/english-version/, accessed 5 July 2018. This is expected to result in a cultural change, and have already been adopted by the INTERPOL as best practice guidelines. See https://www.interpol.int/Crime-areas/Crimes-against-children/Appropriate-terminology, accessed 26 July 2018.

9 The Child Pornography Prevention Act 1996, which was struck down as unconstitutional by the courts, generated a scholarly debate on virtual child pornography in the United States. On the categorisation of virtual child pornography into the three sub-sets, see S Liu, '*Ashcroft*, Virtual Child Pornography and First Amendment Jurisprudence' (2011) 11(1) *US Davis Journal of Juvenile Law and Policy* 1–54.

10 There are wide variations and interesting issues surrounding the definition of what constitutes virtual child pornography. See Gillespie (n 6) Ch.5 for a detailed analysis.

11 Coroners and Justice Act 2009, s 62.

material.[12] The most important factor that distinguishes virtual pornography is that this is non-photographic material depicting no real children, whereas pseudo pornography would normally involve the use of photographic material of real persons. The classification into pseudo and virtual pornography is the correct approach as they raise slightly different legal issues, as readers will see from the discussion that follows in this book.

Child pornography and the internet

Child pornography is not a creation of the internet. The exploitation of children, including 'child prostitution' and depiction of children in a sexualised context, dates back to ancient times.[13] The internet has, however, transformed the way child pornography is produced, distributed and accessed[14] and has contributed to its exponential growth.[15] There are many reasons for this. First, the internet has made it easier to *access* child pornography, with relatively low risk of getting caught, when compared to trying to obtain child pornography from a traditional brick and mortar outlet. Second, materials can be uploaded and shared from around the world, which substantially increases the *volume* an individual is able to access from their location. Third, the internet and computer technology generally has also made it much easier to digitally alter and *create* pseudo images (for instance, blending the face of a child to the body of an adult in the image) of child sexual abuse, without having to invest in expensive technology. Pseudo and virtual child pornography raise a number of legal and ethical issues which are examined in some detail in Chapters 3 and 4, but as these images essentially portray children in an inappropriate sexualised context they are treated as illegal in many jurisdictions. Fourth, the internet has made the *distribution* of child pornography a lot easier compared to traditional forms of media; perpetrators use a range of different ways to distribute child pornography, including websites, social media, peer-to-peer file-sharing sites, and also the 'dark web'.[16] Finally, the practical difficulties in identifying and prosecuting offenders based in other

12 Protection of Children Act 1978, s 1. It is however the case that sentencing could be less severe for pseudo-photographs compared to images involving real children.

13 See Suzanne Ost, *Child Pornography and Sexual Grooming: Legal and Societal Responses* (Cambridge University Press 2009) 25; Chad M Steel, *Digital Child Pornography: A Practical Guide for Investigators* (Lily Shiba Press 2013) 6.

14 See Yaman Akdeniz, *Internet Child Pornography and the Law: National and International Responses* (Ashgate 2008).

15 Max Taylor and Ethel Quayle (n 5). In relation to how the internet contributes to the trade in child abuse images, Max Taylor and Ethel Quale, 'Criminogenic Qualities of the Internet in the Collection and Distribution of Abuse Images of Children' (2008) 29 *The Irish Journal of Psychology*, Issues 1–2. See also, for a history of how the internet started to be used of child pornography, Philip Jenkins, *Beyond Tolerance: Child Pornography on the Internet* (New York University Press 2001) Ch 3.

16 'Dark web' refers to parts of the internet that cannot be found using ordinary search engines, some of which are used for criminal activity, including child pornography.

jurisdictions have also created a number of challenges for combating child abuse imagery on the internet. Whilst the difficulties in relation to jurisdiction are not unique to child pornography, as there are numerous other areas of the law that have faced problems due to the global nature of the internet, content offences are particularly problematic. The substantial variations in the way the child pornography is regulated across different countries and pornography's status generally as a form of expression create numerous challenges for the law, in particular for the regulation of virtual child pornography where direct harm to children is more difficult to establish, as discussed in Chapter 4.

The growing availability of child pornography on the internet therefore naturally raised concerns at national and international level. The International Conference on Combating Child Pornography on the Internet, held in Vienna in 1999, called for the worldwide criminalisation of the production, distribution, exportation, transmission, importation, intentional possession and advertising of child pornography, and emphasised the need for greater cooperation and partnership between governments and the internet industry. Whilst a number of countries already had legislation in place which criminalised the production of child pornography, a fundamental change, which the internet arguably necessitated, was criminalising not just the production and distribution of such images, but also its simple possession. In many liberal Western democracies, the regulation of obscene material traditionally focused on controlling its publication and distribution rather than criminalising consumption. The internet and digital technologies prompted a fundamental re-think of this model and there are a number of reasons for this change in the focus of regulation. This is analysed in more detail in Chapter 3, but at this stage it will suffice to say that the global nature of the internet and the consequent difficulties in identifying and prosecuting the publishers and distributors of illegal child pornography based in foreign jurisdictions, combined with the practical difficulties in getting the content removed at source, meant that a regulatory model focusing on the point of supply was no longer adequate (or practical) for effectively addressing the problem. In addition, the vastly different approaches among different countries in relation to the specific legal age of a 'child' for the purpose of pornography also made the effective regulation of child pornography problematic. The challenges stemming from jurisdiction and the difficulties in relation to determining a definitive internationally agreed age for construing a person as a child for the purpose of illegal pornography are considered in more detail in the following sections.

Jurisdictional issues

Problems arising from jurisdiction and conflict of laws are neither new in relation to the internet, nor unique to child pornography. The *Yahoo! v LICRA* case is a classic example of how jurisdiction can pose problems on the internet where material (albeit in a different context) considered to be criminally illegal in one country was deemed to be within constitutionally protected right to free speech in another, which on the facts of this case meant that a court order in France would potentially not be enforced in the United States.[17] As far as child pornography is concerned, owing to the vastly different legislative approaches to 'child pornography' internationally, a regulatory model based on adult obscene material that criminalises publication and distribution would inevitably lead to difficulties. For instance, UK law treats anyone under the age of 18 as a child for the purpose of child pornography legislation. If pornographic material is published on the internet from a country where the permissible age threshold is lower, say 16, it would lead to a situation where the same material is legal in the jurisdiction where it is uploaded, but would be classed as illegal child pornography in the UK if the person depicted is under 18. The difficulties arising specifically from the lack of consensus regarding age is discussed in more detail in the next section below. If the UK were to prosecute the publisher it would be unlikely to yield any positive results if the material is regarded as legal within the other jurisdiction, as extradition is likely to be unrealistic in such instances. Publishers are unlikely to be deterred from publishing material on the internet for fear of prosecution from a foreign country if the material is legal within their own jurisdiction. A content-related offence emanating from a foreign jurisdiction is unlikely to command obedience or respect in the home jurisdiction provided that the material is legal within their own jurisdiction. For example, publishers based in a country where virtual child pornography that does not feature real children is permitted are not likely to be concerned about the laws of another country where such material is illegal. Most countries will be unwilling to enforce foreign judgments that are decided based on principles contrary to their own local laws and fundamental rights. The tension between English and US defamation laws, where the former has traditionally had a stricter approach to defamatory speech and the US courts have refused to enforce English libel judgments in the US, offers a good example for this.[18] It is unlikely that a possible legal

17 *Yahoo!, Inc. v La Ligue Contre Le Racisme et L'Antisémitisme*, 169 F. Supp. 2d 1181, 1194 (N.D. Cal. 2001). The District Court in California granted a declaration that the French judgment should not be enforced in the USA on free speech grounds. This was later overturned on appeal (379 F 3d1120 (9th Cir, 2004) on the basis that the District Court had no jurisdiction to hear the matter as enforcement in the US had not been sought in the first place, but the merits of the decision itself were not commented on. The civil litigation was eventually resolved when Yahoo! banned the sale of Nazi memorabilia (which was the basis for the dispute) on its auction sites. For a good discussion on the case, see M Greenberg, 'A return to Lilliput: The LICRA v Yahoo! Case and the Regulation of Online Content in the World Market' (2003) 18 *Berkeley Tech. L.J.* 1191. Also see, on internet jurisdiction generally, U Kohl, 'Eggs, Jurisdiction and the Internet' (2002) 51(3) *International and Comparative Law Quarterly* 556–582.

18 For example, see *Bachchan v India Abroad Publications*, 585 NYS 2d 661 (NY Supp Ct, 1992). For a discussion on the problems with enforcement, see KH Youm, 'The Interaction between American and Foreign Libel Law: U.S. Courts Refuse to Enforce English Libel Judgments' (2000) 49(1) *International and Comparative Law Quarterly* 131–165.

action from a foreign jurisdiction will act as a deterrent for anyone from publishing material online from within jurisdictions where such material is perfectly legal.

Furthermore, even if the material is regarded as illegal in the other jurisdiction, there are a number of practical difficulties that could pose hurdles to successful prosecution. Cooperation between the law enforcement authorities of both countries and, more importantly, a certain degree of will and resolve to assist with the case, are sometimes dependent on the local resources available. It may be that the local police could charge the offender based on the local laws rather than extraditing to the other country, but in the event that the offender needs to be extradited (provided that there is an extradition agreement in place that would facilitate this) it would be next to impossible to gather sufficient forensic computer evidence without the assistance of the local police force. In any event, transferring sensitive evidence from a foreign country with the associated costs involved in the participation of any foreign witnesses, etc. could make prosecution a daunting and expensive affair.

In addition to the jurisdictional constraints mentioned above, there is the problem with the lack of harmonisation of certain aspects of substantive law internationally, including a standard definition of a 'child' for this purpose. The problems caused by the lack of consensus regarding the definition of a child in relation to pornography are discussed in more detail in the next section. Whilst child pornography involving real children is broadly recognised as illegal in many jurisdictions,[19] there is a striking lack of consensus internationally when it comes to the legality of virtual child pornography.[20] This is partly due to the apparent lack of 'direct harm' caused to children during production, which has made it difficult to criminalise virtual child pornography in some jurisdictions, for example where the right to free speech is broader in scope.[21] Representing young adults in a sexualised context in comics and cartoons may fall within 'artistic expression' in some societies, for instance some Japanese manga and anime feature children in sexually explicit scenarios, which is not illegal

19 According to the International Centre for Missing and Exploited Children (ICMEC) 'Child Pornography Model Law and Global Review' in 2016, there are 35 countries that do not yet have legislation specifically addressing child pornography. This is, however, a significant improvement over the position in 2006 when the corresponding number was 95 countries without specific legislation addressing child pornography. For the full report, see http://www.icmec.org/wp-content/uploads/2016/02/Child-Pornography-Model-Law-8th-Ed-Final-linked.pdf, accessed 5 July 2018.

20 Of the countries that have specific legislation addressing child pornography, there are still 26 that do not have provisions for 'computer-facilitated' offences. See ICMEC global review, ibid.

21 For example, the Child Pornography Prevention Act 1996, which was enacted with a view of criminalising pseudo and virtual child pornography, was struck down as unconstitutional in *Ashcroft v Free Speech Coalition* in the United States on First Amendment grounds. This is examined in further detail in Chapter 4.

in Japan,[22] whereas all sexual representations of children including wholly computer-generated images are illegal in the UK.[23] Such differences in substantive law at international level are obviously problematic and will inevitably raise jurisdictional difficulties should a dispute arise at transnational level.

Content regulation generally and pornography in particular is very jurisdiction-specific owing to the vastly different perceptions and norms regarding what is permissible or repugnant content as construed by different societies internationally. It is well accepted that the regulation of pornography generally imposes a level of constraint on the right to freedom of expression (as 'normal' pornography, unlike obscenity, forms part of protected speech); and jurisdictions with broader free speech rights will naturally protect a wider range of material, including some forms of pornography that may be regarded as illegal elsewhere in other jurisdictions. Virtual child pornography is a classic example of this. States are well within their sovereign right to make laws that legalise or criminalise pornography within their borders. The internet has effectively undermined the ability and power of states to regulate content that in the pre-internet age was regulated within their geographical borders. The disappearance of physical boundaries in cyberspace has also rendered the traditional customs and importation rules practically obsolete, as content originating from abroad could be easily accessed on the internet, bypassing borders. Therefore, states invariably had to think about newer forms of regulation in order to reinstate the traditional control they exercised over the publication, distribution and importation of pornography within their respective home jurisdictions. In other words, the traditional focus of the law on the publisher and distributor of content inevitably had to change if child pornography were to be effectively addressed on the internet. The increasing levels of criminal liability imposed on the consumers of child pornography need to be examined in this context. In addition, states also had to adopt a level of extraterritoriality in terms of the scope of domestic legislation pertaining to child pornography in order for it to be effective in cyberspace. These developments, and how child pornography laws have evolved significantly in the internet age, are discussed in the next chapter.

Who is a child? The age (old) problem

Determining the age threshold for a person to be classed as a child for the purpose of child pornography is problematic on many counts, particularly in the

22 Japan banned the possession of child abuse images featuring real children in June 2014, but despite calls to also ban virtual sexual images of persons under 18, which would address the sexual representation of children in manga and anime, the Parliament decided against this. The decision to exclude virtual pornography drew international criticism from child protection advocates both within and outside Japan.

23 Coroners and Justice Act 2009, s 62.

global context of the internet. It is the case that, even within the same jurisdiction, the definition of a child can vary depending on the context and purpose. For example, in the UK the age of consent for sex is 16, whereas the age for consent to pose for a sexually explicit image is 18.[24] The age of criminal responsibility generally is much lower, being 10 years. It is generally recognised that, as growing up is a constantly evolving process, children will demonstrate different levels of maturity at different ages, and children are able to take responsibility for some of their actions.

The legal age of consent for sex varies from country to country. There are countries where the minimum age of consent for sex is lower than 16, for instance in Germany and Italy it is 14, and in other countries such as India and Iraq the age of consent for sex is 18. In the United States and Australia, there is no uniform age of consent as it a matter for each state or territory to set its own threshold.

The minimum age of consent to pose for sexually explicit images also varies across jurisdictions. Even within the same jurisdiction, the legal age of consent for sex is not necessarily the same as the age of consent to pose for sexually explicit images, as noted above in the case of the UK. The difference in the age threshold between these two categories is perhaps understandable: physical sexual activity is a private act, whereas sexual images could have wider implications owing to their nature of permanence, especially in the context of the internet. It is therefore reasonable to require a higher level of maturity for providing consent to creating sexually explicit images compared to sexual activities.

In terms of the international legal instruments relating to child sexual exploitation and child pornography, whilst the recommended age limit to construe a person as a child is 18 years, there is still some flexibility allowed for individual states. For example, the United Nations Convention on the Rights of the Child defines anyone under the age of 18 as a child, but leaves room for Signatory States to set a different age within domestic legislation.[25] The European Directive on Combating the Sexual Abuse and Sexual Exploitation of Children and Child Pornography defines a child as 'any person below the age of 18 years' for the purpose of child pornography and leaves it to national legislation to determine the legal age of sexual consent.[26] The Council

24 Section 7(6) of the Protection of Children Act 1978 as originally enacted defined a child as a person under the age of 16. This was later amended under s 45(2) of the Sexual Offences Act 2003, which changed the definition of a child to anyone under the age of 18 for the purposes of child pornography, and in line with the international treaties of which the UK is a signatory.

25 The Optional Protocol to the United Nations Convention on the Rights of the Child on the sale of children, child prostitution and child pornography (A/RES/54/263) also sets the age of a child as below the age of 18, effectively by referring to the definition provided in the UNCRC itself.

26 Art 2, Directive 2011/92/EU of the European Parliament and of the Council of 13 December 2011, which replaces the Council Framework Decision 2004/68/JHA.

of Europe Convention on Cybercrime[27] also defines a child as under the age of 18, but with a provision that allows signatories to reduce this to 16 under national law. The flexibility provided within these instruments essentially recognises the social and cultural variations among different societies in construing a child, but it also has the effect of rendering the regulation of child pornography in cyberspace more complex.

Setting a definite age of consent for pornography is far from straightforward. It is well known that children of the same age group may have different levels of maturity: this is more problematic with respect to borderline age groups, for instance some 17-year-old children may well have greater mental maturity to fully comprehend the ramifications of being photographed in a sexual context than some who are slightly older and above the legal age for this purpose. This makes it difficult to accept physical maturity as the solemn standard for consent. In addition, it is also the case that children attain puberty at slightly different ages and there are variations depending on genetic build, body type, diet and lifestyle, as well as social factors, which render it difficult to assess the age of a child by looking at an image.[28] Physical maturity as a criterion for consent is problematic in any case: in the absence of a prescribed age threshold, courts would still need to assess whether the child depicted also had the mental maturity to give consent, as biological growth on its own cannot determine a child's capacity to give consent to sex or to producing sexual images. Gillespie attributes this to our 'moral and cultural tradition', that puberty cannot on its own set the point at which children can consent to sexual intercourse.[29] Furthermore, the viewer of the image will have no way of knowing whether the person depicted had the sufficient level of (mental) maturity to be classed as an adult for the purpose of the image. This is in fact impossible for a third party to judge, and if maturity were to be the sole criterion for defining a child it would lead to inconsistent and undesirable results. Gillespie therefore rejects maturity as a method of construing childhood for the purpose of pornography.[30]

There are also other facets of law where a physically mature child benefits from additional protection of the law. For example, in English contract law the general

27 Convention on Cybercrime of the Council of Europe (CETS No.185).

28 See for example, E Sthathopulu, J Antony Hulse, D Canning, 'Difficulties with Age Estimation of Internet Images of South East Asian Girls' (2003) 12(1) *Child Abuse Review* 46–57. Also see C Cattaneo, S Ritz-Timme, P Gabriel, D Gibelli, E Guidici, P Poppa, D Nohrden, S Assmann, R Schmitt, M Grandi, 'The Difficult Issue of Age Assessment on Pedo Pornographic Material' (2009) 183 *Forensic Science International*, Issues 1–3, e21–e24.

29 Gillespie (n 6). This would be inevitable given the special status afforded to children generally because of the recognition that their level of maturity is lower than that of adults. This is widely recognised not just in the context of age of consent for sex or pornography, but also under other areas of law, for example, contracts entered into by minors are voidable in many situations under English law.

30 For an excellent analysis on the definition of a child, see Alisdair A Gillespie, 'Legal Definitions of Child Pornography' (2010) 16(1) *Journal of Sexual Aggression* 19–31. Also see Gillespie (2011), *supra*, n 6, 13–20.

rule is that a person is not bound by a contract which he enters into during his minority.[31] A minor for this purpose is anyone under the age of 18. In the contract law context, the law is essentially seeking to protect children from the consequences of their inexperience. The law recognises that children are in a weaker position in terms of capacity to enter into voluntary obligations – this special treatment is granted purely on the basis of their mental maturity (or more accurately, lack of it) rather than physical. This not to suggest that not all children attain a level of maturity required to be treated as fully capable of entering into legal obligations on (or only on) their magical eighteenth birthday. Notwithstanding the subjective variations in the levels of mental maturity attained by individual adolescents, the law here simply recognises that a reasonably higher and uniform age threshold of 18 is in the interest of the larger group, and protects all children. It should be no different for child pornography – the consequences of posing for a sexually explicit image while young and lacking experience could be profound, with potential long-term implications.

It seems fairly pragmatic that the law has to be somewhat prescriptive and specify an age threshold for the purpose of child pornography. Whilst this may not be the perfect solution it does contribute to offering more clarity for all involved – the participants, producers, viewers as well as for law enforcement authorities. Adhering to a prescriptive age limit, although pragmatic, still leaves some issues unresolved, for instance where the person/s depicted look younger than 18 but are in fact over the age of 18 it could still lead to a prosecution. This is not always easy to establish, especially when the content originates abroad. The capability of digital technology to modify images in order to make the person depicted look younger (pseudo-imagery) raises further challenges for the law: these are complex issues and are discussed in more detail in Chapter 3.

The lack of consensus internationally regarding the definition of a child means that the traditional regulatory model for pornography that focused on the point of supply would be difficult to enforce, especially when the publisher's jurisdiction has a lower age threshold for defining a child. For example, if the minimum age of consent for pornography is 16 in a particular jurisdiction, publishing a sexually explicit image of a 17-year-old would obviously be permissible in that jurisdiction, but the same image will be classed as child pornography in other jurisdictions where the minimum age is 18. In light of cases such as *R v Perrin*,[32] if the image is accessible in the UK it would be deemed to be 'published' here and therefore the publisher will have committed an offence under UK law. In practice, if the webpages were merely accessible from the UK, just as they would be from anywhere in the world, it would be very difficult, if not impossible, to prosecute the publisher who has acted entirely lawfully in their own jurisdiction.

31 Subject to some exceptions, for instance a beneficial contract of employment or where the contract is to supply him with 'necessaries' where the contract as a whole is for the benefit of the minor.

32 *R v Perrin* [2002] EWCA Crim 747.

A universally agreed minimum definitive age of consent for child pornography would have remedied this situation. As this was not the case, states that wished to control the dissemination and access to 'child pornography' – defined according to the age threshold in national law – within their geographical boundaries naturally had to think about newer regulatory strategies that are workable in the internet environment.

An examination of how child pornography laws have evolved in the internet age would reveal significant changes in substantive laws as well as enforcement strategies. Shifting the focus of regulation away from the publisher and distributor and targeting the end user by imposing higher levels of criminal liability for consumption is one of the step changes seen in this context.

The next chapter examines how child pornography laws have undergone a transformation in the internet age, and specifically analyses the various production, distribution and possession offences in relation to real and pseudo child pornography and the complexities of applying these laws to the internet. Virtual pornography is examined separately in Chapter 4, owing to the slightly different set of issues raised. Robust and fit-for-purpose legislation is only the first step – the challenges of online child pornography have also resulted in states having to formulate a range of co-regulatory and self-regulatory measures involving non-state actors, which complement state-level legislation for the identification and removal of child pornography from the internet. The arrival of private actors into the regulatory framework is another radical change necessitated by the internet, which has resulted in the imposition of a level of *de facto* liability on intermediaries, as explored in Chapter 5.

3 Transformation of child pornography laws

It should be fairly clear from the discussion so far that a new regulatory strategy that goes beyond focusing on publishers and distributors was inevitable in order to combat child pornography on the internet. It is pertinent to outline briefly the relevant international instruments before examining the legislative framework at national level in order to fully understand how the regulatory landscape has evolved as a result of the internet and digital technologies. The key international instruments that are relevant to child pornography are briefly discussed at the outset in this chapter. It is not the intention of this book to provide a detailed list of legislation in every jurisdiction. UK law is used as the 'platform' for examining the legal developments and relevant issues. References are made to other jurisdictions where relevant in order to draw comparisons as well as to highlight key differences in the law and regulation. For example, whilst the UK criminalises all forms of child pornography, including pseudo and virtual images, the position is less clear in the US when it comes to fictitious representations of children (virtual child pornography). Notwithstanding such differences, the jurisdictions referred to in Part 1 of this book are examples of regulatory models that are widely regarded as relatively successful in combating child pornography online. It will be clear from the discussion in this chapter that the internet and digital technologies have had a significant role in the evolution of laws and regulatory strategies to combat child pornography. The pressure on other governments to adopt similar models will naturally follow, which to a certain extent has already begun over the last ten years or so, and it is only a matter of time before further countries will be persuaded to reform their national laws.

The chapter will demonstrate how child pornography laws have undergone a transformation over the last four decades. Child pornography was traditionally regulated under obscenity laws which merely focused on the effect of the image on the viewers, but it eventually gave way to specific laws that recognise the harm inherent in the creation and distribution of child pornography. The arrival of the internet and advances in digital technology meant that the distribution and access models for child pornography underwent a radical change, necessitating a number of further changes to the substantive legal framework. Law progressively adapted and evolved over this time: the internet and digital technologies have meant not only that new laws had to be enacted, but the courts have also interpreted some of these laws in innovative ways in the process of responding to the challenges raised by the internet.[1] In this process, increasing levels of liability have been imposed on consumers of child pornography, marking a step change in the traditional focus of the law on controlling the publication and distribution of content to a more specific approach targeting end users. This was achieved in two ways: first, through specific statutory provisions that criminalise the simple possession of child pornography, regardless of intention to distribute. Second, by means of liberal interpretation of the law by courts, which resulted in the consumers of content being made criminally liable for 'producing' child pornography.

Whilst the overall objective of child pornography laws, regardless of whether the material in question is real, pseudo or virtual imagery, is the protection of children from sexual abuse and exploitation, each category raises different sets of issues and challenges for the law. This chapter analyses the various justifications and arguments for specifically criminalising the production and distribution, as well as the simple possession of real and pseudo child pornography, and examines the complexities of applying these laws to the internet. It will be examined whether the various prohibitions and constraints that are imposed by the law, most notably the increasing use of simple possession offences that prohibit the private consumption of content, which is essentially conduct carried out in private, are proportionate and fit for purpose. In particular, what constitutes 'possession' in the context of the internet users raises pertinent issues and merits analysis. Similarly, culpability for illegal content received unsolicited or unbidden, for example by email or inadvertent browsing, is also analysed in the chapter.

My analysis in the chapter will reveal that robust legislation that specifically criminalises the ***production and distribution*** of child pornography in all its manifestations – be it real or pseudo child pornography – is a legitimate and proportionate response for a number of reasons. As for criminalising simple ***possession***, I argue that the current law is appropriate and proportionate for real child pornography as well as for pseudo-imagery, regardless of whether a child suffered any physical harm during its creation. I also argue that there is sufficient legal basis for criminalising the possession of pseudo child pornography featuring young adults. Finally, the issues stemming from self-generated images by children ('sexting') are also examined. It should be noted that virtual pornography and the issues stemming from the various enforcement models are not covered in this chapter in any detail, but are discussed separately in the following two chapters owing to the different set of issues raised.

1 The Court of Appeal decision that interpreted the 'making offence' in *R v Bowden* offers a good example for this, discussed later in the chapter.

International initiatives

There are at least three international instruments that specifically address child pornography, worthy of consideration here, in addition to the European-level initiative in the form of a Directive, discussed further below.[2]

United Nations Convention on the Rights of the Child 1989

The United Nations Convention on the Rights of the Child 1989 (UNCRC), which is acclaimed as the most widely ratified international human rights treaty in history, has a specific provision that requires signatories to adopt appropriate measures to address the sexual exploitation of children:

> 'States Parties undertake to protect the child from all forms of sexual exploitation and sexual abuse. For these purposes, States Parties shall in particular take all appropriate national, bilateral and multilateral measures to prevent ... (c) the exploitative use of children in pornographic performances and materials.'[3]

The UNCRC establishes a broad set of principles aimed at the welfare of children and reflects the need to extend particular care to the child in accordance with various international treaties and agreements such as the Geneva Declaration of the Rights of the Child 1924, Declaration of the Rights of the Child adopted by the UN General Assembly in November 1959, Articles 23 and 24 of the International Covenant on Civil and Political Rights, the International Covenant on Economic, Social and Cultural Rights and other relevant statutes and instruments of international organisations and specialised agencies concerned with the welfare of children.[4] Article 34 of the Convention specifically mentions child pornography, but has been criticised for being imprecise and inadequate in terms of extent, definition and efficacy.[5] Nevertheless, the UNCRC has certainly provided the basis for further developments in the protection of children from sexual exploitation, such as the Optional Protocol, and was probably not intended to be an all-encompassing legal response to child sexual exploitation. It should also be noted that the Convention pretty much pre-dates the internet in its current form, and therefore it is unlikely that the drafters would have envisaged the scale of the threat posed by online child pornography.

2 Directive 2011/92/EU of the European Parliament and of the Council of 13 December 2011 on combating the sexual abuse and sexual exploitation of children and child pornography, and replacing Council Framework Decision 2004/68/JHA.

3 United Nations Convention on the Rights of the Child 1989, Art 34.

4 As stated in the Preamble to the United Nations Convention on the Rights of the Child 1989.

5 Alisdair A Gillespie, *Child pornography: Law and Policy* (Routledge 2011), 290.

The Optional Protocol

The Optional Protocol to the Convention on the Rights of the Child on the sale of children, child prostitution and child pornography was adopted by General Assembly resolution A/RES/54/263 on 25 May 2000, which builds on the general provisions within the UNCRC on child sexual exploitation and strengthens the obligations that signatories should undertake in order to guarantee the protection of children in this context. The role of the internet and modern technologies in the increasing availability of child pornography is specifically acknowledged in the Optional Protocol, which refers to the conclusions drawn at the International Conference on Combating Child Pornography on the Internet held in Vienna in 1999. The conference had recommended the 'world-wide criminalisation of the production, distribution, exportation, transmission, importation, intentional possession and advertising of child pornography' and called for closer cooperation between governments and the industry to combat child pornography. Accordingly, the Optional Protocol stipulates a number of provisions specific to child pornography, including a wide definition of child pornography under Article 2(3):

> 'Child pornography means any representation, by whatever means, of a child engaged in real or simulated explicit sexual activities or any representation of the sexual parts of a child for primarily sexual purposes.'

The reference to 'any representation, by whatever means' is significant in the context of digital technologies as it would encompass a broader range of sexualised representation of children, including digitally enhanced material. The Optional Protocol requires signatory states to criminalise child pornography within their domestic law, regardless of whether the offence is committed domestically or transnationally, or on an individual or organised basis.[6] This extraterritoriality aspect is significant in relation to online child pornography. Owing to the variations in the definition of a child for the purposes of child pornography among different nations, combined with the principle of dual criminality that many jurisdictions still follow, lack of extraterritorial reach of domestic law can pose problems for prosecutions. The principle of dual criminality generally requires that, for offences committed abroad, the act should be an offence in both the jurisdiction where it occurred and where the perpetrator is normally resident (this could be citizenship, or in some cases ordinary residence would suffice). For instance, it is possible that someone travels to another jurisdiction with a lower age threshold of consent, for instance 16, whereas the age of consent for pornography in his home jurisdiction is 18, and produces a sexually explicit image of a 16-year-old. In this case the person would have committed an offence of producing an indecent photograph of a child as per

6 Art 3.

the law of his home jurisdiction, but would have committed no offence as per the law of the other country where the photograph was taken. The person would, of course, still be responsible for possessing an indecent image under the law of his home jurisdiction, which usually carries a lesser sentence than that for producing child pornography.[7] Strictly applying the traditional dual criminality rule would mean that it would be difficult to prosecute this person in his home jurisdiction, and given that there was no offence committed as per the law of the other jurisdiction there would obviously be no prospect of a prosecution in that country either. The requirement of extraterritoriality of relevant national laws as envisaged in the Optional Protocol would assist states to prosecute their citizens who travel with the intention of sexually abusing children to other countries where the laws are less developed or more lax. The UK, for instance, made some significant amendments to its domestic law in order to treat certain offences under section 72 of the Sexual Offences Act 2003 committed by UK nationals abroad to be treated as if they were committed within the UK.[8]

The Optional Protocol also requires states to criminalise the production, distribution, dissemination, importation, exportation, offering, selling or possession for the above purposes of child pornography.[9] It recommends international cooperation with governments, *vide* Article 10(1) which calls for multilateral, regional and bilateral agreements for the detection, investigation, prosecution and punishment of offenders guilty of child sexual exploitation. As with the UNCRC itself, the Optional Protocol also has proved to be a popular instrument, with 172 countries having signed and ratified it as of March 2016.[10]

The Cybercrime Convention

The Convention on Cybercrime of the Council of Europe[11] is a leading international legal instrument which contains specific provisions[12] to combat child pornography. The Convention is open for signature both by EU Member States and non-Member States which have participated in its elaboration, and for accession by other non-Member States. Article 9(2) stipulates that child pornography should be defined to include 'pornographic material that visually depicts … a minor engaged in sexually explicit conduct, a person appearing to be a minor engaged in sexually explicit conduct; and realistic images representing a minor engaged in sexually explicit conduct'. A 'minor' is defined as to include all persons under the age of 18

7 For example, in the UK the maximum penalty for the possession of child pornography is five years' imprisonment, whereas production is punishable up to a maximum of ten years. The relevant laws are discussed in more detail later in the chapter.

8 The amendments were made through the Criminal Justice and Immigration Act 2008, s 72.

9 Art 3(c).

10 See http://indicators.ohchr.org/, accessed 5 July 2018.

11 Convention on Cybercrime of the Council of Europe (CETS No.185), also known as the Budapest Convention.

12 These can be found under Title 3, 'Content related offences'.

years; if, however, a signatory state requires a lower age limit, there is some flexibility up to a lower limit of 16 years. Article 9(1) requires States Parties to criminalise

- the intentional production of child pornography for the purpose of its distribution through a computer system;
- offering or making available child pornography through a computer system;–
- distributing or transmitting child pornography through a computer system;
- procuring child pornography through a computer system; and
- possessing child pornography in a computer system or on a computer data storage medium.

As outlined in the Explanatory Report to the Cybercrime Convention, the provisions under Article 9 on child pornography are intended to 'strengthen protective measures for children, including their protection against sexual exploitation, by modernising criminal law provisions to more effectively circumscribe the use of computer systems in the commission of sexual offences against children'.[13]

> 'This provision responds to the preoccupation of Heads of State and Government of the Council of Europe, expressed at their 2nd summit (Strasbourg, 10–11 October 1997) in their Action Plan (item III.4) and corresponds to an international trend that seeks to ban child pornography, as evidenced by the recent adoption of the Optional Protocol to the UN Convention on the rights of the child, on the sale of children, child prostitution and child pornography and the recent European Commission initiative on combating sexual exploitation of children and child pornography (COM2000/854).'[14]

Whilst many states already had provisions that criminalise the production of child pornography within their domestic law, the role of the internet as the 'primary instrument' for trading such material and the need to incorporate specific provisions to combat the sexual exploitation of children within an international legal instrument was something which was recognised by the drafters of the Cybercrime Convention. Accordingly, the Convention stipulates specific offences for the production, offering and distribution of child pornography. In addition, the term 'procuring for oneself or for another' in para 1(d) is intended to also cover downloading of child pornography from the internet.[15]

The offence of possession of child pornography, regardless of the intention to distribute, is a significant step achieved by the Convention. This seems to be an

13 Council of Europe, *Explanatory Report to the Convention on Cybercrime* (2001) Budapest, para 91.

14 Ibid, para 92.

15 Ibid, para 97.

acknowledgement that possession of child pornography is very much an important aspect of effective regulatory strategy to combat its proliferation.[16] However, Article 9.4 also allows signatory states to opt out of criminalising the possession or the procurement of child pornography, which left a fairly sizeable gap given the importance of criminalising possession to meaningfully combating child pornography, particularly in the context of the internet – the significance of possession offences for combating online child pornography is discussed later in the chapter.

The Cybercrime Convention is one of the earliest international legal instruments to create specific criminal offences related to the production, distribution, accessing and possession of child pornography using a computer or the internet. The popularity and significance of the Convention is evidenced by the fact that a number of countries outside the Council of Europe have ratified it, which should in theory mean a wider harmonisation of the law internationally but for the exceptions contained within it.[17] For instance, whilst the criminalisation of simple possession is envisaged by the Convention, this is not mandatory as signatory states have the choice of opting out of this provision, which leaves a lacuna in terms of providing a consistent, robust regulatory framework to fight online child pornography internationally. A further drawback of the Convention is that it only specifically deals with child pornography in the context of computers and the internet, and offline versions are not within its remit.

The Lanzarote Convention

The Council of Europe, continuing its work in the important area of child protection, subsequently passed another Convention on the Protection of Children Against Sexual Exploitation and Sexual Abuse,[18] also known as the 'Lanzarote Convention', with a wider remit to address the various aspects of child abuse and sexual exploitation going beyond just child pornography. There are provisions within the Convention that criminalise the distribution and possession of child pornography (both online and offline),[19] including 'knowingly obtaining access, through information and communication technologies, to child pornography'.[20] The provision referring to 'obtaining access' should cover cases where someone does not download child pornography to the computer, but merely views or browses it using the computer. Whilst UK courts would regard accessing or browsing as 'making' child pornography, it is good practice for substantive law to

16 See para 98, '... the possession of child pornography stimulates demand for such material. An effective way to curtail the production of child pornography is to attach criminal consequences to the conduct of each participant in the chain from production to possession.'

17 For an up-to-date list, see https://www.coe.int/en/web/conventions/full-list/-/conventions/treaty/185/signatures?p_auth=KcDod03x, accessed 5 July 2018.

18 CETS 201.

19 Art 20.

20 Art 20.1(f).

be broader in scope and as technology-neutral as possible in terms of the activities that are criminalised.[21] In light of the different ways in which pornography can be accessed on the internet, it is pertinent to criminalise any form of intentional viewing, for example by browsing or accessing video streaming sites, without the requirement of active downloading to the computer.[22]

The Convention allows a signatory state to opt out of criminalising the production and possession of virtual child pornography defined as 'simulated representations or realistic depictions of a non-existent child' and the possession of pornography that was created by children who are above the age of consent, as long as the material was produced and possessed by them with their consent and solely for their private use.[23] This effectively makes the criminalisation of virtual child pornography optional for signatory states. The latter provision protects those who are under 18 but above the age of consent for sex (which is lower in many jurisdictions) in a relationship, who will not be prosecuted for taking or sending each other private pictures that would otherwise be regarded as child pornography. This would include what is commonly referred to as 'sexting', and the issues raised in the context of self-generated child pornography are examined in the final section of this chapter.

Article 21 requires signatory states to criminalise recruiting or coercing a child into participating in pornography and knowingly attending pornographic performances involving the participation of children. In addition, the Convention stipulates an offence titled 'corruption of children', to cause a child to witness sexual abuse or sexual activities regardless of having to participate themselves.[24] The Convention also addresses the potential for predators using the internet and communications technologies to groom children. Article 22 (solicitation of children for sexual purposes) criminalises any 'proposal through information and communication technologies' of an adult to meet a child for the purpose of engaging in sexual activities, where such proposal has been followed by 'material acts leading to such meeting'. The threat from paedophiles using the internet and information and communications technology (ICT) to groom children is a matter of grave concern for states and some jurisdictions had already legislated, including the United Kingdom, which created a specific offence of 'child grooming' through section 15 of the Sexual Offences Act 2003.[25] The Convention aims to combat child sex tourism, and to this end

21 UK courts have interpreted the term 'making' child pornography as encompassing downloading images to a computer as well as calling an image to the computer screen without the requirement of active downloading. See *R v Bowden* [2000] QB 88; *R v Smith; R v Jayson* [2003] 1 Cr App R 13. These cases are discussed in some detail later in the chapter.

22 Some countries already have specific 'access offences' which do not require active downloading, for example Canada and the United States, as discussed later in the chapter.

23 Art 20.3.

24 Art 22.

25 The accuracy of the term 'child grooming' for this offence is actually disputed. Section 15 of the Sexual Offences Act criminalises intentional meeting, or travelling/arranging to travel to

establishes that individuals can be prosecuted for some offences even when the act is committed abroad. The Convention also establishes victim support programmes and requires states to set up internet and telephone helplines for children.[26]

The Convention entered into force on 1 July 2010 and is an important source of international law in the context of child sexual exploitation. It enhances the protection afforded by the United Nations Convention on the Rights of the Child and its Optional Protocol on the sale of children, child prostitution and child pornography.

European Union

At the European level, a significant legal instrument relevant to child pornography is the European Union Directive on Combating the Sexual Abuse and Sexual Exploitation of Children and Child Pornography (Directive 2011/93/EU). The Directive replaced the Council Framework Decision 2004/68/JHA and in many ways builds on the Council of Europe Convention on the Protection of Children Against Sexual Exploitation and Sexual Abuse discussed above. The Directive specifically acknowledges the role of the internet and ICT in facilitating the increase of child pornography and child sexual exploitation.[27] In particular, the Directive acknowledges the use of social networking sites and chatrooms for the online solicitation of children for sexual purposes,[28] and requires Member States to criminalise such conduct.[29]

The Directive provides a broad definition of 'child pornography', which includes:[30]

- (i) any material that visually depicts a child engaged in real or simulated sexually explicit conduct;
- (ii) any depiction of the sexual organs of a child for primarily sexual purposes;
- (iii) any material that visually depicts any person appearing to be a child engaged in real or simulated sexually explicit conduct or any depiction of the sexual organs of any person appearing to be a child, for primarily sexual purposes; or
- (iv) realistic images of a child engaged in sexually explicit conduct or realistic images of the sexual organs of a child, for primarily sexual purposes;

meet a child following previous communication to commit a sexual offence under part 1 of the Act. This, in itself, is incapable of addressing child grooming. A new s 15A offence was subsequently added through the Serious Crimes Act 2015, criminalising 'sexual communication with a child', which addressed the gap in the law.

26 Art 13.
27 Recitals 3 and 12.
28 Recital 12.
29 Art 6.
30 Art 2(c).

Article 2(c)(iii) clearly covers pseudo-imagery, although Member States have discretion not to criminalise this category of material where the person featured in the image is actually 18 years of age or above *at the time of* depiction.[31] Article 2(c)(iv) would imply that the material needs only to convey a realistic impression that the person is a child, or sexual organs depicted are of a child. This would encompass material produced using computer technology, i.e., virtual child pornography, as long as it is realistic. There is, however, a 'private use' exception provided under Article 5(8) whereby Member States have discretion to criminalise such material produced or possessed solely for the producer's private use, provided that there is no risk of dissemination of the material. The flexibility generally afforded to criminalising virtual pornography in the instruments noted above can therefore also be seen in the Directive. The reasons for the slightly different treatment of virtual pornography are explored in further detail in Chapter 4.

The Directive aims to be otherwise comprehensive in that it criminalises the production, acquisition, possession, knowingly obtaining access by means of ICT, distribution, dissemination or transmission, and offering, supplying or making available of child pornography.[32] In addition, the Directive requires the criminalisation of causing, recruiting, coercing or forcing a child to participate in pornographic performances, or profiting from exploiting a child, and knowingly attending pornographic performances by a child.[33]

The key provision in the Directive, however, can be found in Article 25, aimed at websites containing child pornography. It calls for 'necessary measures to ensure the prompt removal of webpages containing or disseminating child pornography hosted in their territory' and 'to endeavour to obtain the removal of such pages' hosted abroad. In addition, the Article stipulates that access to such webpages should be blocked for internet users within the Member State's territory. Blocking as a regulatory tool, examined in further detail in Chapter 5, is naturally subject to controversy even in the context of child pornography. The safeguards that need to be adopted in conjunction with blocking access to webpages are set out in Article 25(2) which requires Member States to establish 'transparent procedures and provide adequate safeguards, in particular to ensure that the restriction is limited to what is necessary and proportionate, and that users are informed of the reason for the restriction' and to include the possibility of judicial redress. In light of the current regulatory model in many European states that largely adopt an 'identification and blocking' strategy, these provisions are particularly pertinent, as will be demonstrated in Chapter 5.

31 The exception is found in Art 5(7).
32 Art 5.
33 Art 4.

National law

A number of countries have enacted specific legislation to combat child pornography. Whilst some of these actually pre-date the internet, many regulatory initiatives were to respond to the challenges raised by the internet and digital technologies as well as to meet the obligations under the international instruments noted above. The standards, however, vary considerably around the globe. As of 2016, there were at least 35 countries that had no legislation at all specifically addressing child pornography.[34] This, whilst offering depressing news, is still a significant improvement compared to a decade ago: there were 95 countries in 2006 with no legislation in place specifically addressing child pornography.[35] As for the countries that have specific legislation, the nature and scope of legislation varies considerably. Of these, legislation in 60 countries does not define 'child pornography'[36] (for example, Thailand, Spain, Sri Lanka, Slovenia, Singapore, Qatar, Portugal, Pakistan, Lithuania, Indonesia, Kuwait, China, Egypt, Armenia), and there are 50 countries where the possession of child pornographic material regardless of intention to distribute or profit from it is not criminalised by legislation (for example, Russia, Malaysia, Mauritius, Paraguay, Saudi Arabia, Singapore, Rwanda, Tanzania, Tunisia).[37]

The United Kingdom is in many ways a pioneer in establishing a robust and comprehensive regulatory framework to combat child pornography on the internet, which criminalises the production, distribution and possession of all forms of child pornography including real, pseudo and virtual imagery. UK law will form the primary basis for my analysis in this chapter in order to examine how child pornography laws have evolved in the internet age.

Evolution of child pornography laws

Child pornography laws in the UK as we see them today have evolved over the last four decades, and to a significant extent in response to the challenges presented by the advent of the internet and advances in digital technology. In the UK, prior to the enactment of the Protection of Children Act 1978 (PCA), the primary basis for prosecuting child pornography cases was under the provisions of the Obscene Publications Act 1959, which was mainly concerned with the 'obscenity' of the material and was not specifically designed for combating child pornography. In other words, the focus of the law was on the images as such and their effect on the viewer, rather than the underlying harm caused to the child featured in the image. The law in this sense did not, for all practical

34 See International Centre for Missing & Exploited Children (ICMEC), *Child Pornography: Model legislation & Global Review*, 8th edn, 2016. Available at http://www.icmec.org/wp-content/uploads/2016/02/Child-Pornography-Model-Law-8th-Ed-Final-linked.pdf, accessed 5 July 2018.

35 Ibid.

36 For the full list see the ICMEC Model Legislation & Global Review, ibid.

37 Ibid.

purposes, differentiate between adult and child pornography. In fact, the Williams Committee Report,[38] which reviewed existing legislation on obscenity and indecency in 'publications, displays and entertainment' excluding broadcast material, did not find any evidence that child pornography was a growing issue at the time to merit *sui generis* legislation.[39] There were, however, calls from other quarters for specific legislation, including from the press and influential activists like Mary Whitehouse, then Chairperson of the National Viewers and Listeners Association, in 1977,[40] particularly following concerns in the United States about the rising problem of child sexual exploitation including the use of children in pornography. There was growing recognition that the existing legislation, the Obscene Publications Act 1959, was inadequate to respond to the specific problem of child pornography due to the Act concerning itself primarily with the effect of the material on the viewer (the 'deprave and corrupt test' for judging obscenity) rather than the effect that creating such images might have on the (child) participants themselves. Specific legislation to address child pornography was needed not only to prevent any indirect harm caused to the viewers (as is the case with the Obscene Publications Act 1959), but primarily to prevent the direct harm caused to the young and underage participants. Following the enactment of the PCA, it could be said that the law was no longer just concerned about the obscenity of the images *per se*, but it aimed to address the inherent harm caused to the child in the making of the image itself.[41]

Whilst the PCA specifically criminalised the production and distribution of child pornography, a possession offence targeting the viewer was not envisaged by this legislation, except for possession with intention to distribute further. It was only later, in 1988, that a simple possession offence was introduced through the Criminal Justice Act 1988, which made it an offence to possess child pornography regardless of intention to distribute further.[42] The definition of 'child pornography' at the time only covered real, and not computer-modified images of children. This left a loophole in light of the advent of the internet and digital technologies in that the law was not capable of addressing pseudo-images, for instance when images of the face of a child is digitally morphed onto the (nude) body of an adult to give an overall impression of a child posing nude or appearing in a sexualised context. Whilst pseudo child pornography may not cause actual physical harm to a child, in that there was no physical exploitation

38 Williams Committee Report, *Obscenity and Film Censorship* (Cmnd 7772, 1979) HMSO.

39 For a good overview of the recommendations of the Report see, Colin Manchester, 'A note on England's Proposals for Restricting and Prohibiting Pornography' (1979) 14 *University of Western Australia Law Revie*, Issues 1 & 2, 172–183.

40 *The Sunday Times*, 19 June 1977, as cited in Yaman Akdeniz, *Internet Child Pornography and the Law: National and International Responses* (Ashgate 2008) 18.

41 Prevention of harm as a justification of specific child pornography legislation is analysed in further detail later in the chapter.

42 Criminal Justice Act 1988, s 160.

involved during production, it could nonetheless result in mental and emotional harm due to the depiction of the child in such a grossly inappropriate manner, as discussed later in this chapter. In addition, the indecency of the image itself, due to the portrayal of a child in an abhorrent way, arguably justifies its prohibition.[43] In light of this, the UK extended the possession offence to pseudo photographs through the Criminal Justice and Public Order Act 1994.[44]

The latest change in the substantive law relating to child pornography occurred in 2009 with the enactment of the Coroners and Justice Act 2009, section 62 of which criminalised the possession of non-photographic sexualised representation of children. The new law was not intended to include real or pseudo-images of child sexual abuse (as these were already covered under existing law, mentioned above), but covers entirely non-photographic and computer-generated images. The virtual pornography offence has been subject to some criticism, particularly in light of the fact that there are no real children involved in its production (nor the face of a real child, as might be the case with pseudo photographs). The lack of any actual direct harm caused to a child therefore raised questions regarding the proportionality of criminalising its possession.[45] As discussed in Chapter 4 in greater detail, there are divergent views on the regulation of virtual child pornography and the law varies in different jurisdictions – for instance, an attempt to criminalise the possession of virtual child abuse imagery in the United States through the Child Pornography Prevention Act of 1996 resulted in the US Supreme Court, in *Ashcroft v Free Speech Coalition*,[46] holding the section criminalising computer-generated child pornography as unconstitutional due to the absence of actual direct harm caused to children.

There are different rationales and arguments for prohibiting the production, distribution and possession of child pornography and each of these merits separate analysis. As will be clear from the discussion below, the internet and digital technology has played a considerable role in what has now become a rather irreversible transformation of child pornography laws. It has, in the process, imposed unprecedented criminal liability on individual end users rather than just the publishers and distributors as was previously the case with

43 Suzanne Ost, 'Children at Risk: Legal and Societal Perceptions of the Potential Threat that the Possession of Child Pornography Poses to Society', (2002) 29(2) *Journal of Law and Society* 436–460.

44 Section 84 of the Criminal Justice and Public Order Act 1994 amended the Protection of Children Act 1978 which brought pseudo-photographs on a par with indecent photographs of children. It also amended the Criminal Justice Act 1988, thereby criminalising the possession of indecent pseudo-photographs.

45 See e.g., Brian Simpson, 'Controlling Fantasy in Cyberspace: Cartoons, Imagination and Child Pornography' (2009) 18(3) *Information and Communications Technology Law* 255–271; Suzanne Ost, 'Criminalising Fabricated Images of Child Pornography: a Matter of Harm or Morality?' (2010) 30(2) *Legal Studies* 230–256. For a discussion from a US perspective, see Paula Bird, 'Virtual Child Pornography Laws and the Constraints Imposed by the First Amendment' (2011) (16)(1) *Barry Law Review* 161–176.

46 *Ashcroft v Free Speech Coalition* 535 U.S. 234 (2002).

traditional forms of media. The following sections analyse the different stages of evolution of child pornography law, looking at the laws that specifically criminalise the production, distribution and possession of child pornography.

Production and distribution

Production

In terms of how the law relating to the production of child pornography has evolved, two key points are worth noting: first, by criminalising the production of child pornography the law has gone beyond focusing on the indecency or obscenity of the image, and recognised the harm inherent in creating child pornography. Whilst this aspect pre-dates the internet, as legislation addressing the production of child pornography already existed before the internet became 'main-stream', the rationale and importance of specifically criminalising the production of child pornography was nevertheless strengthened by the internet. Second, in what could be called as a classic example of the law adapting to the internet, judicial interpretation of production has meant that viewers of child pornography have effectively been rendered potentially liable for 'making' child pornography and not just 'possessing', as demonstrated in *R v Bowden*.[47] Both points are explored further below.

The law that specifically criminalises the production and distribution of child pornography in the UK is found in section 1 of the PCA, which creates a number of offences:

> (1) It is an offence for a person —
>
> (a) to take, or permit to be taken or to make, any indecent photograph or pseudo-photograph of a child; or
> (b) to distribute or show such indecent photographs or pseudo-photographs; or
> (c) to have in his possession such indecent photographs or pseudo-photographs, with a view to their being distributed or shown by himself or others; or
> (d) to publish or cause to be published any advertisement likely to be understood as conveying that the advertiser distributes or shows such indecent photographs or pseudo-photographs, or intends to do so.

Section 1 (a) is essentially the 'production offence' – i.e., taking or making an indecent photograph or pseudo-photograph of a child. This version of the section stated above is slightly different from the original wording as enacted in 1978, following a series of amendments made in response to the challenges raised

47 *R v Bowden* [2000] QB 88.

by the internet and digital technologies. An examination of the wording of section 1 will reveal that there is no reference to the term 'child pornography' – the relevant term for this purpose is 'indecent photographs' and 'indecent pseudo-photographs'. 'Indecent' is also not defined in the Act, but it is settled law that it is broader than the traditional concept of 'obscenity'. In *R v Kerr*[48] the Court of Appeal provided clarity to the meaning of the word 'indecent': a photograph will be indecent if ordinary people would consider it as such, by applying recognised standards of propriety. 'Photograph' has a wide meaning – it can include an indecent film, a copy of an indecent film, and an indecent photograph contained in a film.[49] A film for this purpose includes any form of video-recording.[50] References to a photograph include the negative as well as the positive version, and data stored on a computer disc or by other electronic means capable of conversion into a photograph.[51] 'Pseudo-photograph' is defined as an image, 'whether made by computer graphics or otherwise howsoever, which appears to be a photograph'.[52]

There are compelling reasons for criminalising the production of child pornography. As noted earlier, the focus of the Obscene Publications Act 1959 (and equivalent law elsewhere, for e.g. the *Miller*[53] test in the United States) is on the effect of the material on the viewer. In order to be treated as obscene, the material should be of such nature as to deprave and corrupt those who are likely to come across such material.[54] The possibility of any harm caused to the participants featured in the material itself was not the concern of traditional obscenity laws. This would generally work for adult pornography, where the participants are usually adults who are capable of consenting to the acts portrayed in the materials. There are, of course, instances where actual harm may have been caused or consent not provided in adult pornography, but such cases are left for other branches of the criminal law to deal with (for instance, the criminal law offence of assault or rape) and not envisaged within the remit of content offences as contained within the Obscene Publications Act 1959. Child pornography is fundamentally different in this context, in that the participants, being children, are not capable of providing consent to sexual acts (under UK law, where the participant is between the ages of 16 and 18, whilst they are of legal age of

48 *R v Kerr* [1988] 1 WLR 1098–1106.
49 Protection of Children Act 1978, s 7(2).
50 Protection of Children Act 1978, s 7(5).
51 Protection of Children Act 1978, s 7(4). The definition of 'photographs' was amended by s 84 (3)(b) of the Criminal Justice and Public Order Act 1994 to cover data stored on a computer disc/by electronic means.
52 Protection of Children Act 1978, s 7(7). Section 7(8) goes on to state that, 'If the impression conveyed by a pseudo-photograph is that the person shown is a child, the pseudo-photograph shall be treated for all purposes of this Act as showing a child and so shall a pseudo-photograph where the predominant impression conveyed is that the person shown is a child notwithstanding that some of the physical characteristics shown are those of an adult'.
53 *Miller v California* 413 U.S. 15 (1973).
54 Obscene Publications Act 1959, s 1.

consent for sex, the age of consent for sexually explicit photographs is 18, save for some limited exceptions). Therefore, as far as pornography involving real children is concerned, production would essentially involve the actual abuse of a child, which in itself justifies strong punitive measures in the form of substantive laws. In addition, there is evidence to suggest that recording the physical abuse aggravates the psychological harm suffered by the child.[55] The internet has exacerbated the possibility of such psychological harm. In the pre-internet era, an image or video in most cases would remain in the hands of the perpetrator, or at most distributed to a relatively small group of people. The potential for further global distribution on the internet at a previously unimaginable scale aggravates the psychological harm further, rendering it a matter of more serious concern. Apart from the potential for instantaneous distribution to a global network, there is also the risk of permanence in that once the material is made available on the internet, it could possibly remain somewhere forever, for instance in the hands of someone who has already downloaded it even if the material is successfully removed from all websites.[56] The potential risk of a permanent record of the abuse being left in the public domain for others to view for sexual purposes could mean a more long-lasting and severe psychological trauma for the child victims.[57] In this sense, the internet has necessitated a much stronger case for criminalising the production of child pornography due to the continuing harm it causes to the (child) victims of sexual abuse and exploitation. Producing child pornography, therefore, must be treated as a serious offence as stipulated by the various international instruments noted earlier. This position is generally reflected in the relevant national laws in many, if not all, jurisdictions.[58] It is perhaps fair to state

55 See Jennifer Martin and Ramona Alaggia, 'Sexual Abuse Images in Cyberspace: Expanding the Ecology of the Child' (2013) 22(4) *Journal of Child Sexual Abuse* 398–415; Max Taylor and Ethel Quale, *Child Pornography: An Internet Crime* (Brunner Routledge 2003) 24; Tink Palmer, 'Behind the Screen: Children who are the Subjects of Abusive Images', in Ethel Quayle and Max Taylor (Eds), *Viewing Child Pornography on the Internet: Understanding the Offence, Managing the Offender, Helping the Victim* (Russell House 2005) 61–74; Marcella Mary Leonard, '"I did what I was directed to do but he didn't touch me": The Impact of being a Victim of Internet Offending' (2010) 16(2) *Journal of Sexual Aggression* 249–256.

56 With advances in technology, such as Microsoft PhotoDNA, which uses a PhotoDNA signature, this works like a 'fingerprint' for an image and can be used to find copies of a particular image. Whilst such technology has the potential to identify copies of a particular image by matching the 'fingerprints', and therefore substantially reduce its availability on the wider internet that may otherwise go undetected, it cannot obviously stop an image being reproduced in the first instance, especially if a hard copy has already been made. PhotoDNA is used by leading hotlines such as the Internet Watch Foundation in the UK as well as by the National Centre for Missing and Exploited Children in the United States.

57 See Marcella Mary Leonard (n 55). See also Julia von Weiler, Annette Haardt-Becker and Simone Schulte, 'Care and Treatment of Child Victims of Child Pornographic Exploitation (CPE) in Germany' (2010) 16(2) *Journal of Sexual Aggression* 211–222.

58 See ICMEC report (n 34).

that in the internet age it is simply reckless and irresponsible for any state not to specifically criminalise the production of child pornography.

Pseudo-photographs

Digital technologies and the internet have contributed to the growth of pseudo child pornography, which, as noted earlier, has necessitated amendments to the law. Creating an indecent pseudo-photograph is now something within the reach of the non-expert individual with the assistance of the technology and the internet – for example, initially by downloading the pictures of a child and an explicit image of an adult on to one's computer and then using software (which ranges from basic 'Photoshop' to more sophisticated (and expensive) specialist software) to combine both images to create a new indecent photograph. Whilst creating a pseudo-photograph was still possible in the pre-internet era, for instance by simply pasting two photographs together with the face of a child and body of an adult, this was far from sophisticated. In addition, the potential for distribution would also have been rather limited at that time: the creator will in all likelihood keep the image for his/her own personal consumption or circulate it within a small group of like-minded individuals. The internet has obviously changed this by making it a lot easier to share the material anywhere in the world, necessitating a more robust legal response.

Pseudo-photographs were brought within the remit of child pornography offences through amendments made by section 84 of the Criminal Justice and Public Order Act 1994, following a Home Affairs Committee recommendation that advances in technology had left a loophole in successfully prosecuting child pornography cases where the images were pseudo-photographs not involving real images of children.[59] The amendment inserted the words 'to make' into section 1 (1)(a) of the PCA alongside the offence of 'to take' (an indecent photograph of a child). The scope of 'photographs' was also extended to include 'pseudo-photographs', thereby bringing pseudo-photographs on a par with real photographs of children.[60] Whilst the amendment was intended to specifically address pseudo-photographs, it has had some significant implications, with the courts interpreting the term 'to make' child pornography broadly to encompass downloading of images to the computer (including temporarily to the Random Access Memory or temporary internet cache) – practically rendering viewers liable for 'producing' pornography.[61] Following this legislative change, UK law now treats the production of pseudo child pornography on a par with real child pornography, although it may carry a lighter sentence. It is generally the case with pseudo-imagery that the child depicted will not have suffered any physical abuse during its production,

59 See Home Affairs Committee, *First Report on Computer Pornography*, London: HMSO 1994.

60 Protection of Children Act 1978, s 7.

61 This has been the position following the Court of Appeal decision in *R v Bowden* [2000] QB 88, discussed below.

as the images are typically created using computer modification or alteration of existing photographs. Therefore, it can be asked whether it is justifiable to criminalise pseudo-imagery on the same lines as real child pornography. Whilst it is true that there might not have been any physical abuse perpetrated on the child depicted in the image during its creation, it cannot be disputed that there is still clear *exploitation* due to the child's being portrayed in an inappropriate sexually explicit manner. It can result in psychological harm to the child, which would justify criminalising the production of such material.[62] It is, of course, arguable that if the victim is not aware of the existence of the photograph, it cannot result in any psychological harm to the child. However, as Wolak et al argue, child pornography is not a victimless crime and the children pictured in the images are victims of exploitation.[63] In the case of pseudo imagery, a child is being used, without his/her knowledge, in producing child pornography. In this sense, pseudo-imagery is a product of a form of sexual exploitation.[64] There is an element of harm inherent in the image, which subsists regardless of whether the child is aware the image was made or circulated. As Rogers points out, 'those who create, trade, and view child pornography harm the child's inherent right of human dignity not to be viewed in this fashion', which is 'violated each and every time an image is made and circulated'.[65] Some commentators also argue that the creation of 'inherently private images of children undermine the sexual autonomy and identity of the child', which justifies making this an offence.[66] The justifications for criminalising indecent pseudo-photographs of children are examined later in the chapter in the context of possession offences, where some of these issues will be explored further.

The UK position is essentially that the lack of physical abuse in producing pseudo-photographs does not necessarily diminish the gravity of the offence – pseudo-pornography still portrays children in an abhorrent manner with a real risk of psychological harm to the child.

62 See Max Taylor and Ethel Quayle, *Child Pornography: An Internet Crime* (Brunner-Routledge 2003). See also Ethel Quale, Lars Loof and Tink Palmer, *Child Pornography and Sexual Exploitation of Children Online* (ECPAT International 2008); Tink Palmer, 'Behind the Screen: Children who are the Subjects of Abusive Images', in Ethel Quale and Max Taylor (eds) *Viewing Child Pornography on the Internet* (Russell House 2005); Peter J King, 'No Plaything: Ethical Issues Concerning Child-Pornography' (2008) 11(3) *Ethical Theory and Moral Practice* 327–245.

63 See Janis Wolak, Marc Liberatore, Brian Neil Levine, 'Measuring a Year of Child Pornography Trafficking by U.S. Computers on a Peer-to-Peer Network' (2014) 38 *Child Abuse and Neglect* 347–356. See also Janis Wolak, David Finkelhor, Kimberly J Mitchell, 'The Varieties of Child Pornography Production', in Ethel Quale and Max Taylor (Eds) *Viewing Child Pornography on the Internet* (Russell House 2005).

64 See Audrey Rogers, 'The Dignitary Harm of Child Pornography – From Producers to Possessors', in Carissa Byrne Hessick (Ed.), *Refining Child Pornography Law: Crime, Language and Social Consequences* (University of Michigan Press 2016) 171.

65 Ibid, 177.

66 Gillespie (n 5) 31.

The 'making' offence: consumption constituting production

Producing child pornography in its literal sense should mean the creation of entirely new material, but in what appears to be a classic example of law adapting to the challenges raised by technology, the courts have accorded a broad interpretation to the meaning of 'to make' an indecent photograph under section 1 of the PCA. *R v Bowden*[67] is the landmark case in this regard, which effectively extended the scope of the production offence with the result that those who had nothing to do with the original creation of the material can be held liable for 'making' child pornography for simply downloading from the internet. *Bowden* has also arguably blurred the distinction between the offences of 'making' an indecent photograph and the (separate) offence of simple possession, as examined further below.

In *Bowden*, the accused had downloaded indecent photographs of children from the internet, some of which he stored on disc and some he printed. He was convicted in the Crown Court at Cambridge on a guilty plea to the 'making' of indecent photographs of children contrary to section 1(1)(a) of the PCA. He later appealed against his conviction on the ground that the judge was wrong to rule that he was guilty of 'making' photographs, contending that he was merely in possession of the photographs. The Court of Appeal dismissed the appeal, holding that the PCA was concerned not only with the original creation of indecent images, but also with their proliferation. The appellant argued that the word 'make' should apply only to pseudo-photographs, i.e., a 'true construction' of section 1(1)(a) should mean that the conduct criminalised is either 'taking' a photograph; or 'making' a pseudo-photograph. It was also argued, alternatively, that the verb 'make' is used in the sense of 'create', and should not therefore be interpreted to encompass mere down-loading or printing out of computer data.[68] During the trial, the agreed statement of facts said that 'it is not part of the Crown's case that the defendant created for the first time any image that did not already exist in a visually identical form'. A key argument of the appellant, therefore, was that he was not guilty of 'making' photographs contrary to section 1 of the Act.

The Court of Appeal found these to be interesting arguments, but declined to accept them. The court took the view that the amended section was clear and unambiguous in its true construction as it simply renders the making of a photograph or pseudo-photograph unlawful. The words 'take' or 'make' are not defined in the legislation, and the court therefore would construe the words upon their natural, literary meaning. Citing the Oxford English Dictionary, which defines the verb 'make' as 'to cause to exist; to produce by action, to bring about', the court observed that such a meaning applies not only to original photographs, but by virtue of section 7 also to negatives, copies[69] of photographs

67 *R v Bowden* [2000] 2 All ER 418.

68 Ibid, para 443.

69 Section 7(2), 'References to an indecent photographs include ... a copy of an indecent photograph'.

and data stored on computer disk. As the definition of an indecent photograph also encompasses copies of an indecent photograph, a liberal interpretation of section 1(1) would mean that one could be 'making' an indecent photograph by creating a new copy of that image. The court accepted the submission of the counsel for the respondent:

> A person who either downloads images onto a disk or who prints them off is making them. The Act is not only concerned with the original creation of images, but also their proliferation. Photographs or pseudo-photographs found on the Internet may have originated from outside the United Kingdom; to download or print within the jurisdiction is to create new material which hitherto may not have existed therein.[70]

The appeal was therefore dismissed, thereby establishing that downloading an image meant that an image was being *made* (stored in the hard disk on defendant's computer) contrary to section 1 of the PCA.

Bowden has been subject to some academic criticism.[71] The significance of the decision in *Bowden* is that it effectively rendered the relevance of the (separate) offence of possession under the Criminal Justice Act 1988 unclear, at least in the context of the internet and computers. If it is possible to interpret the downloading or accessing of child pornography as 'making' child pornography, why have a separate offence for possession in the first place? Akdeniz is critical of this outcome[72] and argues that extending the scope of 'making' to encompass downloading images is problematic – Bowden did not 'create' the images himself as he did not take the photographs, but was merely accessing them on the internet and making copies of *existing* images. Akdeniz is uncomfortable, therefore, with regarding Bowden as the original 'creator' of images and suggests that, citing relevant Parliamentary discussion, the intention of Parliament was mainly to criminalise the 'making of pseudo-photographs' and there was nothing to suggest that making a copy of an existing indecent image by downloading would be encompassed within the new section 1 offence.[73] He concludes that *Bowden* should have been treated as a case of possession, and due to the approach the court has taken, the case has effectively blurred the distinction between simple possession offences and the more serious offence of production.

Gillespie, however, rationalises *Bowden* as a policy decision.[74] At the time *Bowden* was decided, the maximum punishment possible for possession under

70 *R v Bowden* [2000] 2 All ER 418, para 445

71 See for example David Ormerod, 'Indecent Photographs of Children: Making an Indecent Photograph of a Child whether Breach of European Convention on Human Rights, Articles 8 and 10' (2001) *Criminal Law Review* 657–659.

72 Yaman Akdeniz, *Internet Child Pornography and the Law: National and International Responses* (Ashgate 2008) 50.

73 Ibid.

74 Gillespie (n 5) 122.

the Criminal Justice Act 1988 was only six months, whereas the 'making' offence under the PCA provided for a maximum sentence of three years. He argues that *Bowden* was a decision influenced by a desire to award an appropriate sentence.[75] This must be correct. Simple possession now carries a maximum sentence of five years' imprisonment following amendments made by the Criminal Justice and Courts Services Act 2000. The current guidelines by the Sentencing Council for England and Wales for child pornography offences recommend that making an image by simply downloading should be treated as possession for the purpose of sentencing.[76] Whilst sentencing is a complex matter as part of which courts consider a range of factors, it is also true that not awarding a sentence that reflects the gravity of the crime carries the risk of trivialising the offence. This would be most counter-productive in relation to child pornography, something which the court may have rightly factored in whilst reaching its decision in *Bowden*.[77]

The insertion of a 'making' offence was in all likelihood intended to address directly the specific issue of pseudo-photographs, as argued by Akdeniz. The court seems to have responded to new challenges and threats emanating from technological innovation by being innovative itself in applying the law. In many ways, the decision in *Bowden* demonstrates that the judiciary are not willing to tolerate child pornography and tend to make full use of existing legislation to send a strong message to society regarding the unacceptability of such material. In the process, *Bowden* has effectively rendered the end consumer liable for 'production', without actually 'producing' child pornography, leaving the distinction between a traditional 'producer' and 'consumer' of content blurred in the context of the internet. The onus imposed on the consumer of content was unprecedented – viewers of child pornography are no longer passive recipients of content, but in the eyes of the law are now treated as active 'creators' of indecent images, which marks a step change in the overall regulatory approach.

Email communication and browsing

Whilst *Bowden* involved active downloading and/or printing of images, merely viewing images without actively downloading it to a computer, for example on

75 Ibid. The Criminal Justice and Court Services Act 2000 subsequently amended the possession offence by extending the maximum sentence to five years, which means that courts can now pass longer sentences for simple possession.

76 Sentencing Council, *Sexual Offences Definitive Guideline*, April 2014, at 76. See https://www.sentencingcouncil.org.uk/wp-content/uploads/Aug-2015-Sexual-Offences-Definitive-Guideline-web.pdf, accessed 6 July 2018.

77 It is also worth noting that there are counter-arguments in relation to the severity of sentencing, mostly from a US perspective where the federal sentencing guidelines have progressively created harsher sentencing regimes for child pornography offences. See M Hamilton, 'The Efficacy of Severe Child Pornography Sentencing: Empirical Validity or Political Rhetoric?' (2011) 22(2) *Stanford Law and Policy Review* 545–585; Carisa Byrne Hessick, 'Post-*Booker* Leniency in Child Pornography Sentencing' (2011) 24(2) *Federal Sentencing Reporter* 87–92.

video streaming websites, raises further issues. A further question to consider is in relation to indecent photographs received by email – following *Bowden*, is it possible that someone who receives an email attachment is guilty of making child pornography? It is interesting to note how the law has treated these two issues, which were addressed in the case (conjoined appeal) of *R v Smith; R and Jayson*.[78] In both cases the appellants were convicted of the offence of making an indecent photograph of a child under section 1(1) of the PCA.

Email communication

In *Smith*, the appellant had opened an email attachment sent to him containing the indecent image of a child. Smith argued that he did not 'make' the image within the meaning of section 1(1), as all he had done was merely to open the attachment to the email and look at the images, without doing anything beyond 'an intentional act in simply accepting the e-mail and opening the attachment'. Even though the image was not saved to a file or directory, it was nevertheless saved in the temporary internet cache owing to the way the computer functions. He argued that the offence of making an indecent photograph could not be committed merely because the computer automatically downloaded a copy to the cache of the computer, where no 'conscious or deliberate downloading' took place.

The court considered the *mens rea* of the offence at some length. Whilst the fact that Smith had on previous occasions solicited such images pointed to evidence that he had an interest in 'the material of the kind received by way of the attachment', there was nothing to suggest that he had, in fact, sought the particular images in question. The court noted, citing Simon Browns LJ in *Atkins v DPP*,[79] that the offence of making an indecent photograph under section 1(1) of the PCA and the offence of possession under section 160(1) of the Criminal Justice Act are not absolute offences.[80] Therefore,

> 'if the appellant had not known that the attachment contained or was likely to contain indecent photographs of pseudo-photographs of a child, he could not be guilty of the offence of making those photographs or pseudo-photographs when he opened the e-mail and its attachments. Nor could he have been guilty of making the photographs by the automatic storing of them in the cache if he was unaware of the existence of the cache'.[81]

78 *R v Smith; R v Jayson* [2003] 1 Cr App R 13.

79 *Atkins v Director of Public Prosecutions; Goodland v Director of Public Prosecutions* [2002] 2 Cr App R 248.

80 It was held in *Atkins* that the offence of making did not encompass the unintentional making of copies by images being automatically stored in the cache; and the offence of being in possession did not encompass having images stored in the cache, the existence of which was unknown to the appellant.

81 *R v Smith; R v Jayson* [2003] 1 Cr App R 13, para 19.

However, as there was evidence that Smith had in the past solicited and shared images of such nature, which was exacerbated by the fact that he had not deleted any of the images in question and left these in his inbox, the court was reluctant to consider him as an unsuspecting, innocent person who opened an unsolicited email or attachment unaware of what it contained. The court also rejected his argument in relation to automatic downloading, by noting that the matter was settled, correctly, in *Bowden*. The appeal was therefore dismissed.

The decision settled the law in relation to indecent photographs received by unsolicited emails. It is clear following *Smith* that whether an offence was committed under section 1(1) of the PCA or section 160(1) of the Criminal Justice Act 1988 will depend on the recipient's knowledge of the actual, or likely, nature of the contents. If an innocent person opens an attachment without such knowledge, no offence of making an indecent photograph or a pseudo-photograph contrary to section 1(1) of the PCA, nor the offence of possession contrary to section 160(1) Criminal Justice Act 1988 is committed by opening the attachment, or by the automatic storing of the content in the cache if the person is unaware of the existence of the cache. In practice, this would mean that it would be more difficult for someone to avoid liability if they stored the email upon discovering its content rather than deleting it.[82]

Browsing

In *Jayson*, the appellant was convicted on seven counts of making an indecent photograph of a child. The images were not specifically actively downloaded to a folder in the hard disk, but were found in the temporary internet cache of his computer, which was downloaded automatically when the images appeared on the screen while browsing. Jayson deliberately sought the images in question, and admitted that he was aware of how the internet cache operates. The prosecution based its argument on two counts: searching the World Wide Web and selecting images to appear on the computer screen was sufficient to amount to 'making'; or, the fact that images were stored automatically in the temporary internet cache amounted to 'making' an indecent photograph of a child.

A central argument advanced by Jayson focused on section 7(4)(b) of the PCA, which refers to a photograph as including 'data stored on a computer disk or by other electronic means which is capable of conversion to a photograph'.[83] His contention was that the word 'stored' implies a requirement that the electronic data be retained for future use and in order to enable subsequent retrieval. He argued that in order to be guilty of the offence of making a photograph or pseudo-photograph by causing data to be stored on a computer disk, it is necessary that there be *mens rea*, i.e. the intention to store and subsequently to retrieve the material. He pointed out that the images that

82 For a case comment, see David C Ormerod and Glenda Vencatachellum, 'Indecent of Children' (2002) *Criminal Law Review* 659–663.

83 Protection of Children Act 1978, s 7(4)(b).

appeared on the screen would remain in the computer's random access memory only while they were being viewed, and in relation to the images stored in the temporary cache, as these were not saved in a specific directory no intention could be inferred to retrieve them subsequently – and therefore it could not be said that he intended subsequent retrieval in relation to either of the methods relied on by the prosecution. Citing *Atkins v DPP*, he argued that *Atkins* was decided on the basis that Atkins had 'made' the photographs by actively downloading them into a directory and into the cache, but not merely downloading them on to the screen, although it was undoubtedly the case that the images had appeared on the screen (a deliberate act) when he was browsing the internet. The Court of Appeal rejected these arguments and held that the act of voluntarily downloading an indecent photograph from a website onto the computer screen is an act of making a photograph (or pseudo-photograph) following *Bowden*. The court went on to say:

> 'We reach that conclusion as a matter of the ordinary use of language, and giving to the word "make" its ordinary and natural meaning, as did this court in Bowden. By downloading the image, the operator is creating or causing the image to exist on the computer screen. The image may remain on the screen for a second or for a much longer period. Whether its creation amounts to an act of making cannot be determined by the length of time that the image remains on the screen.'[84]

It should be noted that in *Atkins* it was not at issue whether the mere act of downloading the images on to the screen in itself was an act of 'making' the photographs. The allegation in Atkins was that he had made the photographs by downloading them into a directory and into the cache, not by downloading them on to the screen. The court in *Atkins*, therefore, did not have to consider whether downloading the photograph to the screen amounts to 'making' an indecent photograph contrary to section 1(1) of the PCA. The decision in *Jayson* brought clarity in this regard, thereby extending the scope of 'making' an indecent photograph to encompass browsing material on the internet without the requirement of active downloading.

On the point of storage of data as per section 7(4) PCA, the court rejected Jayson's argument and held that it is merely a part of the definition of a photograph and has nothing to do with what constitutes making a photograph, which is a separate question altogether. The *mens rea* necessary to constitute the offence is, in fact, that the act of making the photograph should be deliberate and intentional with knowledge that the image is, or is likely to be, an indecent photograph or pseudo-photograph of a child.

> 'We note in any event that the requirement in s. 7(4)(b) is that data stored on a computer disc or by other electronic means "should be

84 *R v Smith; R v Jayson* [2002] EWCA Crim 683, para 33.

capable of conversion into a photograph". It is not a requirement that the data should be retrievable.' (Para 35)

'We conclude, therefore, that the trial judge was right to rule that the act of downloading the images from the Internet to the screen of the appellant's computer was an act of making an indecent photograph provided that the requisite mens rea was present. That mens rea was as we have described; it did not require an intention on the part of the maker to store the images with a view to future retrieval.' (Para 36)

The appeal was therefore dismissed. Both *Smith* and *Jayson* confirmed the previous broad interpretation of the 'making' offence in *Bowden*. It does not seem plausible that the lawmakers had envisaged such a wide interpretation of the offence by inserting the word 'make' to section1(1) of the PCA, which was primarily done to respond to the new challenges raised for child pornography by the internet and digital technologies. It is perhaps inconceivable that, prior to this amendment, courts would have been able to rule that downloading an image on to the screen (or the cache), or even actively to a computer would amount to a production offence. It is certainly the inclusion of the word 'make' that has given the courts such flexibility, as the word 'take' (an indecent photograph) is unlikely to be accorded such wide meaning on a literal construction.[85] These developments mean that those who consume child pornography on the internet are, from a legal perspective, effectively treated as producers of content regardless of their physical involvement in its production.

The approach in *Bowden, Atkins,* and *Smith* and *Jayson*, however, raises the question: what is the purpose or relevance of a simple possession offence, at least from an internet or computer perspective, if existing legislation governing the production of child pornography has already been interpreted so broadly? A separate offence for simple possession is still extremely important, the justifications for which are considered later in the chapter. It should also be noted that the broader interpretation of the 'making' offence is the invention of courts in the UK and may not necessarily be followed in other jurisdictions. In practice, however, prosecutors tend to prefer charging on the basis of a 'making' offence rather than on the basis of simple possession. The reason for this will be explained later, and will be easier to decipher once we understand how the offence of possession works in practice.

Distribution

It should be clear by now why the production of child pornography should be specifically criminalised, and also how the law has evolved in this respect in light of the challenges posed by the internet and digital technologies. It is only logical

85 Interestingly, there is no corresponding 'making' offence for virtual child pornography or for adult extreme pornography in the UK, which raises another set of issues – these are discussed in Chapters 4 and 6 respectively.

that the act of dissemination of child pornography should also be criminalised owing to the continuing harm that further distribution would cause to the subject of the image. The harms stemming from recording the sexual abuse and exploitation of children and the psychological harm associated with the images perpetuating on the internet has already been discussed and will not be repeated here. Distributors are complicit in the continuing harm caused to the child. Each act of distribution contributes to the collective harm to which all distributors and downloaders contribute. This is regardless of whether a victim is aware of a particular act of distribution; victims live with a constant, overwhelming realisation that 'many people have access to the images', and that 'anyone could be viewing them at any time of the day'.[86] Distribution of child pornography is not a victimless crime – the children depicted in the image are victims of abuse or, in the case of pseudo-imagery, exploitation.[87] In addition, Ost argues that distribution amounts to an intrusion upon the victim's privacy and dignity, and the wrong which occurs when distributors exploit the child's abuse by making it available for others to view and download is irrespective of the victim's being aware of them.[88] The internet enables instantaneous distribution of content globally which can be done using various methods ranging from email communication, peer-to-peer technology, as well as by posting the material on websites, social media and shared on the 'dark web'. As technology continues to evolve, the law has to ensure that its remit encompasses not only the current distribution models, but also those that will inevitably evolve in the future. It is important, therefore, that the legal definitions are technology-neutral and flexible in order to accommodate any changes in technology that may impact on the methods of distribution.

In the UK, material depicting real children in a sexual context will certainly be classed as 'obscene' and the its publication and distribution was therefore already an offence under the traditional Obscene Publications Act.[89] A more specific offence addressing the distribution of child pornography was necessary for similar reasons, outlined earlier in the context of criminalising production, and in particular in order to prevent secondary harm caused to the child depicted in the image. This was achieved under section 1(1)(b) of the PCA, which makes it an offence to 'distribute or show' indecent images of children. In addition, section 1(1)(c) of the Act makes it an offence to be in possession of indecent images with a view to distributing or showing to others. There is an overlap between the offences in section 1(1)(b) and section 1(1)(c), and as Gillespie has pointed out, it is the latter that seems to be the more frequently

86 See Leonard, (n 55) 252.

87 See Janis Wolak, Marc Liberatore, Brian Neil Levine, 'Measuring a Year of Child Pornography Trafficking by U.S. Computers on a Peer-to-Peer Network' (2014) 38 *Child Abuse and Neglect* 347–356.

88 Suzanne Ost, 'A New Paradigm of Reparation for Victims of Child Pornography' (2016) 36(4) *Legal Studies* 613–638 at 619.

89 Obscene Publications Act 1959, s 1.

applied in cases.[90] 'Distribution' is provided with a broad and technology-neutral definition in section 1(2):

> For the purposes of this Act, a person is to be regarded as distributing an indecent photograph if he parts with possession of it to, or exposes or offers it for acquisition by, another person.

It is worth briefly examining how the law addresses the different methods of distribution that the internet facilitates. The offence of 'showing' has been interpreted by the Court of Appeal as the act of displaying the material to another, and is therefore fairly straightforward.[91] It would also be relatively uncomplicated to apply the offence where someone sends an image to another by email. A particular issue to consider, however, is how the law has responded to instances of simply making the material available for others to access, rather than actively sending it. This is pertinent especially in the context of peer-to-peer technology where one does not need to actively send files to another person, but only makes them available by placing the files in their 'shared folder' from which others can download the material. Peer-to-peer networks are considered to be a major source of distribution of child pornography.[92]

A leading case in this context is *R v Fellows and Arnold*,[93] where the first appellant stored indecent images of children in a data archive on his employer's computer. The images could be accessed by a password which the first appellant provided to other users who could then access the archive through the internet. He chose the recipients on the basis of those who were vouched for by existing password holders, or who provided additional similar images for the archive. The first appellant was convicted of four offences of having in his possession indecent photographs of children with a view to their being distributed or shown by himself or others, contrary to section 1(1)(c) of the PCA, and of one offence of publishing an obscene article contrary to section 2 (1) of the Obscene Publications Act 1959. The second appellant was convicted of three offences of distributing or showing indecent photographs of children contrary to section 1(1)(b) of the PCA. They appealed on the ground, *inter alia*, that simply making the images available for other users to download does not amount to 'distributing or showing' as there was no positive action from their side to distribute or show the material. The Court of Appeal held that by permitting others to access the database containing child pornography operated by the appellant, he was effectively taking a positive action to show and distribute the material contrary to section

90 Gillespie (n 5)130.
91 *R v ET* [1999] Crim LR 749.
92 See Wolak, Liberatore, Levine (n 87) 347–356.
93 *R v Fellows and Arnold* [1997] 1 Cr LR 524.

1(1)(c) of the PCA.[94] The court agreed with the analogy drawn by the trial court that this was similar to providing a key to a library displaying pictures, which amounts to 'showing' –

> 'giving the password enabling others to have access to the archive was equivalent to giving them the key to a library where the picture was exposed, so that the recipients could enter the library in order to look at the picture, and that this would amount to "showing" the picture to those persons, and perhaps "distributing" it also, although for the purposes of distribution some more active participation might be required.'[95]

In the later case of *R v Dooley*,[96] the Court of Appeal held that distribution need not be the sole or primary reason for leaving the images in the shared folder, as long as one of the reasons is to enable others to access the images. For someone who knows how peer-to-peer technology works, it would be fairly evident from the fact of having left the images in the 'shared' folder that the purpose is to allow others to access the files and this is therefore the correct approach.

The intentional distribution of child pornography should undoubtedly be treated as a serious offence, especially in light of the multiple modes of distribution facilitated by the internet, and the continuing and aggravated harm it causes to children. Courts in the UK have taken a strict approach in interpreting and applying the law to the internet environment. For example, section 1(d) of the PCA criminalises the publishing or causing to publish any advertisement likely to be understood as conveying that the advertiser distributes or shows such indecent photographs or pseudo-photographs. Courts have accepted the common law offence of incitement[97] as the basis to convict someone who placed an order in response to an advertisement which offered the supply of child pornography, regardless of the willingness of the advertiser to supply them[98] or whether the order was processed entirely automatically by means of a computer.[99] In both cases the businesses were based abroad, and the court was willing to 'stretch the law' of general incitement for what some commentators consider 'public policy reasons'.[100]

In spite of robust responses by the law, challenges do remain, especially in relation to content distributed through the dark web and encrypted email services

94 Ibid.
95 For an excellent analysis of the (unreported) trial court's ruling, see Colin Manchester, 'More about Computer Pornography' *Criminal Law Review* (September 1996) 645, which the Court of Appeal cited extensively in their judgment.
96 [2005] EWCA Crim 3093.
97 The common law offence of incitement has now been replaced by the Serious Crimes Act 2007, Part 2.
98 See *R v Goldman* [2001] EWCA Crim 1684.
99 *R (on the application of O'Shea) v Coventry Magistrates Court* [2004] EWHC 905 Admin.
100 For a good analysis see Gillespie (n 5)133–137.

(for example, 'protonmail'). The increasing use of mobile devices to exchange child pornography and the development of advanced and default encryption also make it more difficult to detect content and identify offenders.[101] Some of the issues related to identification are considered in Chapter 5 in the context of enforcement of child pornography laws.

Possession

It should be clear by now that the law relating to the production and distribution of child pornography have undergone considerable changes in light of the challenges posed by the internet and digital technologies. Criminalising the possession of indecent images of children, however, is perhaps the most significant change seen in the legislative landscape of pornography. The possession offence for pornography is a relatively new concept as traditionally obscene material was regulated at the point of supply rather than consumption. As noted earlier, when legislation was introduced in England and Wales for child pornography in the form of the PCA, a simple possession offence was not envisaged. Whilst it was an offence to be in possession of indecent images of children with a view to distribute, as discussed earlier, merely possessing it for private consumption was not an offence.[102] It was not later until the late 1980s that the mere possession of child pornography, regardless of intention to distribute, was criminalised under section 160(1) of the Criminal Justice Act 1988. The law for the first time imposed criminal liability on the consumer of obscene content, thereby criminalising conduct essentially carried out in private.

It is not clear whether the internet itself was the reason for introducing a possession offence for child pornography in the United Kingdom as the internet had not yet become so widely used back then in terms of dissemination and sharing of child pornography. A Parliamentary Home Affairs Committee which inquired into the newer threats raised by 'computer pornography' did not specifically assess the impact of the internet, as the main concern at the time was the circulation of obscene and illegal material through the then common methods of storage and distribution such as floppy discs and CD-ROMS and publications in electronic format. The Committee reported back to Parliament recommending a series of changes to existing legislation.[103] Existing laws were accordingly amended subsequent to the Report. The Criminal Justice Act 1988 was amended to extend the simple possession offence to pseudo-photographs,

101 US Department of Justice, *The National Strategy for Child Exploitation Prevention and Interdiction: A Report to Congress*, April 2016, Washington DC. The report identifies that the anonymity offered by 'the dark internet' 'emboldens users to commit more egregious offences than are seen on traditional platforms' (at 71). Available at https://www.justice.gov/psc/national-strategy-child-exploitation-prevention-and-interdiction, accessed 6 July 2018.

102 Protection of Children Act 1978, s 1(1)(c).

103 Home Affairs Committee, *First Report on Computer Pornography*, London HMSO, 1994.

and the definition of indecent images of children within the PCA was amended to include computer-generated photographs and images of children, as noted earlier.[104] Whist these changes in the law were more in response to challenges raised by broader 'computer pornography' rather than the internet *per se*, this turned out to be a timely legislative initiative as the internet had started becoming more popular in the 1990s, and the availability and distribution of child pornography also became more prevalent and a growing concern for the law enforcement authorities.[105]

There are a number of reasons why the possession of child pornography should be criminalised, which are discussed in more detail later in the chapter. Establishing meaningful and enforceable substantive law that sends a strong message to society that child pornography is unacceptable is one of the main purposes of a possession offence. Whilst legislation is not the only solution for effectively combating child pornography in cyberspace, it nevertheless remains an indispensable regulatory tool. Clear, proportionate and enforceable laws supported by appropriate criminal sanctions are quintessential for meaningful regulation of illegal content in cyberspace, and simple possession offences for child pornography should be examined in this context.

Meaning of 'possession'

The offence of simple possession is contained within section 160(1) of the Criminal Justice Act 1988, which reads:

> (1) Subject to section 160A, it is an offence for a person to have any indecent photograph or pseudo-photograph of a child in his possession.

The definitions for 'photograph', 'pseudo-photograph', and 'child' are the same as in the PCA.[106] Whilst the law criminalised simple possession, the word 'possession' itself is not defined within any legislation pertaining to child pornography. In the days following the introduction of the offence there was a fair amount of confusion and lack of clarity as to what exactly constitutes possession in a digital context. In the tradition of common law, early cases attempted to provide clarity on the meaning of 'possession' in the context of digital imagery, as set out below.

Knowledge

Logic dictates that actual knowledge of possession of the offending material should be a key element of the offence. This is particularly so in relation to information received

104 Criminal Justice and Public Order Act 1994, s 84(4).
105 For an analysis of the statistics of prosecutions under the new offences, see Akdeniz (n 72).
106 Section 160(4), Criminal Justice Act 1988.

unbidden on a computer device, for example by way of unsolicited communication, or illegal content inadvertently stumbled upon while searching for lawful material online, copies of which would nevertheless be stored by the browser software in the cache of the computer. It would be harsh if the law would punish those whose computers may have stored transient copies of illegal content in such cases.

The law recognises these possibilities and has provided certain defences under section 160(2) of the Criminal Justice Act 1988. It is a defence if the person 'had not himself seen the photograph or pseudo-photograph and did not know, nor had any cause to suspect, it to be indecent'.[107] Case law has provided further clarity for this provision in *Atkins v DPP*,[108] by holding that the unknowing possession of images can be a legitimate defence, where Simon Brown LJ noted (referring to section 160(2)(b)):

> '... it seems to me indeed that the very fact that Parliament created a defence for those possessing photographs reasonably not known to be indecent, strongly suggests that there was no intention to criminalise unknowing possession of photographs in the first place.'[109]

This would mean that for possession of an indecent photograph to be proved, it is necessary to establish some knowledge of its existence. If images are automatically stored without the defendant's knowledge in the cache of the computer, of which he is also unaware, no knowledge could be inferred merely because the images are retrievable by someone who possesses the skill to do it.

A further defence is available in relation to material received by means of unsolicited communications, where 'possession' depends on two factors: (i) whether the material was actually received without any prior solicitation by or on behalf of the defendant, and (ii) the defendant does not keep it for an unreasonable time.[110] *R v Smith and Jayson*[111] clarified that it would be a valid defence if the recipient was, before opening the attachment, unaware that it contained or was likely to contain, an indecent image.[112] This means that if the recipient did not possess actual knowledge of the existence, or of the likelihood of the existence, of child pornography within an email attachment, it would provide a valid defence for the offences of being in 'possession' as well as 'making' an indecent photograph.[113]

107 Section 160(2)(a).
108 *Atkins v DPP; Goodland v DPP* [2000] 2 Cr App R 248.
109 Ibid, para 262. See also *R v Collier* [2004] EWCA Crim 1411.
110 Criminal Justice Act 1988, s 160(2)(c).
111 *R v Smith and Jayson* [2002] EWCA Crim 683.
112 See also, *R v Skinner* [2005] EWCA Crim 1439. For a case comment, see David C Ormerod, 'Case Comment on *R v Smith (Graham Westgarth)*' *Criminal Law Review* (August 2002) 659–663.
113 The reference to the offence of 'making' is relevant because following *R v Bowden* the offence of 'making' child pornography could also be made out if an image is accessed by opening an attachment.

'Custody and Control'

The second element of 'possession' is physical in nature and requires that the person must have custody and control of the images stored on a device in order to possess them. Clarity and standard in this respect was provided in the significant case of *R v Porter*.[114] The facts of this case are slightly complex, and it is pertinent to provide a brief overview of the facts in order to contextualise the reasoning of the court. The appellant, who worked in the field of information technology, was charged with being in possession of 3575 still images and 40 movie files of child pornography contrary to section 160 (1) of the Criminal Justice Act 1988. The images and movie files were found in the hard disk drives of two computers built by the appellant. Of the 3575 still images, 875 had been deleted in the sense that they were placed in the 'Recycle Bin' of the computer which was then emptied. The remaining 2700 still images were saved in a database of a program called ACDSee, which was a specialist programme designed for viewing graphical images and was generally used by photographers. The program creates thumbnail images of the pictures viewed when opened in the 'gallery view', but all of the larger images had been deleted, which meant that the thumbnails could no longer be viewed in the gallery view. A trace of each thumbnail, however, remained in the database of the program. In terms of the movie files, of the 40 files 7 had been deleted as above, i.e., placed in the 'Recycle Bin', which was then emptied. The remaining 33 files had not been saved as such, but were recovered from the cache of the two computer hard disk drives.

The prosecution conceded that the appellant had deleted all the items before the computers were seized on the 5 November 2002 and that he did not have the software (nor there was any evidence that the appellant had attempted to obtain such software) to retrieve the deleted images or movie files. In addition, the thumbnail metadata that remained in the database of the ACDSee program could be retrieved only by using specialist forensic techniques and equipment provided by the US Government, and was not available to the public.

At trial stage, the appellant had argued that he had no case to answer in relation to the files he had deleted as he had done all that he could do in order to divest himself of possession. He conceded that the 33 movie files that were in the cache were retrievable and thus were in his possession. The trial judge rejected this argument and held that the fact that the image was held in a deleted file rather than an active file did not mean that the user was not in possession, if the file (deleted or otherwise) was on a hard disk or computer in his possession.

On appeal, the appellant argued that there is no offence of possession of indecent photographs or pseudo-photographs unless the images are 'readily

114 *R v Porter* [2006] EWCA Crim 560. See also later case of *R v Leonard* [2012] 2 Cr App R 12.

accessible to the accused for viewing at the time when they are said to be possessed or capable of being made so accessible without the need to obtain additional specialist software'. [115] He also argued that if a person has taken all reasonable steps to destroy the images or make them irretrievable by deleting them (after emptying the 'Recycle Bin'), the images should be regarded as no longer being in that person's possession. The prosecutors took the view that so long as the images remain on the hard disk drive and are recoverable and capable of being viewed, they should be deemed to be in the possession of a person who has control of the hard disk drive. In other words, the prosecution argument was that if the images were on a person's hard disk drive within the *computer* which was in his custody and control at the relevant time, possession should be automatically inferred by virtue of section 160(1). This would mean that there is no need to consider whether the files themselves were accessible to the accused as long as the *device* that held the files were within the 'custody and control' of the person.

The court went into some detail in order to interpret the meaning of 'possession'. Analogies were drawn to previous cases such as *DPP v Brooks*,[116] which related to the unlawful possession of drugs rather than pornography, that focused on the concept of 'custody and control' in order to determine possession: 'one has in possession whatever is, to one's knowledge, physically in one's custody or control.'[117] The concept of having possession of something with the knowledge that one has it in one's physical custody and control was also followed in the subsequent case of *R v Boyesen*.[118] Acknowledging that the context of possession of pornography is different from the unlawful possession of drugs, the court nevertheless found no difficulty in importing the concept of 'custody and control' to the possession of indecent images. The court did not, however, accept the Crown's argument regarding physical custody of the computer and instead focused on the actual images themselves and held that if a person cannot retrieve or access the deleted images on a computer, then he no longer has control or custody over such images. The appeal was accordingly allowed.

Porter is the right decision and mitigates some of the harshness of the strict application of a simple possession offence. If the court were to rule otherwise following the trial court's interpretation of 'possession', it would lead to an absurd situation in that inadvertent or unsolicited exposure to indecent photographs on a computer will inevitably lead to a possession offence as the images will be retrievable from the cache or hard disk using specialist software regardless of the person's taking all reasonable steps to delete them (as far as a non-professional person can). Therefore, all that needs to be proved would be that the person had custody and control of the device and also had the knowledge

115 Ibid, para 9.
116 *DPP v Brooks* [1974] AC 862.
117 Ibid, 866H, *per* Lord Diplock.
118 *R v Boyesen* [1982] AC 768, 773H.

that such images would remain on the hard disk of their computer despite their actively deleting them, which some people would know anyway. It would be impossible to evade the offence even in cases where the legislation provides legitimate defences as per section 160(2), i.e., where the person has received the images unsolicited by email or inadvertently come across such images and has taken all reasonable steps to delete them within a reasonable time, merely because the images could be retrieved using specialist software. The Court of Appeal has rightly settled this issue and averted the unwelcome consequences of the trial court's earlier interpretation of 'possession'.[119]

Making or possession?

It was noted earlier that there is some overlap between the offences of 'making' an indecent photograph under section 1 of the Protection of Children Act 1978, and 'possession' under section 160 of the Criminal Justice Act 1988, and in particular why both offences exist despite arguably blurred boundaries. A difficulty with the operation of the possession offence in practice is that it would not always be straightforward for prosecutors to establish 'possession' following *Porter*. Successful prosecution for a charge of possession will very much depend on where the files are stored within the device (for example, whether they are in the cache or in an easily retrievable folder) and whether they are easily retrievable without specialist knowledge or software. If content is automatically cached on to the computer's memory, it needs to be proved that the viewer knew of the cache. Similarly, for downloaded images which have been deleted from the computer (i.e., also from the Recycle Bin) it will need to be proved that the relevant person has the knowledge and ability to retrieve it. Such evidentiary burden for establishing 'possession' under section 160 of the Criminal Justice Act 1988 has led to the Crown Prosecution Service actually preferring the charge of 'making' an indecent photograph under section 1 of the PCA over a charge of simple possession under the 1988 Act. In light of the wide interpretation of 'making' afforded by the cases noted above, opening email attachments or the act of viewing images on the internet without active downloading is safer to prosecute as a 'making offence', provided that the necessary mental element is present.[120] The 'making' offence therefore would assist in the cases where the requirements of 'custody and control' cannot be met and serves to fill a gap in the law. However, might a separate 'access offence' for intentionally accessing child pornography be more desirable to fill this lacuna?

119 It is to be noted that the issue arose mainly because the prosecution charge was based on possession of images *at the time* when the computer was seized by the police; if the charge was on the basis of possession at an earlier time (before deleting the images) it would have been a different outcome as the images would have been well within his custody and control in this case.

120 This also reflects the current legal guidance issued by the Crown Prosecution Service.

Access offence

The UK does not currently have an offence that specifically criminalises knowingly accessing child pornography, without the requirement of active downloading. Some countries have followed this route and created a specific offence for intentional access. Canada, for example, criminalised 'accessing' child pornography to include the act of 'knowingly causing child pornography to be viewed by, or transmitted to, himself or herself'.[121] In the United States, a Federal amendment in 2008 criminalised knowingly accessing child pornography, in addition to the existing offence of possession contained in USC § 2252A(a)(5).[122] Had the United Kingdom adopted a similar approach and enacted an 'access offence', it would perhaps have avoided the courts' having to take the inventive step of interpreting the 'making offence' to encompass (knowingly) browsing the internet for child pornography without actively downloading content to the computer.[123] An access offence would also assist in cases where possession is difficult to prove, as per *Porter*, for example, where somebody uses a public internet café to view images stored in the cloud, without actively downloading it into their own storage devices. In this case it could be argued that the person does not have control or custody of the images. It is, of course, still possible to rely on the 'making' offence as the image will have been called upon the screen of the computer, but it is perhaps more logical to treat these as 'access offences', thereby avoiding the general criticism of 'making offences'. In addition, as Horsman argues, access offence could help overcome some of the difficulties with obtaining forensic digital evidence on user devices when offenders use private browsing or encryption to view child pornography.[124] In cases where the device cannot be decrypted, or where sufficient forensic evidence cannot be found from the device, he points out that evidence can still be obtained with the assistance of internet service providers – who are now required to retain Internet Connection Records (ICR) of users for a period of 12 months under the Investigatory Powers Act 2016. Whilst this sounds like a sensible suggestion, as Horsman points out himself, relying on ICR retained by internet service providers for evidence-gathering purposes carries the risk that those who access the material unintentionally may be under suspicion, potentially leading to erroneous prosecutions.[125] The fate of the Investigatory Powers Act 2016 itself (or any other similar legislation that require mandatory data retention) is uncertain in

121 Section 163.1(4.1) of the Criminal Code. The definition of 'access' is found in s 163.1(4.2).

122 This closed a gap in the law following *US v Stulock* 308 F.3d 922 where the Court of Appeals for the Third Circuit held that merely viewing images on websites does not constitute possession.

123 The requirement to prove intention for access offences would be essential, in order that inadvertent exposure to child pornography does not constitute an offence.

124 Graeme Horsman, 'Combating those who Intentionally Access Images Depicting Child Sexual Abuse on the Internet: A Call for a New Offence in England and Wales' (2018) 34 (1) *Computer Law & Security Review* 111–124.

125 Ibid.

light of the recent CJEU decisions in *Tele2 Sverige and Tom Watson and Others*,[126] and the previous decision in *Digital Rights Ireland* that invalidated the Data Retention Directive.[127]

Refocusing the law

Whilst *Porter* had the right outcome in the end, it also highlighted some of the problems with how the society and judiciary generally perceive child pornography offences. A criticism levelled by Gillespie is that the law has focused on the wrong issue, i.e., rather than focusing on the actions of the offender the law seems to focus on the images. This is a valid criticism. The initial approach of the trial court in *Porter* offers an example for this – the focus was purely on the presence of images on the hard disk of the computer regardless of the actions (i.e., emptying them from the recycle bin) of the defendant. There are other commentators who are critical of the tendency of the law to not focus on the main issue. For instance, Williams is critical of the law generally being primarily interested in the image, and thinks it fails to sufficiently consider the suffering of the child.[128] The tendency of the law to focus on the wrong issues has been highlighted by Wall in the context of cybercrimes generally, where he argues that the discussion in cybercrime tends to be offence-based without due consideration given to offender behaviour and other characteristics of cybercrime.[129] In the context of child pornography, the law should be primarily offender-focused, rather than merely focusing on the existence of an indecent image on a computer – the latter could result in overzealous prosecutions that could lead to disproportionate outcomes, including the possibility of innocent people who accidentally stumble across child pornography being subjected to the trauma of an unnecessary prosecution. It is worth noting that due to the very nature of child pornography offences, the media – and consequently the public – are usually quick to condemn the accused and pronounce them 'guilty' even before the due process of the law takes it course and finds the person guilty beyond reasonable doubt. In the event that the accused turns out to be innocent following trial, the damage to their reputation (and in many cases their careers and family) will have already been caused, in some cases irreparably so. Far from being granted the presumption of being treated as innocent until proven guilty, a person in such a situation will often be condemned as guilty from the outset, which goes against the principles of fair trial and due process of the law.

It is also important to ensure that legal responses are proportionate and stem from reasoned and evidence-based assessment of the threats and challenges.

126 Joined Cases C-203/15 and C-698/15.

127 Joined Cases C-293/12 and C-594/12.

128 Katherine S Williams, 'Child pornography law: Does it Protect Children? (2004) 26(3) *Journal of Social Welfare and Family Law* 245–261.

129 See David Wall, *Cybercrime: The Transformation of Crime in the Information Age* (Polity Press 2007).

Child pornography is a very serious issue and ought to be met with a robust response. At the same time, there is no place for knee-jerk reactions or measures that are a result of 'moral panic', as it risks undermining the legitimacy of the laws that are meant to protect children. Ost points out the existence of a moral panic about child pornography by examining the way in which the media, the public, the police, politicians and the judiciary have responded to the problem. [130] She reaches this inference by applying the concept of 'moral panic' as conceived by Jock Young and Stan Cohen[131] in light of the reaction by each of the above parties and concludes that there are grounds to indicate the existence of a moral panic in our society about child pornography and its possession. This, Ost argues, has the potential to distort our perceptions of the actual, credible threat posed by child pornography. This is, however, not a view shared by all commentators. For instance, Gillespie is of the opinion that whilst there are some exaggerated claims about the prevalence of child pornography, the evidence is less convincing to establish the presence of a moral panic surrounding child pornography.[132] Whilst evidence of 'moral panic' is harder to establish, it is true that the public perception of the prevalence of child pornography has led to legislative action that criminalises a broader category of content, for example virtual pornography, and sometimes the debate surrounding the regulation of adult pornography tends to get conflated and linked with 'child pornography'. The latter is particularly dangerous – not just for the right of adults to consume (lawful) adult pornography, but also for the respect-worthiness and legitimacy of child pornography laws itself. These themes are explored further in Chapters 4 and 7.

Rationale of possession offences

The discussion so far has focused on aspects of the interpretation and operation of possession offences from a UK perspective. It was noted earlier that criminalising simple possession marked a significant change in the overall regulatory approach for combating child pornography in the digital era. It is pertinent to examine the rationale of simple possession offence in more detail in order to appreciate why it has become such an indispensable tool in the broader regulatory framework to combat child pornography on the internet.

There are various justifications for criminalising the possession of child pornography. It should be noted that criminalising the private consumption of

130 Suzanne Ost, 'Children at Risk: Legal and Societal Perceptions of the Potential Threat that the Possession of Child Pornography Poses to Society' (2002) 23(3) *Journal of Law and Society* 436–460 (see 443–447 in particular for this analysis).

131 Ibid, citing J Young, 'The Role of the Police As Amplifiers of Deviance, Negotiators of Drug Control as Seen in Notting Hill' in Stanley Cohen, *Images of Deviance* (Penguin Books 1971) and Stanley Cohen, *Folk Devils and Moral Panics: The Creation of the Mods and Rockers* (Paladin 1973).

132 Gillespie (n 5)11.

pornography is slightly controversial, especially when the harm that law is seeking is prevent is less apparent, for example virtual child pornography that may not cause direct harm to children. As already stated in Chapter 2, criminalising possession offers a solution to the complex practical problems of jurisdiction as it is a lot easier to identify and prosecute the possessor based in the home jurisdiction compared to the uploader or producer of the material based abroad. The challenges in relation to jurisdiction have already been noted and will not be repeated here. It is acknowledged that a possession offence cannot be justified solely on the basis of practical convenience, but as will be seen from the discussion below, there are a range of compelling reasons for criminalising the possession of child pornography. Production of child pornography causes harm to children and in that sense it can be argued that possessors are also complicit in the abuse and exploitation of children. In addition, the possession offence for child pornography is generally supported by a range of other arguments and justifications including that it curtails the demand for child pornography, minimises the risk of possession leading to contact offending, and addresses the secondary harm caused to the victims as well as indirect harm to wider society stemming from possession. Each of these different possible justifications is considered below.

Curtailing demand

The basic premise of this rationale is that by criminalising simple possession the market for child pornography itself can be destroyed. This is a fairly incontrovertible argument – if people are deterred from seeking and possessing child pornography with the threat of criminal sanctions, it should have a detrimental effect on the demand for such content, which will in turn have an impact on the trade itself, resulting in fewer people producing child pornography.[133] Consequently, if there is a reduction in demand for child pornography, fewer children will be abused for the purpose of producing the material, so ultimately it benefits children. This would be undoubtedly true for commercial child pornography. Whilst there seems to be no evidence for a large commercially profitable market for child pornography, a commercial market nevertheless does exist. The Internet Watch Foundation Annual Report of 2016 sheds some light on the extent of commercial child pornography websites.[134] In 2016, out of a total of 57,335 webpages confirmed as containing child sexual abuse material, 5452 were assessed as being commercial in nature. In other words, 10 per cent of all

133 The link between criminalising possession and market reduction was held out to be a key justification for criminalising extreme pornography in the UK, which raises a separate set of issues to child pornography and is examined separately in Chapter 6.

134 Internet Watch Foundation, *Annual Report 2016*, available at https://www.iwf.org.uk/report/2016-annual-report, accessed 9 July 2018. Commercial child abuse imagery is defined as imagery which is produced or is being used for the purpose of financial gain by the distributor.

webpages assessed were commercial webpages.[135] There is some evidence that a number of websites on the open internet (as opposed to the 'dark web') provide lists of URLs which enable the download of child pornographic material using BitTorrent technologies.[136] The report also raised concerns about newer forms of commercial distribution of child pornography such as the use of disguised websites[137] and the use of alternative payment mechanisms, for instance cryptocurrencies such as Bitcoin. Therefore, it appears that commercial child pornography remains very much a challenge and, as technology develops newer forms of accessing and delivering content, also continues to evolve.

The market influence argument, however, is not specific to commercial child pornography. It may also apply to non-commercial producers of child pornography where more demand from other people could encourage the producer to produce more material in light of the social relationships that may have developed among a group of people facilitated by an interest in the use of child pornography.[138] The internet allows paedophiles to communicate with one another, build social cohesion and to obtain 'hierarchical' status within online communities reflected in the volume of content collected and distributed.[139] Further, there is also the possibility that those who already are in possession of child pornography may seek more and new images, which is supported by some evidence suggesting that downloading behaviour and the fantasies that are fuelled by it do not remain a static response, and more images will be sought, thereby fuelling further demand for child pornography.[140] Whilst this might be the case for those who are already in the habit of viewing and possessing child pornography, it is unclear whether viewing child pornography has an addictive effect in that it can actually lead people who are new to child pornography to become regular viewers and seeking more material. There is, however, some research that points to a Guttman-like progression, whereby individuals who start watching adult pornography at a younger age are more likely to progress to engage in deviant pornography, including child pornography and bestiality, compared to those

135 This actually showed a decrease from previous year – in 2015, 14,708 (21%) webpages were identified as commercial in nature. However, the IWF report suggests that this could be due to newer methods adopted by distributors to share child pornography, in particular by using disguised websites.

136 Ibid.

137 These refer to commercial websites that display lawful adult content when loaded directly into the browser, but when accessed through a link on a particular gateway site, display illegal child pornography.

138 See Gillespie (n 5) 38.

139 Ethel Quale and Max Taylor, 'Child Pornography and the Internet: Perpetuating a Cycle of Abuse' (2002) 23(4) *Deviant Behaviour* 331–361.

140 See Ethel Quayle, Marcus Erooga, Louise Wright, Max Taylor and Dawn Harbinson, 'Abuse Images and the Internet', in Ethel Quayle, Marcus Erooga, Louise Wright, Max Taylor and Dawn Harbinson (eds) *Only Pictures? Therapeutic Work with Internet Sex Offenders* (Russell House Publishing 2006) 61.

with a later 'age of onset'.[141] There is also evidence that some paedophiles obtain pleasure from collecting pictures as part of a series, to create an archive which can be used for trading for new material.[142]

The link between possession and demand was addressed by the Supreme Court of Canada in the leading case of *R v Sharpe*,[143] where the Court considered the constitutionality of the possession offence for child pornography under section 163 (1)(4) of the Criminal Code. The question before the Supreme Court was whether the possession offence went too far and criminalised the possession of an unjustifiable range of material contrary to the fundamental rights granted under the Canadian Charter of Rights and Freedoms. The Court ruled generally in favour of criminalising the possession of child pornography and noted that possession fuels demand and thereby causes harm to children:

> 'Production of child pornography is fuelled by the market for it, and the market in turn is fuelled by those who seek to possess it. Criminalizing possession may reduce the market for child pornography and the abuse of children it often involve.'[144]

In an ideal world, if all countries in the world have robust laws that criminalise child pornography and effective enforcement regimes are in place, the trade in child pornography will naturally decline. As long as disparities between the laws of different nations prevail in this regard, content could simply move to jurisdictions that have lax laws. Curtailing demand by criminalising possession of child pornography is one way of addressing this, especially in light of the complex jurisdictional hurdles involved in prosecuting perpetrators based in countries with lax or no relevant laws.

Contact offending and grooming

The possible correlation between those consuming child pornography also physically abusing a child sexually is one of the reasons cited to justify criminalising the possession of child pornography. Wolak et al note that one out of every six cases that began with an investigation of child pornography possession involved an offender who also sexually abused a child or attempted to do so, suggesting a correlation between possession/seeking child pornography and

141 See Kathryn C Seigfried-Spellar and Marcus Rogers, 'Does Deviant Pornography Use Follow a Guttman-like Progression?' (2013) 29(5) *Computers in Human Behaviour* 1997–2003.

142 Collecting behaviour is not solely confined to child pornography and for some people it was 'part of a progression through collecting other forms of pornography'. See Quale and Taylor, (n 139) 343. See also Max Taylor, Gemma Holland, Ethel Quale, 'Typology of Paedophile Picture Collections' (2001) 74 *The Police Journal* 97–107.

143 *R v Sharpe* [2001] 1 SCR 45.

144 Ibid, *per* McLachlin CJ, para 28.

actually sexually abusing a child.[145] Commentators like Edwards (2000) contend that possessors of child pornography are more likely to be paedophiles.[146] There are also opposing views in this respect: for example, Ost argues that whilst studies could reveal a correlative relationship between actual child abusers consuming child pornography, it is more difficult to demonstrate a clear correlation the other way round, i.e., between the consumption of child pornography and subsequent physical abuse of a child as a consequence, and therefore, the 'existence of such a relationship' (content leading to contact) is 'far from certain'.[147] Notwithstanding these divergent views,[148] and even if one accepts that there is a lack of clear and conclusive evidence linking previous consumption of child pornography with contact offences, it is certainly possible that those who consume child pornography are those who have a deviant interest in children, and therefore, on a balance of probabilities, pose a *risk* to children generally.

The possibility that consumption of child pornography could lead to desensitisation and a false sense of normalisation of such behaviour for those who regularly view such material also poses a risk. The potential for child pornography to be used to groom children eventually leading to inappropriate contact and sexual exploitation lends weight to the position that its simple possession ought to be criminalised. For instance, Lanning argues that consumption of child pornography poses the risk that, apart from persuading the child by 'normalising' behaviour, it helps the paedophile believe that his activities are normal – behaviour validation for himself.[149] Thus, the risk is not confined to normalisation of behaviour from the child's perspective: it appears that it is very much an issue that directly impacts on the paedophile's

145 Janis Wolak, David Finkelhor and Kimberly Mitchell, 'Child Pornography Possessors: Trends in Offender and Case Characteristics' (2011) 23(1) *Sexual Abuse: A Journal of Research and Treatment* 22–42.

146 Susan SM Edwards, 'Prosecuting "Child Pornography": Possession and Taking of Indecent Photographs' 22(1) *Journal of Social Welfare and Family Law* 1–21, 13–14.

147 Ost (n 130) 450.

148 The literature is varied on this issue where some researchers find a credible link between possession and contact offending but also the existence of a 'distinct subgroup of online-only offenders who pose relatively low risk of contact offending'. Michael C Seto, R Karl Hanson, Kelly M Babchishin, 'Contact Sexual Offending by Men with Online Sexual Offense' (2011) 23(1) *Sexual Abuse: A journal of Research and Treatment* 124–145. See also Matthew L Long, Laurence A Alison, Michelle A McManus, 'Child Pornography and Likelihood of Contact Abuse: A Comparison Between Contact Child Sexual Offenders and Noncontact Offenders' (2013) 25(4) *Sexual Abuse* 370–395; Michelle Ann McManus and Louise Almond, 'Trends of Indecent Images of Children and Child Sexual Offences between 2005/2006 and 2012/2013 within the United Kingdom' (2014) 20(2) *Journal of Sexual Agression* 142–155; Jennifer A McCarthy, 'Internet Sexual Activity: A Comparison between Contact and Non-contact Child Pornography Offenders (2010) 16(2) *Journal of Sexual Aggression* 181–195.

149 KV Lanning, 'Collectors' in AW Burgess and ML Clark (eds) *Child Pornography and Sex Rings* (Lexington Books 1984) 86.

behaviour itself.[150] Either way, it is clear that there is a credible risk to children stemming from the possession of child pornography which the law cannot ignore for the purpose of criminalising possession.

Harm prevention

John Stuart Mill, in his much acclaimed work *On Liberty*,[151] states that 'the only purpose for which power can be rightfully exercised over any member of a civilised community, against his will, is to prevent harm to others'. Whilst Mill's harm principle has been subject to numerous interpretations, it is generally accepted from a criminal law perspective that criminalising conduct ought to be justified by a greater objective of preventing harm to others. A simple possession offence essentially criminalises conduct carried out in private – viewing pornography is usually a private act and strictly speaking is a separate issue from the direct physical abuse caused to the child during production (assuming the possessor was not also the producer). In those cases where the offender merely possesses the material for personal consumption, the state needs to ensure that there is sufficient justification for imposing a restriction on behaviour that would otherwise fall within one's individual liberties (but for the illegality of the content), and the consequent intrusion into one's private sphere must be proportionate to the harm the law is trying to prevent.

It is clear that child pornography involving real children causes direct harm to children, although this is less straightforward to establish with respect to certain types of pseudo child pornography (featuring adults) and virtual child pornography. Does the simple possession of material that did not result in actual physical abuse of a child during its production deserve to be criminalised? By criminalising such material, is the harm caused to the possessor by punishment (this is assuming the possessor did not create the material) greater than the apprehension of harm to the child?[152] These are pertinent questions that need to be examined in some detail in order to determine the proportionality of simple possession offences for child pornography. The analysis here will only consider images that are photograph-based, including original as well as

150 On the potential of the internet offering support to paedophiles for normalisation of behaviour, see Keith F Durkin and Clifton D Bryant, 'Propagandising Pederasty: A Thematic Analysis of the Online Exculpatory Accounts of Unrepentant Paedophiles' (1999) 20(2) *Deviant Behaviour* 103–127. O'Halloran and Quale replicated this study nine years later, where they found that online communities acts as a support mechanism for paedophiles and can promote pro-offending beliefs in socially isolated individuals – see Elaine O'Halloran and Ethel Quayle, 'A Content Analysis of a "boy-love" Support Forum: Revisiting Durkin and Bryant' (2010) 16(1) *Journal of Sexual Aggression* 71–85.

151 John Stuart Mill, *On Liberty and the Subjugation of Women* (Penguin 2006).

152 Criminalisation itself causes harm to the person who carries out the proscribed activity; in this case, a prison sentence.

pseudo-imagery, but will not include entirely computer-created images (virtual pornography), which is dealt with in the next chapter.

'Harm' can be divided into two broad categories for the purpose of this analysis: (1) direct harm, which is caused to the child depicted in the material, and (2) indirect harm, which is caused to the wider society (including other children) as a result of someone possessing the material. Each will be considered in turn.

Direct harm

The prevention of direct harm to children as the basis for criminalising the possession of child pornography is justifiable with respect to material that was created as a result of physical abuse or exploitation of real children. As children lack the capacity to provide consent for pornography, essentially every indecent image of a child constitutes a case of abuse or exploitation, regardless of whether or not the production was, in a non-legal sense, 'consensual'. Therefore, where the material involves the abuse of real children (as opposed to certain types of pseudo-images, as examined later), direct harm in the form of actual sexual abuse and/or exploitation is caused to the child depicted in the image. Tate neatly summarises this as, 'at its simplest child pornography is no more than the permanent recording of a child being sexually abused'.[153] The direct harm caused to the child in this way could provide sufficient justification for criminalising the consumption of material that was produced as a result of sexual abuse and exploitation of a child.

However, it is also arguable that criminalising possession does not directly address the harm caused to the victim, because the law in this instance is specifically targeting the possessor of the image and not the producer or the perpetrator of the abuse who actually inflicted direct harm on the child. In this sense, a possession offence does not really achieve much in terms of punishing those who caused direct harm to the child during production, unless of course the possessor and creator is the same person. The counter-argument to this is that the image would not have been produced in the first place, and a child abused in the process, but for the demand for the material from those who have an interest in such imagery. In this sense it can be argued that the viewer is also complicit in the direct harm caused to the child depicted in the image and therefore should be penalised.

In addition, the knowledge that the image will remain on the internet aggravates the suffering caused to the child. Possessors are also complicit in the direct harm thereby caused to the victim by perpetuating the harm caused by production.[154] The secondary harm thus directly caused to the subject of the image could provide sufficient justification for criminalising simple possession.[155] As Cassell et al rightly

153 Tim Tate, *Child Pornography: An Investigation* (Methuen 1990) 15.

154 See Gillespie (n 5), citing Suzanne Ost, *Child Pornography and Sexual Grooming: Legal and Societal Responses* (Cambridge University Press 2009) 123.

155 Gillespie, ibid, 34.

point out, possession 'scars real-world victims, who live in constant fear of being exposed and humiliated by those who are obtaining sexual gratification through viewing images of their childhood rape ... all possessors are jointly responsible for seriously harming victims and should be held fully accountable through both criminal penalties and awards of full restitution'.[156] Therefore, whilst a possession offence does not specifically target those who actually physically abused or exploited the child during the production of the material, it could nevertheless be argued that it is a proportionate measure that seeks to prevent further secondary harm to the subject of the image.

PSEUDO-IMAGES

Criminalising the possession of pseudo child pornography raises a slightly different set of issues from a prevention of direct harm perspective. There are two categories of pseudo-images worth discussing in this context: first, images that feature actual children, for example where the face of a child is superimposed on the body of an adult in order to give the overall impression of an image of a child. The second category of pseudo-images features young adults who are made to look like children, for example by modifying the image using computer technology. The latter is a more problematic category owing to the fact that the image depicts no actual children, but is nevertheless created or modified with the intention that it conveys the overall impression of an underage person.

In relation to the first category of pseudo-images featuring actual children, it is usually the case that its production would involve no actual physical abuse of a child. Does this mean that criminalising the simple possession of such images is disproportionate? Whilst there may be no physical harm caused to a child during production, it is submitted that it would still be possible to establish direct harm where the image of a real child is used to create the material owing to the potential of psychological harm suffered by the child depicted. Clearly, the degree of harm caused to the subject of the image may not be as severe as would be the case where it was produced as a result of physical abuse, but there is still direct harm caused if the image depicts a real and identifiable child in a grossly inappropriate manner. As noted already, possession amounts to continuing harm to the victim, especially in light of the potential for the images to be redistributed and/or to remain on the internet for long periods of time, which provides a legitimate basis for criminalisation. If the victim is not aware of the existence of the image – and the likelihood of lack of knowledge of the image is much higher for pseudo-photographs than for images that are created by physical

156 Paul G Cassell, James R Marsh and Jeremy M Christansen, 'Not Just "Kiddie Porn": The Significant Harms from Child Pornography', in Carissa Byrne Hessick (ed), *Refining Child Pornography Law: Crime, Language and Social Consequences* (University of Michigan Press 2016) 203–204.

abuse – it can be argued that there is no harm to the child stemming from possession. Whilst this is a stronger argument compared to real child pornography, King makes a persuasive argument:

> '[S]ome degree of harm is almost always done to the subject in the production and distribution of child pornography of all kinds ... and that even if harm is not done in a particular case we can never be sure of that.'[157]

It is difficult for the viewer to know the circumstances in which the photograph was taken – whether the child is aware of its existence or not, how much harm to the victim the image represents or the later effects they suffered. In addition, there is the unacceptable intrusion into the privacy and autonomy of the child depicted – by using the image without consent (albeit consent is irrelevant here in a legal sense owing to the subject being a child) which also arguably causes direct harm to the child. The harm thus caused is regardless of whether the victim is aware of a particular instance of viewing or downloading.[158]

In relation to the second category of pseudo-images, preventing direct harm as a justification for criminalising simple possession is less convincing as the images do not feature any real children. If the material was created by digitally modifying the image of an adult – for example, by reducing the breast and hip size in order to give the overall impression of an underage person, there is no direct harm caused to a real child *per se*, as the subject of the image is actually an adult. Therefore, the direct harm rationale cannot justify the criminalisation of simple possession of such images as none was caused to a child either during the production stage of the material in question, or later in terms of psychological harm, unlike the first category of pseudo-images discussed above.

In most cases, however, it may not be easily discernible for the viewer whether the person depicted in the material is in fact a child or an adult whose image is digitally altered to look like a child. As noted in the discussion on production of child pornography earlier, the existence of child pornography in all its manifestations has the potential to cause further harm to children, but this is essentially general indirect harm rather than the direct harm caused to the subject of a specific image. As far as pseudo-images created using adults are concerned, it might be the prevention of indirect harm that offers a more realistic justification for criminalising simple possession.

It should be clear from the discussion above that preventing direct harm to the subject of the image can offer sufficient justification for criminalising the

157 See Peter J King, 'No Plaything: Ethical Issues Concerning Child-Pornography' (2008) 11 (3) *Ethical Theory and Moral Practice* 327–245. See also Rogers, n 64.

158 See Suzanne Ost, 'A New Paradigm of Reparation for Victims of Child Pornography' (2016) 36(4) *Legal Studies* 613–638. It was also noted in *New York v Ferber* that the recording and distribution of sexual performances of children invade children's privacy interests. See *New York v Ferber* 458 US 747 (1982), 758.

possession of two broad types of image: first, those that were created as a result of actual physical abuse or exploitation, i.e., real child pornographic images, and second, pseudo-images created using a photo of a real child. As for indecent pseudo-photographs featuring adults, we need to explore whether the criminalisation of possession can be justified on the basis of preventing indirect harm, which is explored further below.

Indirect harm

As noted earlier, indirect harm refers to the harm that possessing child pornography causes to the viewer and to the wider society, including other children. Some of the harms of possession have already been discussed in this chapter: there is some evidence that possessors of child pornography could seek more material and thereby fuel demand.[159] In addition, there is also the risk of using child pornography for desensitisation and normalisation of behaviour not just for the offenders themselves, i.e., to convince themselves that viewing child pornography is normal, but also for desensitising children and making them believe that it is normal to have sexual relationships at a younger age, as noted earlier.[160] A further harm from possession is the possibility of contact offending, although, as noted earlier, the evidence that links possession of child pornography leading to actual physical sexual abuse of a child is not always conclusive: whilst there is research that suggests a link, there is also some criticism that it is not necessarily a causal link.[161]

Research does not point to conclusive evidence of harms of the nature outlined above stemming from simple possession. A question that could be asked in this context is whether there is actually the need to search for absolute, conclusive evidence of harm in order to justify criminalising possession. In other words, would a credible *risk of harm*, as opposed to conclusive evidence of harm generally to children, provide adequate justification for criminalising simple possession? Risk of harm as the justification for criminalising conduct is considered in further detail in Chapter 7, while analysing the regulation of adult pornography from the perspective of protecting children from exposure to age-inappropriate material on the internet. A reasonable risk of harm to children has provided sufficient legal basis for regulating conduct with respect to adult pornography – for example, children are not allowed inside a licensed sex shop in the UK. In relation to child pornography, *risk of harm* as providing the basis for criminalising simple possession was considered by the Supreme Court of

159 See nn 140, 141 and 142.

160 See Lanning (n 149).

161 See Katherine S Williams (n 128) citing Jean Proulx, Christine Perreult and Marc Ouimet, 'Pathways in the Offending Process of Extrafamilial Sexual Child Molesters' (1999) 11(2) *Journal of Research and Treatment* 117–129. Also see Tim Tate, *Child Pornography: An investigation* (Methuen 1990); KV Lanning, *Child Molesters: A Behavioural Analysis* (3rd edn, National Centre for Missing and Exploited Children 1992).

Canada in *R v Sharpe*,[162] where the issue of the lack of scientific proof or concrete evidence that the possession of child pornography causes harm to children was directly addressed by McLachlin CJ and Iacobucci, Major, Binnie, Arbour and LeBel JJ as follows:

> In adopting s. 163.1(4), Parliament was pursuing the pressing and substantial objective of criminalizing the possession of child pornography that poses a reasoned risk of harm to children. The means chosen by Parliament are rationally connected to this objective. Parliament is not required to adduce scientific proof based on concrete evidence that the possession of child pornography causes harm to children. Rather, a reasoned apprehension of harm will suffice. Applying this test, the evidence establishes several connections between the possession of child pornography and harm to children: (1) child pornography promotes cognitive distortions; (2) it fuels fantasies that incite offenders to offend; (3) it is used for grooming and seducing victims; and (4) children are abused in the production of child pornography involving real children. Criminalizing possession may reduce the market for child pornography and the abuse of children it often involves.

The Supreme Court was content to rely on the link between possession and harm caused to children: this is not necessarily a causal link based on conclusive evidence, but one that is perceived on the basis of a reasoned risk of harm. This has to be the correct approach. The fundamental purpose of child pornography law is to protect children – it is not simply an instrument to impose moralistic standards on the general public as to what is and is not acceptable content. The state has a compelling interest in the protection of children, which by implication means prevention of harm to children. If there is a reasonable risk of harm to children stemming from the possession of child pornography, it can legitimately be criminalised. This is the essence of the precautionary principle underpinning the laws that relate to children generally – for example, the voidability of contracts by minors in English law seeks to protect minors from the risks and consequences of their actions before attaining the age of majority. Similarly, the regulation of lawful adult pornography with respect to children, for example broadcast regulations that seek to prevent children's exposure to inappropriate content, essentially seeks to prevent a risk of harm to children.[163] These regulatory measures are not always based on conclusive evidence of harm to children: instead, a reasoned risk of harm has provided the legal basis for regulation. Criminalising the possession of child pornography should be no exception. In comparison to exposure to adult pornography, the risk of harm stemming from child pornography is more direct and leaves a much more profound impact on

162 *R v Sharpe* [2001] 1 SCR 45.
163 These are examined in more detail in Chapter 7.

children. It would be illogical if the law recognised the risk of harm in those other areas but did not adopt the same approach for child pornography, which quite reasonably merits stricter regulation.

PSEUDO-IMAGES

It was noted earlier that pseudo child pornography featuring the face of a child should be treated in the same way as real child pornography, in recognition of the direct harm occasioned to the subject of the image. It was also pointed out that the prevention of direct harm does not offer sufficient basis for criminalising the possession of pseudo child pornography created using the photographs of adults. Could the prevention of indirect harm to wider society, including other children, support the criminalisation of this category of pseudo-imagery?

Pseudo-photographs, by definition, mean that the overall impression conveyed by the image would be that of a child.[164] It would be difficult, if not impossible, for the viewer to ascertain the age of the person depicted. If the image appears to be that of a child, those who enjoy viewing such imagery are essentially enjoying child pornography and would presumably use it to fuel their fantasies involving children. In that sense, the image is no different from a pseudo-image featuring a real child, as the effect of the image on the possessor remains the same. Therefore, the same indirect harm that may be caused by pseudo-images featuring real children would also be caused by such pseudo-images created using adults (because the harm being discussed here is not what is caused to the subject of the image, but is a reasoned risk of harm that may be caused to the viewer and wider society, including other children, as a result of possession). In fact, as far as the prevention of indirect harm is concerned, there is no need to distinguish between the two types of pseudo-images; what matters is whether it gives the overall impression of a child and, if so, it should be treated as child pornography regardless of whether the person featured was of legal age. It is clearly the attitudinal harm that the law is trying to prevent in this instance, which is independent of whether actual (direct) harm was caused to a child or not – something which was affirmed by the Supreme Court of Canada and summarised neatly in *R v Sharpe*:

> Child pornography ... is inherently harmful to children and to society. This harm exists independently of dissemination or any risk of dissemination and flows from the existence of the pornographic representations, which on their own violate the dignity and equality rights of children. Although not

164 See for example s 7(8), Protection of Children Act 1978, which states: 'If the impression conveyed by a pseudo-photograph is that the person shown is a child, the pseudo-photograph shall be treated for all purposes of this Act as showing a child and so shall a pseudo-photograph where the predominant impression conveyed is that the person shown is a child notwithstanding that some of the physical characteristics shown are those of an adult.'

> empirically measurable, nor susceptible to proof in the traditional manner, the attitudinal harm inherent in child pornography can be inferred from degrading or dehumanizing representations or treatment. Expression that degrades or dehumanizes is harmful in and of itself as all members of society suffer when harmful attitudes are reinforced. The possibility that pornographic representations may be disseminated creates a heightened risk of attitudinal harm. The violation of the privacy rights of the persons depicted constitutes an additional risk of harm that flows from the possibility of dissemination. Child pornography is harmful whether it involves real children in its production or whether it is a product of the imagination. Section 163.1 was enacted to protect children, one of the most vulnerable groups in society. It is based on the clear evidence of direct harm caused by child pornography, as well as Parliament's reasoned apprehension that child pornography also causes attitudinal harm. The lack of scientific precision in the social science evidence relating to attitudinal harm is not a valid reason for attenuating the Court's deference to Parliament's decision.[165]

It should be clear from the discussion so far that criminalising the simple possession of real and pseudo child pornography is supported by a range of reasons and is a legitimate and necessary step to combat online child pornography. Whilst there is no room for any doubt that the possession of real child pornography ought to be criminalised, there are also pressing reasons for criminalising pseudo-imagery regardless of whether the participants are actual children or young adults who convey the overall impression of underage persons. Possession fuels demand, carries the risk (if not certainty) of contact offending and causes direct or indirect harm to children. In light of the particular challenges raised by the internet in terms of the production and distribution of content at a global scale, criminalising the simple possession of child pornography was an inevitable response from a legal perspective. The significance of simple possession offences for online child pornography naturally means that there is increased and unprecedented criminal liability imposed on the consumer of content, marking a step change in the regulation of pornography.

Webcam performance and live streaming

Apart from traditional static and pre-recorded moving images of children on the internet, live streaming websites and webcam shows also pose particular challenges in relation to the abuse and exploitation of children. Offenders targeting vulnerable children, typically in poverty stricken areas of the world, for live sexual performances and abuse over webcam, are of particular concern. Whilst in such cases the offender may not be directly physically abusing the child, it is nevertheless a form of contact offending, which the law should recognise as such. The

165 *R v Sharpe* [2001] 1 SCR 45, *per* L'Heureux-Dubé, Gonthier and Bastarache JJ.

worldwide demand for such abuse was demonstrated by an operation carried out in 2013: Terre Des Hommes, a Dutch charity that campaigns to end webcam child sex tourism, created a lifelike, computer-generated 10-year-old Filipino girl called Sweetie on a website, which attracted tens of thousands of men from around the world who made approaches to the 'girl'. The charity was able to identify 1000 people willing to pay for Sweetie 'performing' sex acts, including 999 men and one woman from 71 nationalities. It transpired that among those identified, 254 were from the US, 110 from the UK, and 103 were from India, which demonstrates that the issue is global and transcends cultures and jurisdictions.[166]

If the law in the offender's home jurisdiction does not criminalise such behaviour (this would be a 'making' offence or 'possession offence' at the very least, but it should really be a more specific offence that treats such conduct as sexual abuse of children – see the German case discussed further below), it may become very difficult to successfully police and stop the exploitation, for a number of reasons. It would be highly unlikely that the crime would be reported in the first instance, as in many cases the webcam abuse takes place with the knowledge and support of the very people who are meant to care for the child, such as a parent or close relative.[167] As it is an act occurring within the privacy of the child's home, the likelihood of its being reported is often rather bleak. If the case is not reported by the victim, identifying the perpetrators will not be straightforward, especially if payment was made using methods not easily identifiable, for instance cryptocurrencies such as Bitcoin. Assuming that the crime has been reported, and that the offender is identified as being based in a foreign jurisdiction, there is a range of legal and practical hurdles in extraditing the person to the other jurisdiction, especially where there is no mutual extradition treaty. A further hindrance would be the gathering of sufficient evidence that would result in successful prosecution. Computer and digital forensic evidence would be required to prove the guilt of the offender, which is difficult to obtain without the cooperation of law enforcement authorities in their country of residence, all of which make a model based on traditional extradition procedure extremely difficult for cases involving webcam child abuse. In an ideal world, if all countries had adequate legislation to address online exploitation of children, things would be a lot easier in terms of bringing offenders to justice. As it currently stands, however, the laws of individual nations vary considerably, making it crucial that the country where the offender is based criminalises such activities by incorporating a level of extra-territoriality within the relevant domestic laws, as envisaged by some of the international legal instruments discussed earlier. In the UK, a range of different offences would apply in such cases – apart from the offences of making and possessing child pornography, these could also

166 See http://www.bbc.co.uk/news/uk-24818769, accessed 9 July 2018.

167 See Kimberly J Mitchell, David Finkelhor and Janice Wolak, 'The Internet and Family and Acquaintance Sexual Abuse' (2005) 10(1) *Child Maltreatment* 49–60.

be covered under the separate offences of causing or inciting a child to engage in sexual activity (sections 8 and 10 of the Sexual Offences Act 2003)[168] arranging or facilitating commission of a child sex offence (section 14, Sexual Offences Act 2003), or sexual communications with a child (section 15A, Sexual Offences Act 2003). Whilst it is tempting to assume that a content offence would be the appropriate remedy for webcam-based sexual exploitation of children (as it is streamed to the offender as a video online), such cases should actually be treated akin to physical child abuse. The offenders are more directly involved and complicit in the abuse suffered by the child compared to passive consumers of images that are already available on the internet. This was recognised in Germany, where the Federal Court of Justice (Bundesgerichtshof) upheld a Munich District Court's ruling that engaging in sexual activity with children over the internet, for example through webcam or other forms of livestreaming, amounts to child abuse.[169] In this case the defendant was charged with making contact with five children over the internet using webcam and involved indecent exposure of his genitals. The court held that although there was no physical proximity between the parties, an offence under section 176.4(1) of the Criminal Code would still apply as the intention of the legislature could be interpreted in its spirt of protecting children and their overall development without hindrance. The judgment effectively extends the definition of a 'contact offence' in relation to child abuse by effectively extending it to cover virtual sexual activity on the internet, and removing the requirement of physical contact to constitute 'child abuse'. This is a timely and correct decision, one which would hopefully act as a deterrent for those who use the internet to exploit vulnerable children abroad for sexual gratification.

As technology advances, the delivery and access modes of child pornography will continue to evolve. It is imperative that the law catch up with these changes, and that proportionate responses be formulated to reflect the impact on the victim as well as the role of the perpetrator in the abuse of children. Treating live and directed sexual performances of children as content offences trivialises the offence and it is imperative that the law treat these as contact offending.

Self-generated pornography and 'sexting'

The advent of camera-embedded internet-enabled mobile phones has transformed the creation and distribution of self-generated sexually explicit images. This is commonly referred to as 'sexting' – a term originally created by the media in the early 2000s to refer to the sharing of explicit text messages and self-generated images using Multimedia Messaging Service (MMS).[170] There is no

168 Section 8 offence applies to children under 13, and s 10 offence applies to children under 16 years of age.

169 BGH 1 StR 105/09 – Beschluss vom 21. April 2009 (LG München I).

170 Andy Phippen, *Children's Online Behaviour and Safety: Policy and Rights Challenges* (Palgrave Macmillan 2017) 83.

agreed single definition of 'sexting' within academic literature and whilst the term suggests the use of mobile phones to exchange sexually explicit media, it encompasses other modes of communication using a computer or other internet-enabled device.[171] Exchanging naked and sexually explicit images between partners within a relationship has become increasingly common, and is so prevalent among adolescent teenagers that some commentators call it part of growing up in the connected age.[172]

Self-generated images of a sexually explicit nature created by minors raise complex regulatory challenges. Whilst in most cases the images are created with consent (albeit not in a legal sense, given the issue of capacity of minors for consent), there are also cases where children might be coerced (by adults) to produce sexually explicit images – for instance, where one partner is an adult and persuades a child to send naked images. It is also possible that images created within a relationship between adolescents could subsequently be redistributed without consent. The discussion here primarily focuses on the issue of images produced and distributed between those under the age of 18, but it should be noted that the law affords a limited exception to those in a relationship between the ages of 16 and 18, which it is also pertinent to consider.

As discussed in considerable detail earlier in this chapter, UK law makes it an offence to produce, distribute or possess any form of child pornography, and these laws were created with the fundamental objective of protecting children from sexual abuse and exploitation. The law, strictly speaking, does not distinguish between 'indecent photographs' created by adults and those that are self-generated by children themselves. To take an example: if X, a girl aged 16, sends a naked image of herself to her boyfriend Y, aged 17, technically X is committing the crime of producing as well as distributing an indecent photograph contrary to section 1 of the Protection of Children Act 1978. Y would be committing the offence of possessing an indecent photograph under section 160 of the Criminal Justice Act 1988, as well as the offence of potentially 'making' an indecent photograph following *Bowden*, discussed earlier. This scenario does not even consider the possibility of further non-consensual redistribution of the image, and yet what would be a seemingly innocent act between two adolescent children

171 Brian Holoyda, Jacqueline Landess, Renee Sorrentino, Susan Hatters Friedman, 'Trouble at teens' Fingertips: Youth Sexting and the Law' (2018) 36(2) *Behavioural Sciences and the Law*.

172 Andy Phippen (n 170) 96. See, for a good discussion on 'sexting' among young people in Europe, Sonia Livingstone and Anke Görzig, '"Sexting": the exchange of sexual messages online among European youth', in Sonia Livingstone, Leslie Haddon and Anke Görzig (eds) *Children, Risk and Safety on the Internet: Research and Policy Challenges in Comparative Perspective* (The Policy Press 2012). See also danah boyd 'Why youth (heart) social network sites: The role of networked publics in teenage social life' in David Buckingham (Ed.) *MacArthur Foundation Series on Digital Learning – Youth, Identity, and Digital Media Volume* (MIT Press 2007); Julia Davidson, 'Gender, Youth and Intimacy as Seen through the Lens of Sexting', in *Sexting: Gender and Teens*, (Sense Publishers 2014).

– who have attained the legal age of consent for sex – constitutes a criminal act if the law is strictly applied. The only exception provided by the law in the form of a defence is where the couple are married, or are living together as partners in an enduring family relationship.[173]

Current child pornography laws pre-date modern-day smartphones. The laws were enacted to prevent the sexual abuse and exploitation of children by adults: lawmakers could not have envisaged the modern-day prevalence and ubiquity of mobile phones, and the possibility of children voluntarily creating these images themselves (save in cases where a child is coerced by an adult). Lloyd argues that the law should recognise the way mobile phones, which he refers to as the 'quintessential writing machine of the third millennium', have revolutionised our lives in order to 'correctly legislate the act of adolescent sexting'.[174] As times and technology have changed, we find ourselves in a situation where the law that was originally created to protect children from predatory adults could be used against the same children the law seeks to protect. The law in this sense is arguably inconsistent with modern-day realities of life. Whilst the law provides a defence for married couples and those living together in an 'enduring family relationship', this is likely to protect only a small minority of individuals. If 'sexting' has become normative among older adolescents within relationships, the married couple defence in all likelihood will not be available to the vast majority of teenagers. This means that in theory a number of adolescent children would be on the wrong side of the law, having already committed the criminal acts of producing, distributing and possessing child pornography.

This is not to suggest that children are regularly prosecuted for 'sexting' in the UK. In fact, the Crown Prosecution Service Guidelines on Prosecuting Cases of Child Sexual Abuse require that care should be taken with respect to cases involving children, and that 'it would not be in the public interest to prosecute the consensual sharing of an image between two children of a similar age in a relationship'.[175] The prosecutorial discretion available means that the law can be carefully applied in practice, but this does not address the problem with the substantive law itself in terms of its apparent inconsistency with societal realities, which leaves children in a particularly vulnerable position.

This is exemplified when the image is redistributed further without the consent of the person who is the subject of the image – for example, in an act commonly referred to as 'revenge pornography', which typically occurs when the relationship breaks down and one disgruntled former partner disseminates the image to cause distress and harassment to the other. Further redistribution of images

173 Protection of Children Act 1978, s 1A(1).

174 Chris Lloyd, 'The Crime of Sexting: A Deconstructive Approach' (2018) 27(1) *Information and Communications Technology Law* 55–85.

175 Crown Prosecution Service, *Child Sexual Abuse: Guidelines on Prosecuting Cases of Child Sexual Abuse*, para 80, available at https://www.cps.gov.uk/legal-guidance/child-sexual-abuse-guidelines-prosecuting-cases-child-sexual-abuse, accessed 9 July 2018.

without consent of the victim should undoubtedly be subject to criminal liability, as it can result in serious harm to the victim and has led to some tragic outcomes, including suicide.[176] The law, however, is currently failing underage victims of 'revenge pornography'. Whilst the non-consensual disclosure of private images has been criminalised under section 33 of the Criminal Justice and Courts Act 2015 (discussed in more detail in Chapter 7), the substantive laws on child pornography as they currently stand make it very difficult for the victim to report it. To return to the earlier example, if the relationship between X and Y breaks down, and Y subsequently forwards the image to his friends without X's consent, what recourse does that leave for X? X can probably report it to the police as a case of 'revenge pornography' contrary to section 33 of the Criminal Justice and Courts Act 2015, but then, strictly speaking, X herself has committed the crime of producing and distributing child pornography by taking and sending the image in the first place. This does not give X any incentive to report the non-consensual redistribution of the image by Y; far from an incentive, by reporting the incident to the police X risks a crime being recorded against her name. This is not to say that X will necessarily be prosecuted for child pornography offences: since the introduction of the Home Office 'Outcome Code 21' in January 2016, the police have discretion to record that a crime has taken place but that they chose not to take any further action, it being not in the public interest to do so. Whilst this means that the person will not be subject to prosecution, there is no guarantee that an Enhanced Criminal Records Check will not reveal it as the incident will remain on the record as a 'crime' and the child listed as a 'suspect'. In this scenario, the law does not really differentiate between the victim (X) who sent the image to her boyfriend within the security of a relationship, and the perpetrator (Y) who redistributed the image without consent and to cause distress and harassment to the other. Whilst the act of Y should remain an offence – as this would be a clear act of so-called 'revenge pornography' – it is harsh to treat X's act as creating child pornography and this is something for substantive law to address rather than delegating it to police and prosecutorial discretion.

Whilst strong child pornography laws exist for a range of legitimate and compelling reasons, there are some limited circumstances where appropriate defences must be available. The law must reflect modern realities of life and a narrowly drafted defence for consensual sexting between minors of a similar age group should be introduced to existing legislation. The reference to 'similar age-group' is pertinent here – it would be illogical if the defence applied to a 17-year-old who persuaded an eight-year-old child to send a naked image for sexual gratification as it is likely to be exploitative rather than innocent sexting. The law has already been amended in some jurisdictions, including in the state of Victoria in Australia and at state level in the United States. In Victoria, new exceptions were introduced following the

176 See Rayeed Ibtesam, 'On Teenage Sexting and the Law' (2017) 1 *Hamline Journal of Public Law and Policy* 246–277.

recommendations of the Victorian Parliamentary Law Reform Committee's inquiry into sexting through the Crimes Amendment (Sexual Offences) Act 2014.[177] The new exceptions applying to children for the provisions in section 70AAA of the Crimes Act 1958 are intended to protect children from being caught under child pornography offences for the non-exploitative act of sexting. The law provides an exception for self-generated nude images (for example a 'selfie') taken by a child[178] as well as for victims of a criminal offence that resulted in the image (for example, where the image was taken against the will of the subject).[179] In addition, there is a defence available for a person (who is a child) accused of child pornography offences where the images that depict (lawful) conduct with other children where he is not, or he reasonably believed is not, more than two years older than the youngest child depicted in the image.[180] Therefore, if A, a 17-year-old, takes a picture of himself and B, his girlfriend of 16, engaging in a sexual act, the defence allows A to possess a image of the two of them engaging in sexual activity. It is pertinent to note that the law has confined the defence as applicable to images exchanged between peers within a similar age group of two years either way, and that the defence is not available to adults.

There is some progress in the United States in terms of recognition that underage sexting should not be treated on a par with child pornography offences, but state laws vary considerably in this regard. It is still treated as a felony in many states, but there are about 23 states that have adopted sexting legislation or amended existing child pornography legislation for this purpose with lenient penalties amounting to misdemeanour or a minor offence.[181] In Illinois and New Jersey the law does not treat it as a criminal offence, and instead stipulates a counselling programme and/or other informal sanctions. It should be noted that there is also reluctance from some commentators to completely decriminalise adolescent sexting. As argued by O'Connor et al, this is due to 'the long term impact that sexting behaviours can have on young adults', including psychological harm linked to potential cyber bullying, or 'revenge pornography' that may follow the initial act of sexting. They call for 'lesser punishments' such as community services and 'psychological counselling and mandatory relationship education' for images taken consensually. Whilst it is true that consensual 'sexting' carries the risk of misuse of the images in the future, it is absurd to suggest that the law should impose sanctions on consensual exchange of images

177 Victoria Parliament, Law Reform Committee, *Report of the Law Reform Committee for the Inquiry into Sexting*, Parliamentary Paper; Session 2010–13, no 230. Report available at https://www.parliament.vic.gov.au/images/stories/committees/lawrefrom/isexting/LRC_Sexting_Final_Report.pdf, accessed 9 July 2018.

178 Section 51M(1), Crimes Act 1958.

179 Section 51M(2).

180 Section 51N.

181 See Kimberly O'Connor, Michelle Drouin, Nicholas Yergens and Genni Newsham, 'Sexting Legislation in the United States and Abroad: A Call for Uniformity' (2017) 11(2) *International Journal of Cyber Criminology* 218–245.

between adolescents who are of legal age of consent for sex. If revenge pornography is the risk, the conduct that needs to be criminalised is the non-consensual distribution of the image – not the private, consensual taking of the image. Penalising this with 'lesser punishment' would still put the victim in a vulnerable position. Apart from the issue of the conflict it raises between the law and prevailing norms, it will also leave the victim no incentive to report a case of 'revenge pornography' or cyber bullying based on a self-created image, as illustrated in the example above. It should be clear from the discussion in this chapter that the very foundation of child pornography laws is to protect children, who the law has for long recognised are entitled to special care and protection due to their lack of physical and mental maturity. It is ironic that the same laws that were intended to protect them can potentially be used to penalise conduct such as consensual sexting that could, in part, be attributed to the lack of capacity to make informed decisions owing to that same lack of maturity and/or failing to appreciate its long-term consequences. Therefore, if sexting is to be discouraged amongst adolescent teenagers – and this would be a policy decision – measures that seek to achieve this should be outside the strict remit of criminal law and punitive sanctions.

It is perhaps time to consider a carefully drafted exception to child pornography laws in order that children are not persecuted by the very laws that are intended to protect them. This should, at the very least, ensure that consensual and non-exploitative 'sexting' between adolescent children is not criminalised. The law also has an equally important role in ensuring that any further misuse of images that were consensually produced – including non-consensual distribution, cyberbullying or harassment – are criminalised with appropriate sanctions. Needless to say, encouraging responsible 'sexting' behaviour is not something that can be achieved by the deterrence of the law – it requires a holistic approach involving education and awareness at school curriculum level, as well as parental support and guidance.

Concluding thoughts

I have endeavoured in this chapter to outline the different stages of evolution of child pornography laws, focusing on real and pseudo child pornography. It should be clear from the discussion that the law has evolved substantially over the last four decades and has come a long way since the production and distribution of child pornography was specifically criminalised in 1978, recognising the harm inherent in creating the images. The challenges raised by the internet and other digital technologies have necessitated further legislative action, which resulted in new laws being introduced. This has had the result that the focus of traditional laws on the publisher and distributor of content changed, and unprecedented liability was imposed on the end-user of content. This period has witnessed innovative and broad interpretations of the law by the judiciary, effectively rendering the end-user of content criminally liable for making, i.e., producing, child pornography. We have also seen a steady rise in simple possession offences for child pornography, which started with a specific offence focusing on real child pornography, but it was only a matter of time before this was extended to pseudo-pornography, and subsequently to virtual pornography. Laws that impose criminal liability on the consumers of content call for careful scrutiny, as it essentially criminalises conduct carried out in private. As I have demonstrated, there are legitimate reasons for holding consumers of child pornography to account for the harm caused to children, and in this sense the regulatory responses are not only proportionate but indispensable to effectively combat child pornography on the internet. These changes are irreversible and represent a fundamental transformation of child pornography laws, and the overall regulatory approach. The law will no doubt continue to evolve as the distribution and access models for pornography change with further advances in technology.

Legislation, however, is only part of the solution and merely a first step in the broader regulatory framework to combat online child pornography. Laws that cannot be enforced in cyberspace are ultimately bound to fail and therefore effective identification and enforcement mechanisms should be in place alongside robust laws – the subject of analysis of Chapter 5. Chapter 4 considers the legal issues and challenges involved in regulating virtual pornography, which raises a slightly different set of issues.

4 Virtual child pornography

Whilst the term 'virtual child pornography' has often been used to include pseudo photographs, readers are reminded that for the purposes of this book it only includes non-photographic, fictitious images where no real children are depicted.[1] The most important factor that distinguishes virtual pornography from other types of child pornography discussed so far is that it involves no use of photographs at any stage. This would therefore exclude 'indecent photographs' and 'indecent pseudo-photographs' discussed in Chapter 3, and would also naturally mean that the material is not created as a result of causing direct harm to a child. It is, however, possible that the image of a real and identifiable child can be produced as an entirely computer-generated image, in which case psychological harm will indeed be caused to the child, but this should be considered similar to a pseudo-photograph. Derivatives of photographs, such as tracings (for instance where the outline of a photograph is traced manually onto tracing paper or using computer software) are already treated as 'indecent photographs' following a 2008 amendment to the meaning of 'photographs' within s 7 of the Protection of Children Act 1978 to include a 'tracing or other image'.[2] Tracings are therefore excluded from the scope of 'virtual pornography' for the purposes of this chapter. The discussion here is purely focused on non-identifiable fictitious images of children that are computer-generated, but can also include manga images, cartoons and drawings.

Criminalising virtual child pornography has generally been controversial as it raises a number of complex issues. In the absence of real children depicted in the images, what justifies the criminalisation of virtual child pornography? What harms could result from the possession of virtual pornography? Is it really a victimless crime? Could the indecency inherent in the image offer the basis for criminalisation? These are all pertinent questions worthy of examination. This chapter provides an overview

1 There are wide variations and interesting issues surrounding the definitions of what constitutes virtual child pornography. For a detailed analysis, see Alisdair A Gillespie, *Child Pornography: Law and Policy* (Routledge 2012), Ch 5.

2 The amendment was made possible through s 69 of the Criminal Justice and Immigration Act 2008, and came into force in July 2008.

of the legal responses in the UK and the US to regulate virtual child pornography and examines the merits, criticisms and desirability of its criminalisation in light of these questions.

Legal responses

There have been various legislative initiatives to address virtual child pornography both nationally and internationally, but these have also been subject to some controversy. For example, in the United States legislative initiatives to criminalise virtual child pornography date back to 1996, through the Child Pornography Prevention Act 1996,[3] but this was struck down as unconstitutional by the US Supreme Court in *Ashcroft v Free Speech Coalition*.[4] There has been judicial consideration of the application of the law to virtual pornography in Canada by the Supreme Court in *R v Sharpe*.[5] The possession of virtual child pornography has been criminalised in the UK under the Coroners and Justice Act 2009, which remains law.[6]

Internationally, the United Nations Optional Protocol to the Convention on the Rights of the Child calls for the criminalisation of the representation of child pornography 'by whatever means', which could arguably include virtual child pornography.[7] As for other international instruments examined in Chapter 3, the definition of 'child pornography' within the Council of Europe Convention on Cybercrime could encompass virtual child pornography as it refers to 'realistic images representing a minor engaged in sexually explicit conduct'.[8] However, Signatory States have the choice of not applying this provision within their domestic law due to the discretion granted under Article 9(4). Similarly, the definition of 'child pornography' in the Lanzarote Convention is also broad enough to cover virtual pornography: '"child pornography" shall mean any material that visually depicts a child engaged in real or simulated sexually explicit conduct'.[9] Article 20(3), however, grants signatory states the right not to criminalise the production and possession of material 'consisting exclusively of simulated representations or realistic images of a non-existent child'. The EU

3 The Child Pornography Prevention Act 1996 attempted to define 'child pornography' to include any visual depiction, including any photograph, film, video, picture, or computer or computer-generated image or picture, whether made or produced by electronic, mechanical, or other means, of sexually explicit conduct, where such visual depiction is, or appears to be, of a minor engaging in sexually explicit conduct. (§ 121(2), Child Pornography Prevention Act 1996)

4 535 U.S. 234 (2002).

5 *R v Sharpe* [2001] 1 SCR 45.

6 Coroners and Justice Act 2009, ss 62–68. The relevant provisions of the Act came into force in January 2010. The Act does not extend to Scotland.

7 There is, however, some uncertainty as to whether this covers fictional representations of non-identifiable children. See Gillespie (n 1) 104.

8 Art 9(2)(c) of the Council of Europe Convention on Cybercrime (CETS No. 185).

9 Art 20 of the Council of Europe Convention on the Protection of Children against Sexual Exploitation and Sexual Abuse (CETS No 201).

Directive on Combating the Sexual Abuse and Sexual Exploitation of Children and Child Pornography[10] also offers a broad definition of 'child pornography' to encompass virtual representations – 'realistic images of a child engaged in sexually explicit conduct or realistic images of the sexual organs of a child, for primarily sexual purposes'.[11] The Directive allows discretion for Member States not to criminalise such material where it is produced and possessed solely for private use and there is no risk of dissemination of the material.[12] These 'opt-out' provisions are indicative of the difficulties in identifying a universal common standard for regulating virtual child pornography, unlike images involving real children. Whilst there is a certain degree of consensus among countries of the world that real child pornography should be criminalised, the treatment of virtual pornography varies significantly across jurisdictions for a range of cultural, constitutional and political reasons. For instance, certain forms of virtual pornography remain legal in Japan where *manga* (comic books) and *anime* (cartoons) that depict children in sexualised and violent activities remain legal, despite calls to criminalise such material.[13] Some of the challenges of regulating virtual child pornography can be examined through the lens of domestic legislation in the UK, and perhaps more usefully the legislative attempt in the US and the Supreme Court decision that followed in *Ashcroft v Free Speech Coalition*.[14]

UK: Criminalising possession

The UK introduced legislation to regulate virtual child pornography in 2009, more than two decades after the legislative attempt in the US through the Child Pornography Prevention Act 1996. Section 62 of the Coroners and Justice Act 2009 (CJA 2009) created a new simple possession offence for 'prohibited images' of children, punishable by up to three years' imprisonment. The law applies only to images that are non-photographic and specifically excludes indecent photographs and pseudo-photographs that are already covered under existing law discussed in the previous chapter. A 'prohibited image' is defined in section 62 (2) as an image which –

a) is pornographic
b) falls within subsection (6), and
c) is grossly offensive, disgusting or otherwise of an obscene character.

10 Directive 2011/92/EU.
11 Ibid, Art 2(c)(iv).
12 Art 5(8).
13 For a critique see, Cory Lyn Takeuchi, 'Regulating *Lolicon:* Toward Japanese Compliance with its International Legal Obligations to Ban Virtual Child Pornography' (2015) 44(1) *Georgia Journal of International and Comparative Law* 195–236.
14 535 U.S. 234 (2002).

An image falls within subsection (6) if it[15] –

a) is an image which focuses solely or principally on a child's genitals or anal region, or
b) portrays any of the acts mentioned in subsection (7)

The following acts are set out in subsection (7):[16]

a) the performance by a person of an act of intercourse or oral sex with or in the presence of a child;
b) an act of masturbation by, of, involving or in the presence of a child;
c) an act which involves penetration of the vagina or anus of a child with a part of a person's body or with anything else;
d) an act of penetration, in the presence of a child, of the vagina or anus of a person with a part of a person's body or with anything else;
e) the performance by a child of an act of intercourse or oral sex with an animal (whether dead or alive or imaginary);
f) the performance by a person of an act of intercourse or oral sex with an animal (whether dead or alive or imaginary) in the presence of a child.

The CJA 2009 applies to only material that is primarily pornographic in nature. 'Pornographic' is defined within the Act – 'an image is pornographic if it is of such nature that it must reasonably be assumed to have been produced solely or principally for the purpose of sexual arousal'.[17] The relatively clear sets of acts that set out in s 62 (7) should narrow down the scope of the offence considerably, ensuring that other works, for instance artistic expressions, are not penalised. Nevertheless, criticisms and uncertainties remain.

A particular and rather fundamental problem pertains to establishing whether the subject of the virtual image is a 'child'. A 'child' is defined in s 65(5) as a person under the age of 18. Section 65(6) further stipulates that 'an image should be treated as a child if the impression conveyed by the image is that of a child, or the predominant impression conveyed is that of a child despite the fact that some of the physical characteristics shown are not of a child'.[18] Whilst it is relatively less problematic to make a reasonable judgment in relation to a photograph featuring real persons, computer-generated characters or cartoon images are more difficult in terms of ascertaining the age of the character depicted. It will be up to the jury to ascertain this, but due to the very nature of virtual imagery this would not be an easy task. Therefore, there will be a certain level of inherent uncertainty as to the lawfulness of the material, which

15 Section 62(6).
16 Section 62(7).
17 Section 62(3).
18 Section 65(6).

leaves the possessor no clarity as to whether or not he/she is committing a criminal act by virtue of possessing it.

It should be noted that CJA 2009 regulates only the *possession* of virtual pornography. As far as publication and distribution are concerned, the governing law is the Obscene Publications Act 1959, the same legislation that regulates traditional obscenity. If someone creates the material with the intention of publishing, they can be charged under s 2(1) of the Obscene Publications Act 1959, as they would be in possession of the material with a view to publication. If, however, the creator did not have the necessary intent to publish it, they would still (logically) also be in possession of the image and could potentially attract the s 62(1) offence under the Coroners and Justice Act 2009. There is some criticism that relying on traditional obscenity law for the publication of virtual child pornography leads to disproportionate outcomes compared to the offence of possession. The possession offence under s 62(1) CJA 2009 is broader than the 'deprave and corrupt test' under s 1 of the Obscene Publications Act 1959, which means that the person who merely possesses the material is more likely to be committing a criminal offence than the person who actually created it in the first instance. This is because materials that do not necessarily 'deprave and corrupt' according to the obscenity test under the Obscene Publications Act could still be caught under the broader 'disgusting' or 'grossly offensive' standard under CJA 2009.[19]

In addition, the offence under s 62 could theoretically mean that it is a more serious offence to be in possession of virtual child pornography than to produce or distribute it. Any prosecutions for production or distribution will need to be under the Obscene Publications Act 1959. There is no equivalent 'making' offence for virtual child pornography, unlike 'indecent photographs' or 'pseudo photographs' under s1 of the Protection of Children Act 1978. Whilst it is arguable that images that could attract a section 62 offence for virtual child pornography could meet the requirements of 'obscenity' under the Obscene Publications Act and therefore its publication and distribution could be prosecuted on that basis, if the recent outcomes of cases charged using the Act are any indication, this may not necessarily be the case.[20] It is the case that if the image is created by someone they will also logically be in possession, but in theory it raises a peculiar situation where simple possession of virtual pornography is a more serious crime than its production or distribution. In the case of real child pornography producing an image is a more serious offence than its simple possession– which is logical given the possibility of direct harm caused to a child as part of the process. As for virtual child pornography, due to the absence of direct harm caused to children during its

19 See Alex Antoniou, 'Legislative comment: Possession of Prohibited Images of Children: Three Years On' (2013) 77 *Journal of Criminal Law*,337–353 at 351.

20 Prosecutions under the Obscene Publications Act 1959 have been rare in recent times, and there are criticisms that the obscenity provisions under the Act are obsolete. See, for example, Susan M Edwards, 'On the Contemporary Application of the Obscene Publications Act 1959' (1998) 12 *Criminal Law Review* 843–853. These issues are considered in more detail in Chapter 7.

creation it is probably arguable that it does not call for a more serious offence of production. But why, then, is possession treated more seriously? Is it more harmful to possess virtual pornography than to create it?

'Harm' is a rather elusive concept in relation to virtual child pornography. The legislation in the UK was preceded by a public consultation,[21] but the Government's reasoning for criminalising virtual child pornography was never made entirely clear. It was acknowledged by the Government that there was no evidence available to suggest a link between the possession of virtual pornography and an increased risk of harm to children.[22] In fact, one would struggle to find any strong justification for criminalising virtual child pornography in the consultation document. The law has, perhaps unsurprisingly, attracted some criticism and been fairly controversial.[23]

If the images are merely imaginary characters, prevention of direct harm cannot provide the justification for criminalising its simple possession, for none is caused to any real person. The only exception that would apply is where the computer-generated image is indistinguishable from a that of a real child – with advances in technology it is of course possible that an entirely computer-generated image can be created that resembles a real living child. In such cases, the image should, however, be treated like a pseudo-photograph, and the direct (psychological) harm caused to the child justifies its criminalisation as discussed in Chapter 3. As for virtual child pornography that is created purely using imagination, one has to turn to the prevention of any indirect harm stemming from the very existence of the image as a possible justification for its criminalisation.

It is arguable that those who seek and possess such material are people who have a deviant interest in children, and therefore their behaviour itself puts children at risk. A particular concern is that possessors of such images could progress to contact offending and eventually physically abuse a child. However, as noted in Chapter 3, and also acknowledged by the Government in the consultation document itself, there seems to be a lack of empirical evidence in relation to any direct links that possession of images can lead to contact offending.[24] Some commentators support the prohibition of possession of virtual child pornography by those who have a prior history of child sexual molestation on the basis of research evidence that it can

21 Home Office, Northern Ireland Office, Scottish Executive (2007), *Consultation on the Possession of Non-Photographic Visual Depictions of Child Abuse*. Available at http://webarchive.nationalarchives.gov.uk/+/http:/www.justice.gov.uk/docs/consultation-non-photographic.pdf, accessed 19 July 2018.

22 Ibid, 6.

23 See for example, Abhilash Nair, 'When a cartoon or drawing can land you in jail', *The Conversation*, 27 October 2014. Available at https://theconversation.com/when-a-drawing-or-cartoon-image-can-land-you-in-jail-33418.

24 See Ethel Quayle, Marcus Erooga, Louise Wright, Max Taylor and Dawn Harbinson (eds) *Only Pictures? Therapeutic work with Internet sex offenders* (Russell House Publishing 2006). See also the discussion in Chapter 3 in relation to the link between possession and contact offending.

pre-empt recidivist tendencies, rather than a blanket prohibition against the use of virtual pornography for all, including child pornography offenders without a history of contact offending, in light of the lack of evidence of possession leading to contact offending.[25]

There is also an argument that virtual pornography offers an 'outlet' for such people to vent their desire and therefore the possession of such material should be permitted as that reduces the risk to actual children. In addition, it is argued that, if virtual pornography is legal, production of real images of children might decline as producers would prefer to create virtual images rather than producing illegal images involving real children.[26] This argument, however, is not accepted by all, especially in light of the evidence that downloading behaviour and the fantasies that it fuels do not remain a static response, and results in seeking more arousing images.[27] If this is true, it is possible that those who are in the habit of possessing virtual child pornography could eventually progress to seeking indecent images involving real children and therefore it can be argued that virtual child pornography poses a reasonable risk to children.

A further argument that supports criminalising the possession of virtual pornography is that it could be used as a tool in the grooming process to lure children and eventually lead to inappropriate sexual contact. The Home Office Consultation that preceded legislation in the UK pointed to this possibility.[28] There is some merit in this argument, in that an offender could show virtual pornography to the victim in order to persuade the child that such activity is normal.[29] In addition, there is also the risk of normalisation of behaviour for the paedophile itself, as noted in the context of pseudo images in the Chapter 3.[30]

Criminalising simple possession on the basis of these arguments is, however, not supported by all.[31] As research is inconclusive, in order to draw any firm inferences of harm to children from the possession of virtual child pornography, what other justifications might possibly provide the basis for criminalising fictitious virtual child pornography? A possible argument that supports criminalisation is that the

25 See Neil Malamuth and Mark Huppin, 'Drawing the Line on Virtual Child Pornography: Bringing the Law in Line with the Research Evidence' (2007) 42 *New York University Review of Law & Social Change* 773–911.

26 Neil Levy, 'Virtual Child Pornography: the Eroticisation of Inequality' (2002) 4(4) *Ethics and Information Technology* 319–323.

27 Quayle et al (n 24), 61.

28 Consultation (n 21), 6.

29 See generally on child pornography normalising behaviour, Hannah Lena Merdian, Cate Curtis, Jo Thakker, Nick Wilson, and Douglas Pieter Boer, 'The Three Dimensions of Online Child Pornography Offending' (2011) 19(1) *Journal of Sexual Aggression* 121–132.

30 KV Lanning, 'Collectors' in AW Burgess and ML Clark (eds) *Child Pornography and Sex Rings* (Lexington Books 1984) 86. See also Chapter 3, n 150.

31 Suzanne Ost, 'Criminalising Fabricated Images of Child Pornography: A Matter of Harm or Morality?', (2010) 30(2) *Legal Studies* 230–256; Katherine S. Williams, 'Child Pornography Law: Does it Protect Children' (2004) 26(3) *Journal of Social Welfare and Family Law* 245–261.

inherent indecency of the image should justify criminalisation considering that it represents children in an inappropriate sexual context. Whilst this is certainly a good emotive argument, this is fundamentally premised on notions of morality, i.e., that the majority of people would find such representations of children to be disgusting, offensive or abhorrent. The law is therefore arguably not directly seeking to address harm to children, but merely regulating speech that many would find immoral or offensive. It is also arguable that the regulation of virtual pornography is in this sense primarily a 'speech issue'. This is the reason why its regulation is so controversial and particularly problematic. *Ashcroft v Free Speech Coalition*[32] considered some of these issues in detail and is a good reference point to explore the different arguments further.

US: *Ashcroft v Free Speech Coalition*

The arguments for and against the criminalisation of virtual pornography advanced in *Ashcroft v Free Speech Coalition* ("Ashcroft") broadly mirror the existing debates in this area. In this case, the US Supreme Court considered two specific provisions of the Child Pornography Prevention Act 1996 (CPPA), which sought to extend the existing prohibition on child pornography made using actual children to 'any visual depiction including any photograph, film, video, picture, or computer or computer-generated image or picture' that 'is, or appears to be, of a minor engaging in sexually explicit conduct'[33] and any sexually explicit image that is 'advertised, promoted, presented, described, or distributed in such a manner that conveys the impression' that it depicts 'a minor engaging in sexually explicit conduct'.[34]

The first provision banned images created using computer technology, as well as images using adults who look younger and give a realistic impression of minors: collectively referred to as 'virtual child pornography'. As noted before, it should be remembered that 'virtual child pornography' in this regard is broader than the definition in the UK; the latter includes only non-photographic images of children, whereas the former also includes what in the UK would be classed as 'pseudo-photographs'.[35] The Free Speech Coalition, an adult entertainment trade association and others, challenged the CPPA alleging that the provisions 'appears to be' and 'conveys the impression' are overbroad and vague and would cause a chilling effect on protected right to free speech, contrary to the First Amendment to the US Constitution. Although the District Court initially ruled in favour of the Government and granted summary judgment, it was reversed by the Court of Appeals for the Ninth Circuit holding the CPPA invalid on its face, being substantially overbroad and not meeting the

32 535 U.S. 234 (2002).
33 § 2256(8)(B).
34 § 2256(8)(D).
35 Section 1, Protection of Children Act 1978.

criteria of obscenity under *Miller v California*[36] or the prohibition afforded to child pornography under *New York v Ferber*,[37] before eventually being appealed to the Supreme Court.

The Supreme Court held that the material covered under the CPPA goes beyond the categories recognised under *Miller* and *Ferber*. Obscenity is not protected under the First Amendment per *Miller*, and the Court stated that the CPPA does not meet the requirement of the *Miller* test, because its provisions do not require that the work appeal to the prurient interest or be patently offensive as any depiction of sexual activity by those appearing to be minors is proscribed.[38] The Court also found inconsistencies with *Miller* in relation to the contemporary community standards criterion as 'pictures of what appear to be 17-year-olds engaging in explicit sexual activity do not in every case contravene community standards'.[39] In addition, the CPPA did not provide exceptions for serious literary, artistic, political or scientific value (the third prong of the *Miller* test), which the Court was again uneasy about. The Court referred to acclaimed Hollywood movies, such as the Academy Award-nominated film *Traffic* and Academy award-winning film *American Beauty*, both containing scenes of teenage girls engaging in sexual activity. Whilst not specifically holding that the relevant scenes would necessarily violate the CPPA, the Court stated that the films (among many other films and works of art) do explore themes that have been part of art and literature throughout the ages, something which is within the 'wide sweep of the statute's prohibitions'. It would have the result that, if such films have even one scene that depicts sexual activity within the definition of the CPPA, the possessor would be subject to punishment without inquiry into the film's overall redeeming value.[40] The Supreme Court accordingly ruled that the CPPA cannot meet the standards to pass as legislation to address obscenity due to its inconsistency with the well-settled rules in *Miller*.

Child pornography, however, can be prohibited regardless of whether it depicts works of value or falls outside the parameters of obscenity for adult

36 413 U.S. 15 (1973). The three-pronged *Miller* test includes the following criteria:

(a) whether the average person, applying contemporary community standards would find that the work, taken as a whole, appeals to the prurient interest,

(b) whether the work depicts or describes, in a patently offensive way, sexual conduct specifically defined by the applicable state law, and

(c) whether the work, taken as a whole, lacks serious literary, artistic, political, or scientific value.

37 458 U.S. 747 (1982).

38 Under the CPPA, images are prohibited as long as the persons depicted appear to be under 18 years of age, 18 USC § 2256(1).

39 535 U.S. 234 (2002) at 235.

40 The obscenity test under *Miller* requires the work to be considered as a whole to judge the redeeming value; and so, for example, where a single scene is part of the narrative, the work itself does not for this reason become obscene, although the scene on its own might be offensive. This is consistent with the 'deprave and corrupt' test under English obscenity law (s 1, Obscene Publications Act 1959), where the material in question ought to be considered as a whole.

pornography – this was the decision in *Ferber*, which upheld a prohibition on the production, distribution and sale of child pornography. It was acknowledged in *Ferber* that child pornography forms a permanent record of a child's abuse and its continued circulation would harm the child who participated.[41] However, *Ferber* involved real children, whereas the CPPA addressed virtual child pornography which does not involve real children. Drawing a distinction between the two, the Supreme Court highlighted that for child pornography involving actual children the images are themselves the product of child sexual abuse and the state had an interest in preventing such abuse to children without regard to any judgment about its content. This was essentially the main principle in *Ferber*: the target of the New York statute that formed the basis for its legal challenge was to address the production of the work, i.e., the inherent child sexual abuse that forms the basis of production rather than the content itself.[42] In the context of the First Amendment, it is clear that the speech had a direct and proximate link to the crime from which it emanated, which justifies the prohibition. In other words, in order to merit First Amendment protection, speech should not be obscene or the ***product*** of sexual abuse. Similar reasons justified the prohibition on the simple possession of child pornography, which was confirmed by a later decision in *Osborne v Ohio*[43] where it was held that the state has an important interest in protecting the victims of child pornography and for that reason it was justified in 'attempting to stamp out this vice at all levels in the distribution chain', including mere possession.[44]

The Court distinguished between the speech in *Ferber* and that which the CPPA sought to prohibit: in the former, the speech itself is a direct record of sexual abuse, whereas the latter prohibits speech that records no crime and creates no victims by its production. The Government argued that the images can lead to actual instances of child abuse, but the Court rejected this by holding that the causal link is contingent and indirect: 'the harm does not necessarily follow from the speech, but depends upon some unquantified potential for subsequent criminal acts'.[45] Rejecting the argument that paedophiles may use virtual pornography to lure and seduce children, it was noted that 'there are many things innocent in

41 The court, drawing a comparison to defamatory statements, held that each new publication of an image would cause new injury to the child's reputation and emotional well-being (*New York v Ferber* 458 US at 759). The court agreed that the State has an interest in closing the distribution network to address the economic motive in its production, 'the most expeditious if not the only practical method of law enforcement may be to dry up the market for this material by imposing severe criminal penalties on persons selling, advertising, or otherwise promoting the product' (at 760).

42 Note O'Conner J's opinion in his concurring judgment: 'as drafted, New York's statute does not attempt to supress the communication of particular ideas' (*New York v Ferber* at 775)

43 495 U.S. 103 (1990).

44 Ibid at 110, emphasis added.

45 *Ashcroft v Free Speech Coalition* 535 U.S. 234 (2002) at 236

themselves, however, such as cartoons, video games, and candy that might be used for immoral purposes yet we would not expect those to be prohibited because they can be misused'.[46] The Court essentially distinguished between speech and conduct: what the Government is trying to protect children from is not the speech, but from the conduct of those who would commit crimes. The Court took the view that the prohibition imposed on such speech, albeit with the objective to prohibit illegal conduct, was not narrowly drawn and would restrict the speech available to law-abiding adults. If grooming is the threat and main concern of the Government, the law ought to criminalise the conduct – i.e., the act of grooming, rather than the tools that might have been used in the grooming process. Whilst this sounds like a logical approach, it is submitted that virtual child pornography is more than just a tool and the analogy to candy and video games is fraught with difficulties. Virtual pornography does not really fit the description of 'other seemingly innocent items'. Most right-thinking members of society would find sexual representations of children grossly inappropriate and abhorrent. Unlike candy or otherwise innocent tools used in grooming, virtual child pornography is not morally neutral – it has the potential to touch the moral conscience of the average individual. In this sense the analogy is flawed. The inherent *risk* of harm involved in pornographic representation of children and its possession has already been noted in the previous chapter in the context of pseudo-pornography. If there is a genuine risk of harm stemming from possession of virtual pornography, for example by normalising behaviour for children and also for paedophiles as noted in the previous chapter in relation to possession offences, regulation could be justified on this ground.[47]

The Government further argued that virtual child pornography fuels the fantasies of paedophiles, as it has the tendency to 'whet the appetite of paedophiles' and encourages them to engage in illegal conduct. This was rejected by the Court on the ground that 'the mere tendency of speech to encourage unlawful acts is not a sufficient reason for banning it'.[48] The Court was particularly critical that the provisions may amount to controlling a person's private thoughts, which poses a danger to the protected freedoms under the US Constitution. Further, it was noted that there was no real causal link established between speech that might encourage thoughts and impulses and resulting child abuse and without such a strong and direct connection it was not permissible to prohibit speech on the ground that it might encourage paedophiles to abuse children. This position differs from the view taken by the Supreme Court of Canada in *R v Sharpe*.[49] In this case, the child pornography provisions under s 163.1 of the Criminal Code was challenged as unconstitutional and contrary to the fundamental rights granted under the Canadian Charter of Rights and

46 Ibid, at 251.
47 See Chapter 3, page 65.
48 *Ashcroft v Free Speech Coalition*, 535 U.S. 234 (2002) at 253.
49 2001 SCC 2.

Freedoms. It was argued that the breadth of provisions under s 163.1 of the Canadian Criminal Code was too broad as it would cover pseudo images and textual representations of sexual relationships with adults and children, which do not cause direct harm to children and criminalising the possession of such material would amount to a 'thought crime'. Sharpe, whilst conceding that (direct) harm caused to children justifies criminalising possession of some forms of pornography, argued that the other forms of imagery brought within the purview of s 163.1(4), which would include textual representations, pseudo images, etc., goes too far and violates his right to freedom of expression and thought protected by s 2(b) of the Charter. The Court, however, rejected this argument generally, subject to two narrow exceptions, and held that the simple possession of child pornography 'poses a reasoned risk of harm to children': the evidence establishes several links between the possession of child pornography and harm to children and therefore the provisions in s 163.1(4) are constitutional and the restrictions proportionate. The narrow exceptions pertain to two specific categories of material within the offence that raised 'little or no risk of harm to children': (1) written materials or visual representations created and held by the accused alone, exclusively for personal use; and (2) visual recordings created by or depicting the accused that do not depict unlawful sexual activity and are held by the accused exclusively for private use.

It was also argued in support of the CPPA that virtual pornography is indistinguishable from real child pornography and is actually part of the same market; they are often exchanged, one for the other. Therefore, the objective of eliminating the market of child pornography per se should include the elimination of virtual child pornography as the latter effectively promotes the trade in pornography involving real children. The Court rejected this as being implausible because, if the two genres are indistinguishable, it should lead to illegal images being driven from the market and not the other way round, given that pornographers would not risk prosecution by producing child pornography using real children if the virtual variant would suffice. It should be remembered that, at time of going to press, 16 years have passed since *Ashcroft*, and technology has made significant advances since then. It is possible to create virtual pornographic representations that are so realistic that it would be difficult to distinguish between virtual and real images of children – the 'Sweetie' experiment discussed in the previous chapter offers a classic example of how realistic and life-like virtual pornography can be.[50] If the law were to permit virtual pornography on the basis that no child was harmed in its creation, that would be in denial of the possibility that images resembling real and identifiable children can easily be created as 'virtual pornography'. The psychological harm and other justifications supporting the criminalisation of the production and possession of pseudo child pornography discussed in the previous chapter should provide sufficient basis for criminalising this category of material, but then, as noted before, it is arguable that the image should be treated like a

50 See Chapter 3, page 74.

'pseudo-photograph' and not virtual pornography. However, it might still leave a legal loophole for borderline cases where the image may not meet the literal or legal definition of a photograph but yet may resemble a real and living child. In addition, there is as yet no evidence that the volume of real child pornography has declined despite the existence of technology that facilitates the creation of virtual pornography, and with the benefit of hindsight, it is submitted that pornographers have not turned to producing virtual imagery abandoning real child pornography.

The practical difficulty in prosecuting those who produce images using real children due to the indistinguishable effect of virtual pornography was also pointed out in support of prohibition of both categories of image. The Court rejected this on the basis that this would mean that protected speech would also need to be banned as a means to ban unprotected speech, which would be unconstitutional: 'the overbreadth doctrine prohibits the Government from banning unprotected speech if a substantial amount of protected speech is prohibited or chilled in the process'.[51] Laws that aim to control the private thoughts of individuals are impermissible: 'right to think is the beginning of freedom, and speech must be protected from the government because speech is the beginning of thought".[52]

Regulation of virtual pornography law post-*Ashcroft*

Ashcroft demonstrated the biggest challenge for the regulation of virtual child pornography – its conflict with freedom of speech. Whilst courts have been willing to outlaw images that portray real children, owing to the inherent harm to children caused during its creation, the reluctance to extend this to content that did not involve any harm to children is hardly surprising from a US perspective, in light of the First Amendment jurisprudence. Following the striking down of the CPPA by the Supreme Court, the US Government subsequently responded with legislation in the form of the Prosecutorial Remedies and Other Tools to End the Exploitation of Children Today (PROTECT) Act 2003. The PROTECT Act consisted of statues that prohibit the creation, distribution and possession of child pornography,[53] and sought to remedy the criticisms of the CPPA by narrowing the definition of virtual child pornography to include 'indistinguishable' images from that of a real minor.[54] There is specific exemption for 'depictions that are drawings, cartoons, sculptures, or paintings depicting minors or adults'.[55] However, a new statute created in the PROTECT Act limits the scope of this exemption to non-obscene images: s 1466A prohibits images of minors that are 'obscene', regardless of whether the children are

51 *Ashcroft v Free Speech Coalition* 535 U.S. 234 (2002) at 237.

52 Ibid at 253.

53 18 U.S.C. § 2252, 18 U.S.C. § 2252A, and 18 U.S.C. § 2256.

54 Child pornography is defined as any visual depiction of sexually explicit conduct that includes: a) a minor, b) a digital or computer image that is 'indistinguishable' from that of a real minor, or c) an image which has been created or modified to appear to be that of an 'identifiable minor' engaging in sexually explicit conduct (18 U.S.C. § 2256(8))

55 18 U.S.C. § 2256(11).

real and regardless of what form of media, whether it be drawings, paintings, etc. This means that virtual representations that would meet the test of 'obscenity' would come under the purview of the PROTECT Act, even if they are cartoons or drawings.

Whilst at the time of writing the PROTECT Act remains law, there have been doubts raised as to its constitutionality, and whether it is sufficiently distinct from the CPPA in order to withstand constitutional scrutiny on First Amendment ground. Cases such as *United States v Rodrigues-Pacheco*,[56] and *United States v Irving*,[57] considered by the First Circuit and Second Circuit respectively, tried to argue that the Act is unconstitutional and inconsistent with *Ashcroft v Free Speech Coalition*, and the courts upheld the validity of the legislation. In *United States v Whorley*,[58] which involved receiving Japanese anime images of children engaged in sexually explicit acts, the Fourth Circuit ruled that there is no requirement that an actual child be depicted if the requirement that the image is obscene is met as per §1466A(a)(1).[59] Apart from the difficulties of proving obscenity, a further point raised in subsequent cases concerned the constitutionality of a possession offence for obscene material. Whilst obscene speech does not enjoy the protection of the First Amendment, the restriction traditionally applied only to publication and distribution, and not its simple possession.[60] This was raised in *United States v Mees* (Case No. 4:09CR00145 ERW), in which the constitutionality of the PROTECT Act 2003 was challenged before the District Court of Eastern Missouri, but the court rejected the argument, holding that it is not the possession of the material per se that is criminalised by the statute, but through its link to 'interstate commerce', i.e., if the material possessed had travelled by any means of foreign or interstate commerce. It would be inconceivable that material received through the internet will not have an interstate connection, and therefore, in effect, this would for all practical purposes be a simple possession offence. There is academic scepticism regarding the constitutionality of the PROTECT Act for this (and other) reasons, and some commentators think that the Supreme Court may in the future review the Act and find it unconstitutional.[61]

The law that criminalises virtual pornography in the UK law will probably not have the same outcome as *Ashcroft* should it be challenged in courts, owing to the narrower scope of 'freedom of expression' in Europe compared to the First Amendment right in the US. Whilst Article 10 of the European Convention on

56 *United States v Rodriguez-Pacheco*, 475 F.3d 434 at 436 (1st Cir. 2007)

57 *United States v Irving*, 452 F.3d 110 (2d Cir. 2006)

58 *United States v Whorley*, 550 F.3d 326 (4th Cir. 2008).

59 The dissenting judgment of Circuit Judge Gregory is noteworthy in this case, where he expressed strong reservations about the burden it places on protected First Amendment rights (at 353).

60 See *Stanley v Georgia* 394 U.S. 557 (1969).

61 For an excellent analysis of these points in more detail, see Paula Bird, 'Virtual child pornography laws and the constraints imposed by the First Amendment' (2011) 16 *Barry Law Review* 2011.

Human Rights (ECHR) guarantees the right to freedom of expression, this is a qualified right subject to restrictions as set out in Article 10(2). The right can be restricted, inter alia, for the 'protection of morals', and ECHR case law, for example *Handyside v UK*, suggests that it would be within the 'margin of appreciation' of individual states to determine whether a particular measure is necessary to pursue the legitimate aim (in this case, of protecting morals).[62] This would mean that even if the virtual pornography law is challenged on the basis of violation of Article 10 of the ECHR, the chances are that the European Court of Human Rights (ECtHR) is unlikely to deem it incompatible with the Convention. It should be noted that this would not be on the basis of the extent of the restriction placed on the right to freedom of expression per se. The legitimising factor for the law from an ECtHR perspective would be the margin of appreciation available to the UK to decide what is necessary and appropriate for the protection of morals in light of its domestic culture, norms and values. Whilst the law would potentially be ECHR-compatible in this sense, we should not be averse to examining the law in light of the sanctions and restrictions it imposes on individuals and individual freedoms and balance it with the harm – physical, psychological and cultural – it purports to prevent.

Future of regulation

It should be clear by now that there are some strong arguments both for and against the criminalisation of virtual pornography. Whilst it is undisputed that the protection of children is a compelling interest for states, and regulation that seeks to prevent sexual exploitation and harm to children is a priority, when regulating the conduct of adults the restrictions the law imposes on individual freedoms should be balanced against the harm the law seeks to prevent. Such a balancing act is far from straightforward when it comes to fictitious virtual child pornography – evidence of direct causal link to harm is not cogent or conclusive, unlike images featuring real children. Indecency that is inherent in pornographic representations of children – most people would agree that such images fall below the threshold of morally acceptable content – is perhaps the strongest legitimising factor for regulation. Regulating speech on the basis of morality, however, is fraught with difficulties as perceptions of morally acceptable content vary considerably across different societies. Sexualised representations of childlike fictitious characters enjoy a level of acceptance, albeit controversial, and form part of artistic expressions in certain societies, for example Japanese manga and anime. In addition, 'morality' is a fluid concept and is subject to change within the same society itself – the decriminalisation of homosexuality in various jurisdictions offers a good example of this. The risk, therefore, is that it would not be possible to predict the future of regulating virtual pornography on the basis of protecting morality.

62 *Handyside v United Kingdom* (1976) 1 EHRR 737. See also, *Müller v Switzerland* (1991) 13 EHRR 212; *Otto-Preminger Institute v Austria* (1995) 19 EHRR 34.

As technology develops, the challenges and risk to children from virtual child pornography could only grow bigger. Creating life-like images of children by exclusive use of computers is already within the realm of existing technology. In light of advances in 3D printing technology it will only be a matter of time before virtual images can be used to produce three-dimensional products, for instance child sex dolls. There are already concerns about the availability of child sex dolls on the commercial market, and it is fairly conceivable that 3D printers could be used to discreetly produce child sex dolls privately, for which 2D imagery could provide the underlying 'design'.[63] The legality and issues stemming from child sex dolls call for a separate discussion which will not be undertaken here, but the potential use of virtual pornography for creating 3D products in the future cannot be dismissed. In this sense, criminalising virtual pornography may well serve as 'future proofing' the law.

I am in no doubt that the publication and distribution of obscene representations of children should be criminalised, regardless of whether the images depict actual or fictitious children. I was initially torn in relation to whether the criminalisation of possession of virtual pornography featuring entirely fictitious children is a proportionate response in light of the lack of conclusive evidence of harm, as well as the potential interference with individual rights and freedom of expression. Whilst there are supporting arguments for and against criminalisation, I am inclined to conclude that the possession of virtual imagery should also be criminalised. This is obviously not on the basis of conclusive evidence of harm linked to possession, but the law has not always sought to obtain definitive causal links to harm when it comes to regulating content for the purpose of child protection. As noted in *R v Sharpe*, a reasonable risk of harm to children offers a legitimate basis for criminalising sexualised representations of children, and it should logically include virtual child pornography. The laws that regulate content in the offline world, including cinema classification and broadcast regulation discussed in Chapter 7, also follow this logic. In those cases, however, the 'risk' to children is relatively less serious in that what the law is trying to prevent is children's exposure to inappropriate content. The risk of harm to children stemming from the possession of virtual child pornography is comparatively more direct and profound, and it may perhaps be better to err on the side of caution and criminalise it altogether.

63 This is, of course, a simplistic description as 3D printing software is more advanced than just converting an image into a product, but nevertheless the use of virtual pornography for design and development purposes can be reasonably envisaged.

5 Enforcement of child pornography laws

The discussion in the book so far has focused on the various legislative changes in the context of combating child abuse images on the internet. Legislation is merely the first step towards addressing child pornography on the internet. In fact, enacting laws is often the easier part as it is something which can be achieved with some political will. Effective enforcement of the law is the real challenge, which is intrinsically linked to the success of the law itself in cyberspace given the global nature of publication and distribution of child pornography. As noted earlier and eloquently argued by Reed, a law that cannot be enforced in cyberspace will not command the respect of those who are meant to obey it and is ultimately bound to fail.[1] Whilst problems with successful enforcement of the law in cyberspace are not exclusive to child pornography, the vast variations in the legal and regulatory approaches to child pornography internationally make it a particularly challenging area.

There are a number of challenges for states in terms of enforcing the law and protecting victims of child pornography. Once an indecent image is found, the priority ought to be its removal from the internet to prevent further distribution and secondary victimisation to the child. Needless to say, identifying the victim, as well as the perpetrators, is equally important. Possession offences for child pornography mean those who consume it will also need to be tracked down. How is it possible to achieve all this in a timely manner on the borderless, global internet? Whilst child pornography hosted within the home jurisdiction can be tracked down and removed from the source relatively easily with the assistance of law enforcement agencies, this is less straightforward for content originating abroad. It would be pointless merely to target illegal content hosted within the home jurisdiction while material originating abroad remains accessible. A policy of blocking access to child pornographic material hosted abroad therefore inevitably became an integral part of the regulatory framework.

The pressure to respond to online child pornography has resulted in states having to formulate a range of co-regulatory and self-regulatory measures for the identification and removal of child pornography. The regulatory models that have evolved over the last few decades have seen increasing levels of cooperation and

1 See Chris Reed, *Making Laws for Cyberspace* (OUP 2012).

partnership with the police and industry and reporting from the wider public. Such multi-stakeholder model of regulation is perhaps one of the biggest step changes that the internet has necessitated for pornography regulation. The regulatory framework now features prominent non-state actors that serve the role of content assessors and, for all practical purposes, enforces of the law. These regulatory models largely adopt an 'identification and blocking' strategy, whereby content is assessed by a dedicated body and once identified as constituting child pornography the material is taken down where possible and access blocked to internet users with the cooperation of internet service providers (ISPs). Such newer forms of regulation have meant that there is *de facto* liability imposed on intermediaries, in spite of the legal immunity they have enjoyed under various national and international legal instruments. In this chapter, I examine the regulatory framework in the UK to further explore these points, also referring to the models adopted in other countries in Europe and elsewhere. The efficacy of, and legal and policy issues stemming from, such regulatory practices, including its criticisms, are discussed in this chapter.

Regulation and non-state actors

The United Kingdom's regulatory model of identification and blocking is achieved with the help of an independent body called the Internet Watch Foundation (IWF). The IWF was established in 1996 as an independent body which acts as a hotline for reporting online child pornography.[2] The IWF was in many ways a unique model compared to traditional forms of regulation. It is an independent entity, with current legal status of a charity, and is co-funded by the industry and the European Commission. Once the IWF receives a report, the content is assessed by a team of trained analysts and if found illegal the webpage is then added to a block list (called the 'URL list') and passed on to participating ISPs who then block access to the webpage concerned. It should be noted that what is blocked is not necessarily the website as such, but the specific webpage containing illegal images that the uniform resource locator (URL) corresponds to. If the content is hosted within the UK, the IWF alerts the police who will then investigate with a view to tracking down perpetrators and to take down the content at source. If the material is hosted abroad and based in a country where there is an INHOPE[3] member hotline present, a report is made to INHOPE which then forwards it to the relevant hotline in that country. If the content is hosted where there are no partner hotlines, the information is passed on to the INTERPOL through the UK National Crime Agency.

2 See https://www.iwf.org.uk/what-we-do/why-we-exist/our-history, accessed 20 July 2018.

3 The International Association of Internet Hotlines (INHOPE) is an umbrella association of hotlines; it is discussed in more detail later in the chapter.

Initially, the IWF's remit was reactive in nature, i.e., to act upon reports of online child sexual abuse material, with no obligation to proactively monitor and seek out illegal imagery.[4] Its remit has changed over time – for example, it was extended to cover illegal adult pornography ('extreme pornography', discussed below in Chapter 7) following the enactment of the Criminal Justice and Immigration Act 2008 and thereafter to cover non-photographic virtual pornography (covered in the previous chapter) following the coming into force of the Coroners and Justice Act 2009.[5] From April 2014 the IWF was tasked with proactively monitoring child abuse images on the internet following a series of proposals led by the Government.[6] The number of URLs identified by the IWF following their extended remit to proactively seek illegal content has increased substantially according to the IWF Annual Report 2014, which demonstrated the advantages of promoting proactive policing of child abuse imagery rather than adopting traditional reactionary approach based on reports made to the hotline.

The regulatory model in the UK has been hugely successful from a domestic perspective. At the time of inception of the IWF in 1996, about 18 per cent of the world's total online child abuse imagery was hosted in the United Kingdom. In 2016, this figure stood at less than 0.1 per cent of the total global volume of online child pornography.[7] It is clear that the robust legislation in the UK, combined with the concerted effort by the IWF and other partners in law enforcement, have driven websites hosting child abuse imagery almost entirely away from the country. In contrast, the overall volume of child abuse imagery globally has in fact, increased.[8] This does not, however, mean that the total number of children who are exploited for the purpose of producing child pornography has also proportionately risen as a vast number of the images are duplicates of an already existing image. Whilst duplicate images may seem relatively less worrying, in the sense that a child has not been subject to fresh (physical) abuse for its creation, it nevertheless is a serious issue. As discussed in Chapter 3, the existence of an image on the internet causes continuing harm to the victim, and further proliferation of the image should therefore be stopped

4 At the time of its inception, the IWF remit also included developing a content rating system for websites, which was dropped later and the IWF focused on developing as a hotline to combat child pornography.

5 Until 2011, its remit covered material that incites racial hatred. The IWF no longer include extreme pornography within their remit.

6 See, IWF Annual and Charity Report 2013, available at https://www.iwf.org.uk/sites/default/files/reports/2016-03/ar_final_web_low%20res.pdf, accessed 20 July 2018.

7 IWF Annual Report 2016 available at https://www.iwf.org.uk/report/2016-annual-report, accessed 20 July 2018.

8 There were 10,656 webpages confirmed to have child sexual abuse content in 2006 according to the IWF Annual Report 2006. The corresponding figure was 57,335 webpages in 2016, according to the IWF Annual Report 2016. Whilst part of the reason for the increase in number is perhaps due to the proactive searching of images and also increased reporting and wider awareness, the fivefold increase in global volume over a ten-year period is nevertheless concerning.

where possible. Many hotlines now use image hash lists using advanced technology such as the Microsoft PhotoDNA to identify duplicate images and help prevent further redistribution, which importantly also assists law enforcement with victim identification.[9]

There are several hotlines operating in Europe and around the world now, most of which are members of INHOPE (International Association of Internet Hotlines). The first hotline to be established in the world was actually in the Netherlands in 1996, and before the end of that year Norway, Belgium and the UK followed suit by establishing their own hotlines. The need for closer cooperation internationally among hotlines was recognised by Childline International in 1997, which obtained funding under the European Commission Daphne programme to establish a forum for European hotlines to collaborate and work together on common issues. This forum has developed into what is now INHOPE, which was formally established as a Dutch company in 1999. INHOPE has now grown into a global network of hotlines, and following the inception of the INHOPE Foundation in 2010 it helps with the development of new hotlines in countries outside the European Union, particularly in developing countries where there is lack of legislation or expertise.[10] There are 52 member hotlines (including six Foundation hotlines) worldwide under the INHOPE umbrella organisation.

Whilst in the UK the approach is totally industry-led, and the analysis of content and decision as to its potential illegality is made by a private body, many other countries within Europe follow a slightly different approach based on the EU-funded COSPOL Internet Related Child Abuse Material Project (CIRCAMP) which has helped to promote the implementation of the Child Sexual Abuse Anti Distribution Filters (CSAADF) to block child abuse images.[11] Under this model, the analysis of content and decision as to its illegality is actually made by the police (and in that sense by the state rather than a private body) before being passed on to ISPs for blocking access, which do it on a voluntary basis. The CSAADF has been adopted by the national police forces of a number of European countries. A further difference from the system in the UK is that the blocking is actually done at the domain name system (DNS) level rather than just the URL. The domain owner will be contacted under the CIRCAMP model and a 'splash page' that

9 For details of the IWF Image Hash List, see https://www.iwf.org.uk/our-services/image-hash-list. The image hash works something like a unique digital fingerprint for an image, which means copies of the image (even if they have been modified) can then be easily identified and matched to the same victim. See https://www.microsoft.com/en-us/photodna, accessed 20 July 2018.

10 See http://www.inhopefoundation.org/about-us/mission, accessed 20 July 2018.

11 The model adopted in the CIRCAMP project has its origin in Norway in 2004 when a system of blocking at DNS level was developed. The CIRCAMP project aimed to implement access filtering technology (CSAADF) in countries and membership consist of Belgium, Denmark, Finland, France, Germany, Ireland, Italy, Malta, Norway, the Netherlands, Spain and Sweden and are supported by the Interpol and Europol.

provides information to the consumer about the nature of the material being blocked, relevant legislation as well as contact information for making a complaint about the blocking etc. are provided. The provision of such a 'stop' or 'splash' page that gives more information to the consumer about the reasons for blocking makes the process more transparent compared to, for instance, a '404 Error' message that does not really convey any message to the web user for the reasons for the non-availability of the content.[12]

Elsewhere outside the EU, the National Centre for Missing and Exploited Children (NCMEC) has operated a CyberTipline since 1998 in the United States, which functions in a manner similar to the IWF. NCMEC's remit extends beyond online child pornography (it was originally founded as a private foundation focusing on missing children and received a mandate from Congress in 1984, but its remit now covers all forms of child abuse and exploitation both online and offline). CyberTipline is now one of the largest hotlines of its kind in the world and its remit also is broader than the IWF's as it offers

> 'the public and electronic service providers (ESPs) with the ability to report online (and via toll-free telephone) instances of online enticement of children for sexual acts, extra-familial child sexual molestation, child pornography, child sex tourism, child sex trafficking, unsolicited obscene materials sent to a child, misleading domain names, and misleading words or digital images on the Internet.[13]

According to NCMEC's 2015 Annual Report, the CyberTipline received over 4 million reports from the public and electronic service providers in 2014, 99 per cent of which pertained to incidents of child pornography.[14] In the US, electronic service providers (ESPs) are required by law to report suspected child pornographic images to the CyberTipline for investigation by the law enforcement.[15] As the report made by the ESP should also include, as far as reasonably practical, IP addresses, email addresses or other identifying information of the distributor or receiver of child pornography, the remit of CyberTipline actually includes obtaining intelligence on the distributors and consumers of the material for further investigation by law enforcement authorities.

Canada follows a model similar to that of the UK in terms of blocking access to child abuse images originating from abroad. Cybertip.ca, the country's child

12 One of the criticisms of the IWF in the past had been that there was no such mechanism which made the whole process appear to be opaque rather than transparent, but this appears to have been remedied as the IWF now recommends that participating ISPs offer a splash page.

13 See http://www.missingkids.com/gethelpnow/cybertipline, accessed 20 July 2018.

14 National Centre for Missing and Exploited Children Annual Report 2015, available at http://www.missingkids.com/content/dam/ncmec/en_us/publications/ncmec2015.pdf, accessed 20 July 2018.

15 18 U.S.C. § 2258A.

sexual exploitation tipline, was officially launched in January 2005 and works in partnership with ISPs. Project Cleanfeed Canada was launched in November 2006 by Cybertip.ca in partnership with Canada's largest ISPs, modelled after the UK's Cleanfeed initiative. Cybertip.ca receives reports from the public, and the content is analysed by at least two analysts before approved for blocking and URL added to the Cleanfeed distribution list. ISPs then block access to the URL, on a voluntary basis, and without knowledge of the content contained within the sites. There is no further information provided when someone tries to access the page other than a standard message that the internet address is not accessible. In Cybertip.ca's own words, the main purpose of the initiative is 'to reduce accidental access, not to highlight problematic content'.[16] In line with the CIRCAMP and UK models, the system does not log traffic to the filtered sites on the Cleanfeed Canada list and it is stated not to be a 'an investigative tool for law enforcement'. The Canadian model provides for an internal appeal process within Cybertip.ca, and a further appeal by means of a reassessment by the National Child Exploitation Coordination Centre, a national law enforcement entity, whose decision will be final.

There are now several hotlines operating in the world, most of which have followed the IWF institutional model.[17] According to a 2015 study by NCMEC, globally there are at least 48 countries that offer hotline services for reporting child pornography, which leaves about 149 countries worldwide that do not yet have a hotline for reporting child pornography.[18]

A common characteristic of such regulatory models involving identification and blocking strategy is the involvement of non-state actors in the regulatory framework. Whilst the utilisation of the block list compiled by hotlines is voluntary, internet service providers largely tend to participate and have become an integral part of the core regulatory framework for online child pornography. In spite of the legal immunity available for internet intermediaries for illegal content, it will be seen that in reality such regulatory models have imposed a degree of *de facto* liability on them. It is pertinent to briefly examine the role and liability of intermediaries in this context before considering the general criticism of the identification and blocking model as a whole.

16 See https://www.cybertip.ca/app/en/projects-cleanfeed, accessed 20 July 2018.

17 The IWF also launched 'international reporting solution' in 2014 whereby it directly offers use of its existing hotline facilities to other countries. At the time of writing there are twenty international reporting portals in various countries including India, Tanzania, Uganda, Mauritius and Namibia. For a full and updated list, see https://www.iwf.org.uk/what-we-do/how-we-assess-and-remove-content/our-international-reporting-portals, accessed 20 July 2018.

18 Melissa Stroebel and Stacy Jeleniewski, *Global Research Project: A Global Landscape of Hotlines Combating Child Sexual Abuse Material on the Internet and an Assessment of Shared Challenges* (National Centre for Missing and Exploited Children 2015) http://www.missingkids.com/content/dam/ncmec/missingkids/downloads/grp.pdf, accessed 20 July 2018.

Intermediary liability

For the identification and blocking regulatory model to work, the cooperation of intermediaries, in particular ISPs has become indispensable. ISPs, by virtue of their unique position to provide (or block) access to content on the internet, have increasingly become part of the core regulatory framework for combating child pornography. The circumstances in which internet intermediaries become liable for content is set out in law in the EU as well as in the US and is the subject of a fair amount of debate and scholarship. Due to space constraint, a full discussion on the law relating to different types of intermediary liability is not possible in this chapter. It is pertinent to provide an overview of the relevant legal positions in the EU and the US to contextualise their role in regulating online child pornography. It is also important to note that 'intermediaries' is a broad term which in practice encompasses service providers that offer at least three different types of service: (1) at a basic level are 'mere conduits' who merely provide access to the internet'; (2) service providers who also offer storage and caching; and (3) content hosts (for example YouTube, Pornhub, etc.). In Europe, the Electronic Commerce Directive sets out the liabilities of 'information service providers'.[19] Those providers who act as 'mere conduits', i.e., those who do not exercise any control over the content and just make their service available for the transfer of information through their networks enjoy almost absolute immunity from liability. With respect to those who offer storage, liability is dependent on whether they had knowledge of any illegal material before any liability would arise. The position is similar to that of content hosts – where there is no editorial control exercised by the host no liability will apply unless there is actual knowledge of the illegal content. The immunity for content in both cases ceases to exist when they are put under notice of the offending material. Therefore, except for 'mere conduits', the liability of an internet intermediary for content will depend on whether the service provider had knowledge of the offending material.[20] Intermediaries that act as mere conduits enjoy immunity in relation to illegal content under also under US law, s 230 of the Communications Decency Act 1996.[21] Section 230 protects intermediaries from

19 Directive 2000/31/EC, Arts 12, 14, 15 and 19.

20 Whilst search engines have not traditionally enjoyed immunity under the E-commerce Directive and the position as to their liability for third party content is less clear, a level of immunity has been imposed on search engines for privacy and data protection matters following subsequent developments in the EUOn search engine liability. See for example *Google Spain SL and Google Inc. v Agencia Española de Protección de Datos (AEPD) and Mario Costeja González* Case C-131/12 and the 'right to erasure' envisaged within Article 17 of the new General Data Protection Regulation (REGULATION (EU) 2016/679) See also *Metropolitan International Schools Limited v Designtechnica Corporation, Google UK Limited and Google Inc.* [2009] EWHC 1765 (QB) and the CJEU case *Google France, Google Inc. v Louis Vuitton Malletier* Case C-236/08.

21 Section 230 reads, 'No provider or user of an interactive computer service shall be treated as the publisher or speaker of any information provided by another information content provider' (47 U.S.C. § 230). The immunity conferred under s 230 is broader than the European

content-based tortious claims, and the immunity conferred under the provision is underpinned by the First Amendment right to free speech.[22]

Whilst this remains the *de jure* state of affairs, in Europe the *de facto* situation is different: ISPs now play a large and vital role in the regulatory framework of child pornography. For example, in the UK, ISPs accounting for more than 98 per cent of residential broadband connections use the IWF blacklist.[23] There is, strictly speaking no legal obligation on ISPs that act as 'mere conduits' to adopt such a blocking system. That being the legal position, why would ISPs agree to participate actively in what is essentially a self-regulatory framework which has obvious cost implications for them? The answer is twofold: first, there is pressure from governments to adopt self-regulatory mechanisms, with threat of legislation that would impose a legal obligation on them to act.[24] More recently, search engines have also been called upon by the Government to do more to fight child pornography, with threats of legislation if they do not comply.[25] Such measures are perhaps an example 'coerced private regulation', as Black would classify it under his taxonomy of self-regulation.[26] ISPs also have an interest in not losing the current immunity they enjoy for content, for example under the E-commerce Directive. Participating in the voluntary identification and blocking scheme means that ISPs do not have to act as content assessors themselves, and in that sense it is a much more attractive option than facing legislation that would require them to monitor illegal content. It is, in any event, the case that if content assessment is left to individual ISPs, that can lead to arbitrary

provision under the E-commerce directive. For a general comparative analysis, see Broder Kleinschmidt, 'An International Comparison of ISP's Liabilities for Unlawful Third Party Content' (2010) 18(4) *International Journal of Law and Information Technology* 332–355.

22 Section 230 was the only surviving provision of the Communications Decency Act 1996, which was originally enacted to prevent children's exposure to adult content on the internet. The Supreme Court struck down the other provisions of the Act on the basis of First Amendment issues, except s 230 which withstood constitutional scrutiny. The immunity under s 230 has been more or less sacred, until the recent enactment of the Allow States and Victims to Fight Online Sex Trafficking Act 2017 (resulting from the combined SESTA/FOSTA Bill), which makes operators of 'interactive computer services' liable for promoting or facilitating sex trafficking and prostitution. See for an excellent analysis, Mary Graw Leary, 'The Indecency and Injustice of Section 230 of the Communications Decency Act', (2018) 41(2) *Harvard Journal of Law and Public Policy* 553–622.

23 Internet Watch Foundation Annual Report 2013, 27.

24 For example, the Home Office in the UK called ISPs to voluntarily adopt mechanisms failing which a real prospect of legislation that would require them to do so was mooted. See TJ McIntyre, 'Child Abuse Images and Cleanfeeds: Assessing Internet Blocking Systems' in Ian Brown (ed) *Research Handbook on the Governance of the Internet* (Edward Elgar 2013).

25 See, for example William James, 'Cameron urges Google, Yahoo to Act on Child Pornography' *Reuters* 21 July 2012, https://www.reuters.com/article/uk-britain-internet-pornography/cameron-urges-google-yahoo-to-act-on-child-pornography-idUKBRE96K09620130721, accessed 20 July 2018.

26 See Julia Black, 'Constitutionalising Self-regulation' (1966) 59(1)*Modern Law Review* 24–55.

and inconsistent results and would in turn lead to unacceptable levels of censorship. Whilst larger companies (for example, AOL maintains its own blacklist in the US) will have the resources to put in place content analysts, etc., not all companies will be so willing or able to do so. Therefore, a body that is separate from individual ISPs that will analyse the content and make a decision as to its illegality as per the relevant laws of the country would be much more attractive for all parties and less threatening to constitutional rights.

The second factor that leads intermediaries to self-regulate and comply might be the social pressure from consumers generally. For instance, if some ISPs are already participating in such schemes, that might eventually lead other companies to follow suit. Media reports that suggest a causal link between accessing child pornography and contact offending, combined with calls from the Government and child protection activists for intermediaries to do more to prevent access to such material, can influence public perception, which could in turn exert indirect pressure on ISPs to self-regulate.

Relying on intermediaries to block and restrict access to illegal content is undoubtedly a practical option from a regulatory perspective. The technical capabilities of intermediaries to filter content make them a very attractive stakeholder in the regulatory framework. In terms of child abuse images, blocking access to the image would sometimes be the only immediate recourse when the material is hosted abroad and taking it down at source is not a realistic or speedy option. In order that further distribution and downloading is prevented at the point of consumption rather than the point of origin, blocking by ISPs also acts as a situational crime prevention strategy.[27] It should also be noted that the immunity enjoyed by intermediaries stems from laws that are now almost two decades old. Whilst the early position of granting immunity to intermediaries for third party content was to prevent stifling the growth of the internet (and free speech), it is the case that technology has since changed and the capabilities of intermediaries have also changed to assist with detecting and removing illegal content.[28] The debates on the liability of intermediaries in terms of their responsibilities for third party content and to what extent they should assume responsibility by proactively monitoring content have therefore recently been reinvigorated by policy-makers as well as commentators.[29]

27 See TJ McIntyre, 'Child Abuse Images and Cleanfeeds: Assessing Internet Blocking Systems' in Ian Brown (ed) *Research Handbook on the Governance of the Internet* (Edward Elgar 2013), citing John Carr and Zoe Hilton, 'Children's Charities' Coalition on Internet Safety Digital Manifesto' 2009.

28 Microsoft PhotoDNA and other unique hash-identifiers offer a good example for this.

29 See for example, recent European Commission Communication, 'Tackling Illegal Content Online: Towards an Enhanced Responsibilty of Online Platforms' COM (2017) 555 Final. For an academic analysis, see Giancarlo Frosio, 'Reforming Intermediary Liability in the Platform Economy: A European Digital Single Market Strategy' (2017) 112 *Northwestern University Law* 19–46.

Criticisms of 'self-regulation'

The regulatory models involving ISP-level blocking have not been without criticism. One of the main concerns raised against the 'self-regulated' blocking model is that it might result in censorship of speech, without the usual constitutional safeguards that apply to public authorities.[30] Whilst 'proper' government-backed regulation through legislative mandate involves public scrutiny and debates during the legislative process and is subject to judicial oversight, delegating the blocking process to bodies that are non-public authorities could lead to the lack of any such accountability and oversight. [31] Whilst hotlines such as the IWF and CyberTipline are officially non-state entities, critics argue that the line that separates them from being public or private bodies is actually rather blurred. For example, Mueller argues that despite such bodies not being government agencies, they are often funded or supported by governments and 'may be utilised by governments to develop and enforce censorship policies'.[32] According to the NCMEC study, the majority of hotlines (about 70 per cent) identify themselves as non-profit organisations, although 90 per cent of hotlines have received funding from government grants or contracts.[33] Marsden argues that governments tend to favour more private self-regulation/censorship with 'loose – and therefore largely unenforceable links – to the government' but at the same time maintaining strong informal relationships that can influence policy.[34] McIntyre concurs with this criticism and cites the Dutch experience as an exemplar of this policy – when a system adopted in 2007 whereby the ISPs would block access to domains (this involved DNS blocking) based on a list provided by the police was found to be unlawful by a study commissioned by the Government itself, being contrary to Article 10 of the European Convention on Human Rights (ECHR), had to be abandoned.[35] Instead of addressing the concerns raised in the study, the Government response was instead to persuade ISPs to develop a purely self-regulatory mechanism whereby the sites would be identified by a private body rather than the police. This meant that the safeguards that would apply to public bodies in relation to restriction of freedom of expression could be bypassed, being a completely private self-regulatory framework. Bringing the ISPs into the regulatory framework in this manner arguably has the consequence of avoiding existing accountability and constitutional rights that would apply to regulation that directly emanates from the state. It

30 See McIntyre (n 27), 292.

31 For or a critical analysis, see Emily B Laidlaw, *Regulating Speech in Cyberspace: Gatekeepers, Human Rights and Corporate Responsibility* (Cambridge University Press 2015).

32 See Milton Mueller, *Networks and States: The Global Politics of Internet Governance* (MIT Press 2010), Ch 9.

33 Stroebel and Jeleniewski (n18) 23.

34 Chris Marsden, *Net Neutrality: Towards a Co-regulatory Solution* (Bloomsbury Academic 2010) 131.

35 See McIntyre, (n 27).

is perhaps more accurate to call the framework 'co-regulatory' rather than self-regulatory, regardless of how some hotlines/governments describe themselves as 'self-regulatory'.

Another criticism is that private regulation does not comply with fair procedure requirements in that the party affected has not been afforded an opportunity to be heard before a blocking decision is made.[36] This argument should, however, be seen in the context of the realities and complexities raised by images of child abuse. Child pornography, unlike many other forms of speech, including adult pornography, is not just about being unlawful content; as noted before, it represents images of horrific abuse and sexual exploitation perpetrated on a child and its existence on the internet amounts to their continuing victimisation and abuse. It is in the best interests of the child that the proliferation and access to the images are contained as swiftly as possible.[37] Therefore, it is not something that can be seen as purely a 'speech issue', and the wider picture and considerations such as harm, privacy of the victims, etc. need to be considered in formulating regulatory strategies.[38] Nevertheless, it is a legitimate argument that any content regulation should be consistent with constitutional safeguards that exist in the offline world. This should be balanced with the right of the child to be protected from abuse and exploitation and in this sense the test should be whether the best interest of the child depicted in the image can be protected by blocking and removing the material in the swiftest possible manner. Therefore, whilst prior notification to the content owner of a blocking decision may not always be feasible, and in some cases might even jeopardise criminal investigations in terms of tracking down offenders, the opportunity to appeal against a blocking decision should nevertheless be offered even at a later stage in the interest of transparency and fair procedure requirements. This would alleviate some of the concerns surrounding the lack of transparency in blocking potentially illegal content.

There have been some general criticisms regarding the secretive nature of the URL blacklist and the consequent 'distrust' it generates, and also the possibility of the appeals process exposing the complainant's identity and a 'potential for abuse of that individual's rights by the ISPs or the authorities' have been raised in the context of the Canadian regulatory model.[39] The 'secretive' nature of the block list, however, is a practical reality – it would beat the purpose of child

36 Ibid.

37 INHOPE global statistics on European member hotlines suggest that 75% of child sexual abuse material was removed from the internet in less than three days. See, http://www.inhope.org/tns/resources/statistics-and-infographics/statistics-and-infographics-2016.aspx, accessed 20 July 2018.

38 Readers may remember that harm to children inherent in production of child pornography was the essence of the relevant US Supreme Court decisions such as *New York v Ferber* 458 US 747 (1982).

39 See Ronald Reibert, John Palfrey, Rafal Rohozinski, Jonathan Zittrain (eds), *Access Controlled: The Shaping of Power, Rights and Rule in Cyberspace* (MIT Press 2010) 375.

protection if the list of URLs containing child pornographic material is made public. As for the complainant's identity, it is submitted that those who publish pornographic content online are not always entitled to a right of anonymity – and certainly not in legal proceedings. Whilst it is the case that the law seeks to protect the identity of certain vulnerable individuals in the offline world, for instance juvenile offenders, victims of sexual offences, etc., appellants do not usually enjoy a right to anonymity for most legal or criminal proceedings. It is therefore perplexing why complainants against blocking orders should benefit from a right to anonymity online and therefore this criticism does not, in my view, carry much weight.

Critics of the identification and blocking model also raise concern about the possibility of over-blocking.[40] It is acknowledged that over-blocking is a general risk of delegating regulation to private actors due to both legal as well as commercial considerations. The legal consideration that might prompt over-blocking stems from the nature of liability attributed to intermediaries due to the existing legal framework. For example, as noted earlier, under the E-commerce Directive in the EU the immunity that service providers enjoy is subject to their knowledge of unlawful content. Generally speaking, if the service provider is acting as anything other than a 'mere conduit' and is legally subject to a notice and takedown regime, a request from a body like the IWF or other relevant bodies in other jurisdictions would suffice to constitute notice for the purpose of inferring 'knowledge' of the unlawful material. Given the cost implications, it is a much more sensible option, financially, for the intermediary in this instance simply to block the content, rather than diligently examining the material using its own resources. In addition, the risk of legal liability in the event that the content is actually unlawful would mean that it is in the intermediary's best interest to remove the content as expeditiously as possible so as to avoid any potential liability in light of the notice already received. This would potentially mean that intermediaries are more likely to simply block access to the material rather than undertaking an objective independent assessment of the content, which may have implications for free expression. Whilst there is no empirical evidence to support this argument in the context of child abuse images to the best of my knowledge, a 'test-case' conducted in the context of alleged copyright infringement tends to lend some support to this apprehension. Alhert *et al* found that a European ISP was readily willing to block a website that was deliberately set up for the study with no real copyright infringing material when contacted by the researchers with a 'complaint' reporting suspected copyright infringement.[41] The other ISP involved in the study from the US, however, sought further information. Whilst the

40 For example, Mueller is concerned that blacklists raise a serious problem of structural over-blocking. See Mueller (n 32) 198.

41 See Christian Alhert, Chris Marsden, and Chester Yung, 'How "liberty" disappeared from cyberspace: the mystery shopper tests internet content self-regulation', at pcmlp.socleg.ox.ac.uk/wp-content/uploads/2014/12/liberty.pdf, accessed 20 July 2018.

experiment does not contain a representative sample in terms of methodological rigour to draw firm conclusions, it nonetheless supports the perceived risks of private regulation of content in that it may not always adhere to the standards of reasonableness and transparency as required under public law obligations. The fact that the case here involved copyright infringement – primarily with civil sanctions rather than criminal – is also worrying in that a request in relation to illegal content such as child pornography will probably be actioned with even more force and speed.

Fair regulation

Notwithstanding the concerns raised above by critics of the current regulatory model, it would seem that a multi-stakeholder model is a more effective and perhaps the only practical way to enforce child pornography laws in cyberspace compared to traditional policing. Most countries in the world do not have co-regulatory mechanisms such as that of the United Kingdom and still rely on traditional policing methods to deal with child pornography. There are a number of challenges that make the effective policing of online child pornography problematic by relying on the traditional models of regulation. There is obviously the jurisdictional issue of dealing with content originating from abroad: whilst domestic laws may cater for illegal content produced and distributed at national level, the arm of the law does not usually extend to foreign jurisdictions. Blocking access to content hosted abroad would therefore be the only practical way to control the dissemination and access to child pornography within one's home jurisdiction – and industry stakeholders, notably ISPs, have a crucial role to play in this respect. Further, cybercriminals use different tactics that evolve with advances in technology, and child pornography is no exception. For instance, the proliferation of child pornography on the internet takes place not just through the traditional websites and peer-to-peer networks, but newer trends have evolved of disguised websites and paid services using cryptocurrencies.[42] There is also the challenge stemming from the 'dark web', which is harder to police. More recently, secure and entirely encrypted email services such as 'protonmail' also make detecting the distribution of child pornography challenging. Responding to these challenges will require a combination of readily available state-of-the-art technology combined with highly skilled police forces. Technology dependent solutions will invariably require the cooperation of technology stakeholders – the pace at which technology changes and the consequent re-skilling of offenders that would take place would render the challenges above and beyond the scope of, and resources available to, traditional law enforcement agencies. Whilst the UK has dedicated police units to deal with child pornography, such as the Child Exploitation and Online Protection command and specially trained officers, many countries in the world lack trained

42 For the 2016 trends of disguised websites and the use of crypto currencies, see the IWF Annual Report 2016.

specialist units within their police forces. This inevitably means that the law cannot be enforced efficiently: a law which cannot realistically be implemented will eventually lead to the law losing legitimacy and respect.

It should be noted that the majority of criticisms against the current regulatory model are not based on industry participation *per se*, but that the content assessment and subsequent blocking are carried out by private or non-state actors with potential implications for freedom of expression and privacy. As pressure and support for further international cooperation increase, for example through initiatives such as the WeProtect Global Alliance,[43] combined with growing awareness of online child pornography, more countries will soon have their own hotlines. If a state can allocate adequate the resources, training and personnel in order to create a designated 'public authority' that is subject to public law obligations to undertake the content assessment, it would naturally allay some of the fears of the lack of accountability attributed to non-state private institutions offering hotline services. Regardless of whether the content assessor is technically a private body or a government agency, measures that involve regulating content on the internet should be subject to the usual constitutional safeguards to ensure that legitimate content is not blocked in the process and that a regime of private censorship should not dominate the internet. The operation of hotlines should therefore be subject to oversight mechanisms, a meaningful appeal process and judicial scrutiny of its human rights obligations and to ensure that their operations are within strict guidelines of clearly defined substantive laws. The content assessor should be a truly independent body that cannot be influenced by the Government – this is particularly important from the perspective of the misuse of technology for censoring content outside the specific remit of child pornography. Subject to these safeguards, a body independent of the Government and individual companies is perhaps best positioned to act as content assessor, as the identification and blocking model will remain an integral part of the regulatory framework for combating child pornography for years to come.

43 See www.weprotect.org, accessed 20 July 2018.

PART II

6 Extreme pornography

Introduction

The main focus of the book so far has been child pornography, which is perhaps the most despicable of all content on the internet. We now turn to another genre of pornography, referred to as 'extreme pornography',[1] which includes the depiction of varying degrees of violence, ranging from snuff films (where the acts of violence culminate in death of the participant or character), hard whipping and caning of the body including of private parts, sexual intercourse with animals and corpses, to the 'milder' forms of spanking and physical abuse that result in superficial injury. As noted earlier, the regulation of adult pornography was traditionally focused on controlling the publication and distribution of material deemed 'obscene' within the home jurisdiction, something that was relatively enforceable in the pre-internet era through domestic law. The law sought to control the availability and supply of obscene material by imposing the onus on publishers and distributors. The global nature of the internet meant that vast amounts of different types of pornography, including what might be classed as illegal in one's jurisdiction, could be accessed from within the privacy of people's homes, bypassing the need to go to a bricks and mortar outlet or to physically import it from abroad. This has had the effect that states lose their power to control material that is, in their view, harmful to the moral fabric of their societies. It has prompted governments to think about new forms of regulation and means of retaining the traditional control that states had exercised within their physical jurisdictions. As discussed in Part I, newer regulatory strategies were adopted for combating child pornography, including the introduction of simple possession offences in the UK as well as in a number of other jurisdictions. Perhaps drawing inspiration from the success of child pornography regulation, the

1 'Extreme pornography' is defined in s 63 of the Criminal Justice and Immigration Act 2008 (CJIA 2008). 'Extreme pornography' in a non-legal sense has a broader, if not particularly clear meaning and is used as an adjective to describe a broader category of pornographic material. For an interesting discussion on the latter point, see Steve Jones, 'Extreme' porn? The implications of a label' (2016) 3(3) *Porn Studies* 295–307

UK criminalised the simple possession of extreme pornography in 2008. A possession offence for what is essentially adult pornography, albeit in its 'extreme' forms, is a relatively recent phenomenon evidently necessitated by the internet, with the UK being the first country to introduce one for adult pornography in the European Union through the Criminal Justice and Immigration Act 2008.[2]

In this chapter, I examine the extreme pornography offence in the UK in order to consider and analyse the implications of imposing criminal liability on end users for pornography featuring adults, rather than children. A simple possession offence for content featuring adults raises substantially different issues compared to child pornography. A key difference between child pornography and so-called extreme pornography is that the participants of the latter are usually consenting adults, as opposed to children who are incapable of giving consent. I argue that imposing end-user liability for pornography featuring adults sets a bad, and potentially illegal, precedent for internet content regulation.

The chapter begins by briefly setting out the extreme pornography offence. This is followed by an in-depth analysis of whether prevention of harm to participants featured in the material offers sufficient justification for a simple possession offence. Examining the various arguments in this context, including notions of direct and indirect harm, I argue that criminalising the possession of extreme pornography does not actually serve to prevent harm. A possession offence is incapable of addressing any direct harm (caused to participants), and the evidence of indirect (and cultural) harm is too remote in order to justify criminal liability on possessors of content. In other words, the law is simply focusing on the wrong individuals by criminalising the possession of extreme pornography. The chapter then explores other possible justifications for the possession offence, including a discussion of whether morality and notions of profound offence and disgust could legitimise criminalising simple possession. After considering the various arguments in some detail, I establish that it is essentially notions of morality, and the state's desire to retain control over the dissemination of 'morally permissible' content within its geographical borders, that has led to the law. This is not to suggest that protection of morals cannot offer a legitimate basis for content regulation; instead, I argue that criminalising conduct carried out in private, as is the case with 'possession' rather than publication or display (which would be 'public conduct'), should not be solely based on principles of protection of morals. The inherent lack of clarity that morality-based legislation offers to individuals in terms of foreseeability of

2 CJIA 2008, ss 63–67 which came into force in January 2009. Switzerland, which is not in the EU, already had a possession offence for pornography depicting 'acts of violence'. Swiss Criminal Code, Art 135 (inserted by No I of the Federal Act of 5 Oct. 2001 (Offences against Sexual Integrity; Prohibition of the Possession of hard-core Pornography), in force since 1 April 2002 (AS 2002 408 409; BBl 2000 2943)).

one's actions is also problematic. I then briefly explore the issues in the context of individual freedoms, and finally undertake an examination of the law in light of the power imbalance between the state and individuals and how the law risks having no normative influence in cyberspace. Criminalising the possession of adult pornography may well be an example of the 'mission-creep' of possession offences previously applied to child pornography, but raises an entirely different set of issues that cast a shadow on rights, freedoms and sexual autonomy and offers a classic example of bad law-making in cyberspace. It is not my contention that extreme pornography should be left entirely unregulated or encouraged. A possession offence focusing on end users, however, is not an appropriate measure. I conclude that the focus of regulation should be diverted back to the publisher and distributor and therefore alternative regulatory strategies focusing on the distribution and supply rather than consumers should therefore be considered for regulating extreme pornography on the internet.

The law

A triggering event that eventually led to legislation that criminalised extreme pornography in the UK was the tragic murder of a school teacher, Jane Longhurst, by Graham Coutts who, as was established during his trial, had watched violent pornographic material at various stages prior to and after murdering her by strangulation.[3] A campaign was then led by Liz Longhurst, the mother of Jane Longhurst, to ban extreme pornography on the internet: a petition by the Jane Longhurst Trust that contained 50,000 signatures called for the legislation to regulate 'extreme internet sites promoting violence against women in the name of sexual gratification'.[4] The Government issued a Public Consultation in 2005[5] with a view to enacting specific legislation to criminalise the possession of such content. The Consultation received a number of responses, with opinions sharply divided on both ends of the argument; the vast majority of the responses were either strongly in favour of or against the proposed introduction of a possession offence.[6] The Government eventually decided to go ahead with legislation through the Criminal Justice and Immigration Act 2008 (CJIA 2008), creating what was to be the first possession offence for adult pornography in the European Union.[7]

3 *R v Coutts* [2005] EWCA Crim 52.

4 See http://news.bbc.co.uk/1/hi/england/berkshire/5297600.stm.

5 Home Office/Scottish Executive, *Consultation on the Possession of Extreme Pornographic Material*, August 2005 (http://www.gov.scot/Resource/Doc/57346/0017059.pdf, accessed 22 July 2018.

6 Home Office, *Consultation on the Possession of Extreme Pornographic Material: Summary of Responses and Next Steps*, August 2006.

7 Scotland followed suit with separate legislation, see Criminal Justice and Licensing (Scotland) Act 2010, s 42.

The CJIA 2008 made it an offence to be in possession of an 'extreme pornographic image'. It is a primary requirement of the offence that the image must be pornographic, which means it 'may reasonably be assumed to have been produced solely or principally for the purpose of sexual arousal'.[8] Incidentally, this effectively provided a definition for 'pornography' in the United Kingdom in a legal sense. In addition, it is also a requirement that the image must be 'grossly offensive, disgusting or otherwise of an obscene character',[9] and must contain one of the following four acts:

An image is deemed to be extreme if it portrays, in an explicit and realistic way, any of the following acts[10] –

> (a) an act which threatens a person's life,
> (b) an act which results, or is likely to result, in serious injury to a person's anus, breasts or genitals,
> (c) an act which involves sexual interference with a human corpse, or
> (d) a person performing an act of intercourse or sex with an animal (whether dead or alive),
>
> and a reasonable person looking at the image would think that any such person or animal was real.

A further amendment was made to this section by the Criminal Justice and Courts Act 2015, by means of which the possession of images depicting rape and/or non-consensual penetrative sexual conduct was criminalised. This was done following criticisms that the offence contained in the CJIA 2008 as originally enacted did not cover depictions of rape and sexual violence.[11]

> (7A)An image falls within this subsection if it portrays, in an explicit and realistic way, either of the following—
>
> (a) an act which involves the non-consensual penetration of a person's vagina, anus or mouth by another with the other person's penis, or
> (b) an act which involves the non-consensual sexual penetration of a person's vagina or anus by another with a part of the other person's body or anything else,
>
> and a reasonable person looking at the image would think that the persons were real.

8 CJIA 2008, s 63(3).
9 CJIA 2008, s 63(6)(b).
10 CJIA 2008, s 63(7).
11 The Scottish counterpart of the CJIA 2008 was wider in scope and covered 'rape and other non-consensual penetrative sexual activity' from the time it was enacted: s 42 Criminal Justice and Licensing (Scotland) Act 2010.

The punishment for possessing snuff, serious injury and rape fetish images is a maximum of three years' imprisonment and/or a fine; and possession of necrophilia and bestiality carries a prison sentence of a maximum of two years and/or a fine.

The CJIA 2008 does not define the word 'possession'. Therefore, what constitutes 'possession' would be up to judicial interpretation in light of cases such as *R v Porter*[12] that laid down a 'custody and control' test as discussed in Chapter 3. Unlike child pornography, there is no separate offence of 'making' an image, which means that the consumer can be charged only on the basis of the 'custody and control' test as per *R v Porter* to establish 'possession', practically excluding the scenarios in which a 'making offence' as per *R v Bowden* might have come handy.[13]

Defences

There are certain defences available within the CJIA 2008. Section 65 provides a defence if (a) the person had a legitimate reason for possessing the image, (b) that the person had not seen the image and did not know and had no cause to suspect it to be extreme pornography, or (c) that the image was sent without request and that the person did not keep it for an unreasonable amount of time. These are along the lines of the defences available for the possession of child pornography.[14]

There is also a defence available where the possessor can demonstrate that he or she directly participated in the act or any of the acts portrayed, and that no non-consensual harm was caused to any person and, in the case of necrophilia, that the act did not involve a real corpse.[15] 'Harm' in this context is limited to what is permissible by law – this would normally mean harm that does not amount to actual bodily harm under English criminal law.[16] This defence, is however, only available to those who are depicted in the image, which in practice would mean that it will not be available to the production team (the director, producer, etc.) who do not actually feature in the image themselves.

Further, there is a defence for 'excluded images', which is aimed at images that are part of an already classified work, such as a film shown in a cinema.[17] The logic behind this exception is that the British Board of Film Classification (BBFC),[18] an independent body responsible for classifying films in the UK, would not have approved the content had it fallen within the ambit of the extreme pornography law. However, it is not a defence to be in possession of

12 *R v Porter* [2006] EWCA Crim 560.
13 See Chapter 3, page 58 on how the 'making offence' can fill the lacunae of possession offence.
14 Criminal Justice Act 1988, s160(2).
15 CJIA 2008, s 66 (2).
16 *R v Brown* [1993] 2 All ER 75.
17 CJIA 2008, s 64.
18 http://www.bbfc.co.uk/about-bbfc, accessed 22 July 2018.

clips that can 'reasonably be assumed to have been extracted solely or principally for the purpose of sexual arousal', even though the underlying works were classified as a whole for release.[19]

Criminalising possession

Until the enactment of this legislation the regulation of adult pornography, 'extreme' or otherwise, was focused only on the publisher or distributor of content under the Obscene Publications Acts 1959 and 1964, which made it an offence to ***publish*** or ***distribute*** obscene material. It was also an offence to be in possession of obscene material under the traditional regime, but only if the possession was with the intention to distribute.[20] The new extreme pornography law created a simple possession offence which imposes criminal liability on end users regardless of their intention to distribute, marking a fundamental change in regulation by shifting the focus of the law away from the point of supply and distribution to the point of consumption. Whilst the UK and many other countries both inside and outside the EU have had simple possession offences for child abuse images, as discussed in the previous chapters, adopting a similar regulatory approach for what is essentially adult pornography was somewhat novel and has been met with a fair amount of criticism.[21] There are a number of interesting legal issues stemming from this regulatory shift, and the criticism and arguments for and against criminalising the possession of extreme pornography can be grouped into five broad categories:

1. Demand – whether criminalising possession will reduce demand, and thereby destroy the trade.
2. Harm – whether criminalising the possession of extreme pornography prevents harm, either to the participants who created the material or to the wider society by way of possessing such material.
3. Morality – whether the preservation of moral standards could lend support and legitimacy for the law.
4. Individual freedoms – whether criminalising the simple possession is an unacceptable interference with fundamental rights.

19 CJIA 2008, s 64(3)(b).

20 Obscene Publications Act, s 2(1).

21 See for example, Abhilash Nair, 'Caveat Viewer! The Rationale of the Possession Offence' (2008) 22 *International Review of Law, Computers and Technology* 157–164; Andrew Murray, 'The Reclassification of Extreme Pornography' (2009) 72 *Modern Law Review* 73–90; Abhilash Nair, 'Real Porn and Pseudo Porn: The Regulatory Road' (2010) 24 *International Review of Law, Computers and Technology* 223–232; Feona Attwood and Clarissa Smith, 'Extreme Concern: Regulating 'Dangerous Pictures' in the United Kingdom' (2010) 37(1) *Journal of Law and Society* 17–188.

5. Power imbalance and normative force – whether a possession offence for extreme pornography amounts to the state exploiting the vulnerability of weaker individuals, and also whether it acts simply as an ineffective regulatory tool with no normative force.

I will consider each of these in turn below. It will be clear by the end of this chapter that criminalising the simple possession of extreme pornography raises significant issues in relation to all of these different but inter-related issues, and provides a good example of bad law making in cyberspace.

Demand and supply

The justifications for simple possession offences were examined in the context of child pornography earlier in Chapter 3. Readers may remember that one of the key rationales for criminalising simple possession is to break the demand/supply cycle by discouraging people from seeking child pornography in the first place. Echoing a similar rationale, the consultation paper claimed that a possession offence would break the 'demand/supply/demand cycle' by discouraging demand and imposing greater responsibility on individuals (in addition to publishers) for illegal material.[22]

Extreme pornography is not the creation of the internet: it existed in the pre-internet era and in most cases would have been subject to traditional obscenity laws. The advent of the internet, however, meant that the Government lost its ability to control the production and distribution of extreme pornography within the physical boundaries of the UK. Regulating supply of material that is considered obscene according to the prevailing community standards is a legitimate objective for any state. In the pre-internet age, this was achieved through legislation that controlled the publication and distribution of obscene materials (for example, Obscene Publications Act 1959). The importation of material from abroad was also regulated under relevant laws (for example, the Customs Consolidation Act 1876 and the Customs and Excise Management Act 1979). As acknowledged in the consultation document, this ability to control production and supply had previously 'obviated the need for a possession offence'.[23] In the borderless internet, there are obvious practical difficulties in transposing these laws that necessitated further steps to retain this traditional *control* over pornography, which clearly seems to be the driving force behind the legislation. Criminalising the simple possession of content as a means for the state to retain control over what is essentially a genre of adult pornography, albeit in its more 'extreme forms', raises interesting legal issues, as it affects not just conduct carried out in public but also conduct carried out within the private sphere of one's life. Clearly, if the material were of such a nature that viewing it will

22 Home Office/Scottish Executive Consultation (n 5) para 23.
23 Ibid, 1.

inevitably result in harm, either to the viewer or to others, then such a restriction might be justified – this is considered in the next section.

Does a national law in the UK that criminalises the possession of extreme pornography have any impact on its production and supply, let alone leading to the destruction of the industry? The answer is likely to be no, for three reasons. First, it should be noted that very little of such material is produced in the UK – most of this actually originates from abroad.[24] Second, there is little evidence to suggest the existence of a large consumer base in the UK for extreme pornography – as stated in the consultation document, most people would find such material distasteful. By logic, it would mean that there is no sizeable market in the UK for such content in order to have any meaningful impact on the supply by curtailing demand. Third, for the law to succeed, other countries should also have laws that criminalise the kind of material covered under the extreme pornography offence. If the material is hosted in a foreign jurisdiction, would a possession offence in the UK have any significant impact on its trade abroad if the content is lawful in the other jurisdiction? For example, if the content in question is hosted in the fictitious country of Freeland, where it is a perfectly legitimate business, it is inconceivable that a possession offence in the UK would destroy the industry in that country. The law serves no purpose in terms of 'tackling demand at source' if the material is not criminalised in the jurisdiction where it is produced or hosted. In relation to child pornography, possession offences are effective in large part due to many countries having substantive laws that criminalise simple possession, complemented by international co-operation in terms of aspects of enforcement.[25] No such international harmonisation of laws or cooperation can be expected for the wide range of content that is currently covered under the extreme pornography law in the UK. Therefore, if the objective of the law is to address the supply of material, a possession offence at national level is unlikely to achieve this, which effectively renders the law meaningless. As discussed in more detail later, and as argued by Reed, a law that is meaningless and unenforceable is unlikely to command the obedience of cyberspace users.[26] It might be worth considering alternative, more effective, regulatory strategies focusing on the distribution network, for example through internet service providers, in order to regulate and control supply, rather than criminalising consumption.

Harm

Whilst criminalising possession was generally found to be a legitimate response in relation to child pornography owing to the inherent harm it causes to

24 Ibid, para 22.

25 For example the Virtual Global Taskforce (VGT) discussed above in Chapter 5.

26 Chris Reed, *Making Laws for Cyberspace* (OUP 2012).

children, adult extreme pornography merits a fundamentally different treatment. A possession offence for content is intrusive by nature and if inappropriately applied can have the effect of being draconian. By means of a simple possession offence for content, the state is essentially asking its citizens not to view the materials covered under the law even from the privacy of one's home. In other words, the law is regulating conduct which is essentially carried out in private.[27] It is irrelevant whether the viewer has any further intention (for example, acting out the scenes or to cause harm to someone afterwards); the law serves as a complete prohibition on possession even if it is meant purely for private consumption. A question that naturally arises is whether consuming extreme pornography is so harmful that it merits such harsh legislative sanction, along the lines of child pornography. The conditions upon which conduct can be criminalised, and the desirability of so doing, have been the subject of examination by leading philosophers such as Mill and Feinberg, some of which are pertinent to the discussion in this chapter and is undertaken below.[28]

There are important questions that ought to be considered in relation to criminalising the possession of extreme pornography. What is the exact nature of harm addressed by the offence – is it the *direct harm* caused to the participants of the material, or the *indirect harm* caused to the viewer and wider society as a result of possessing those material, or both? The consultation paper pointed to both: in relation to direct harm, one of the stated objectives of the law was to protect the participants of the material from violence, cruelty and degradation.[29] As for indirect harm, a desire to 'protect society, particularly children, from exposure to such material ... which may encourage interest in violent or aberrant sexual activity', is cited as another objective of the law.[30] It is pertinent to examine whether the extreme pornography offence as it currently stands addresses these objectives. In order to enable a structured analysis, issues relating to direct harm and indirect harm are dealt with separately.

Direct harm

The rationale and efficacy of possession offence to address direct harm were examined in relation to child pornography in Chapter 3, where it was established that criminalising possession helps to address the direct harm caused to children. Extreme pornography is fundamentally different from child pornography owing to its participants being adults who, unlike children,

27 This is as opposed to conduct carried out in public, for instance the indecent display of obscene material in public, which existing legislation already prohibits under the Indecent Displays (Control) Act 1981.

28 See Joel Feinberg, *The Moral Limits of Criminal Law: i: Harm to Others* (OUP 1984), and Feinberg, *The Moral Limits of Criminal Law: iv: Harmless Wrongdoing* (OUP 1988).

29 Home Office/Scottish Executive Consultation (n 5) 2.

30 Ibid.

have the legal capacity to consent. The concept of 'direct harm' is therefore less straightforward than in the case of child pornography: it is not possible to draw an automatic inference that direct harm was caused to the participants of every extreme pornographic image, whereas it is a much safer assumption to make in relation to child pornography. In the case of adults, whether harm is caused in a legal sense will depend on the fact of consent, as well as the degree of harm inflicted on participants during the creation of the material, i. e., whether the harm caused was within the limits permitted by law. The discussion of direct harm therefore needs to be subdivided into content that is created with the consent of participants and that produced without. These are examined under the headings 'consensual harm' and 'non-consensual harm', considered in turn below.

Consensual harm

English criminal law does not prohibit the infliction of a certain degree of consensual harm, provided that (subject to certain exceptions) such harm does not exceed the threshold of actual bodily harm.[31] The legally permissible limits of harm in the context of sexual activities were clarified by the House of Lords in *R v Brown*.[32] The appellants were a group of homosexual males, who willingly participated in acts of sadomasochism for sexual pleasure. The acts took place in private, which was recorded using video cameras and the tapes were distributed within the members of the group. Whilst the 'victim' in each case consented to the acts and suffered no permanent injury, the appellants were tried on charges of assault occasioning actual bodily harm, contrary to section 47 of the Offences Against the Person Act 1861, and unlawful wounding, contrary to section 20 of the same Act. The trial judge ruled that consent by the 'victim' provided no defence to the charges and the appellants were sentenced to terms of imprisonment. They appealed on the basis that the offence should not apply to acts carried out in private with the consent of the victim, which was dismissed by the Court of Appeal.[33] The court, however, granted leave to a further appeal to the House of Lords on the basis that a point of law of general public importance was involved in the decision:

> 'Where A wounds or assaults B occasioning him actual bodily harm in the course of a sadomasochistic encounter, does the prosecution have to prove lack of consent on the part of B before they can establish A's guilt under section 20 and section 47 of the 1861, Offences Against the Person Act?'

31 *R v Brown*, [1993] 2 All ER 75.
32 Ibid.
33 *R v Brown* [1992] 2 All ER 552.

The House of Lords affirmed the decision, holding that the consent of the victim does not afford a defence to the offence of assault occasioning actual bodily harm or unlawful wounding that resulted from sado-masochistic activities. [34] It is immaterial that the act took place in private and that there was consent provided for each of the activities involved.

The natural corollary to the ruling in *R v Brown* is that if consent was provided for injury that does *not* amount to actual bodily harm, there is no offence committed.[35] There are also further exceptions in relation to consent even for acts that amount to actual bodily harm or wounding if the injury was a foreseeable incident of a lawful activity in which the person injured was participating. For example, surgery involves violence which can result in actual and sometimes serious bodily harm, but is a lawful activity. There are also other activities where consent by the injured could render the activity lawful, notwithstanding whether actual bodily harm is caused – for instance, piercing, tattooing and sporting activities such as boxing.[36]

The point I wish to make is that it is not unlawful *per se* to engage in sexual activities with full and informed consent that may result in the infliction of a degree of harm within legally permissible limits. It is not the fact that harm was caused *per se* that is the law's main concern – what really matters from a legal perspective is whether consent was provided for the harm sustained, and if so what is the degree of harm caused. Therefore, in order to analyse whether the prevention of direct harm caused to the participants can offer a legitimate basis for criminalising the possession of extreme pornography, it is pertinent to consider both situations – i.e., content that is produced by inflicting consensual harm within legally permissible limits as well as that which resulted in harm that the law will not permit.

CONSENSUAL HARM WITHIN LEGALLY PERMISSIBLE LIMITS

The vast majority of 'extreme pornography' is created by consenting adults, although it is not denied that there may be a small proportion of content created using non-consenting adults. There is little evidence or reliable data currently available to suggest the widespread existence of non-consensual harm inflicted on participants during the production of extreme pornography.[37] If the material is

34 In *R v Donovan* [1934] 2 KB 498, it was clarified that 'bodily harm' has its ordinary meaning and includes any 'hurt or injury calculated to interfere with the health or comfort of the prosecutor. Such hurt or injury need not be permanent, but must, no doubt, be more than merely transient and trifling' (at 509).

35 'In some circumstances violence is not punishable under the criminal law. When no actual bodily harm is caused, the consent of the person affected precludes him from complaining. There can be no conviction for the summary offence of common assault if the victim has consented to the assault.' Lord Templeman, *R v Brown* [1993] 2 All ER 75.

36 Ibid.

37 There is, of course, a wealth of literature generally on pornography's link to exploitation and degradation of women. Mackinnon (2005) in particular argues that the consent to the acts

created by consenting adults and any harm caused was within legally permissible limits, can the state criminalise the possession of a recording of activities that in themselves may not constitute criminal acts?

It is also pertinent to note that the CJIA 2008 does not define what constitutes 'serious injury'. The Crown Prosecution Service legal guidance states it should be constructed in its 'ordinary dictionary meaning'.[38] The lack of definition of 'serious injury' leaves no clarity as to what activities and level of injury would in fact attract a section 63 offence.[39] It should be noted that with existing digital technology it is not difficult to alter or enhance the image or scene in order to magnify the impression of harm caused to the participant(s). It is possible that no actual harm was in fact caused to participants during production, regardless of any realistic impression such digitally enhanced material might convey to the viewer. In such cases, a rather preposterous situation would arise where possessing a recording of the perfectly lawful activities will constitute a crime. It is not an offence to engage in sadomasochistic activities (subject to consent and degree of harm inflicted as noted above). The extreme pornography law would, however, mean that it is permissible and lawful to engage in certain sadomasochistic activities, but a recording of the same activities could attract a possession offence (except for those who participated in it due to the defence under section 64 of the CJIA 2008, but this is obviously a narrow defence). This is an absurdity and criminalising the simple possession of an image of what are essentially legal acts in themselves is criticised even by proponents of the law as an anomaly.[40]

The anomaly of criminalising simple possession of an image of activities that are not in themselves unlawful can also be seen with the provision regarding bestiality in the extreme pornography offence. In the offline world, section 69 of the Sexual Offences Act 2003 (SOA 2003) criminalises (physical) intercourse with an animal. It is an offence for a person to intentionally penetrate the vagina or anus of a living animal with his penis, and he knows that, or is reckless as to

depicted in pornography is only in the 'demented and degraded' sense of the word, and analogises pornography to trafficking. See Catharine A Mackinnon, 'Pornography as Trafficking' (2005) 26(4)*Michigan Journal of International Law* 993–1012.

38 Crown Prosecution Service, *Extreme Pornography: Legal Guidance*, http://www.cps.gov.uk/legal/d_to_g/extreme_pornography/, accessed 22 July 2018. The Scottish offence contains an even wider term, 'severe injury', s 42 of the Criminal Justice and Licensing (Scotland) Act 2010. 'Severe injury' is not defined in this Act.

39 Interestingly, the law only criminalises realistic depictions of 'serious injury' to the breast, genitals and anus. This would imply that harm caused to any other part of the body may not be covered by the provision (although acts that can result in death, such as asphyxiation, could still be covered under the law). It is not quite clear why the law limits injury to these specific parts and nowhere else. For example, hard spanking and caning on the buttocks theoretically will fall outside the remit of the law. If harm prevention was the underlying rationale of the law, clearly the law has not gone wide enough.

40 Clare McGlynn and Erika Rackley, 'Criminalising Extreme Pornography: A Lost Opportunity' (2009) 4 *Criminal Law Review* 245–260.

whether, that is what is penetrated.[41] It is also an offence for a person to intentionally cause, or allows their vagina or anus to be penetrated by the penis of a living animal.[42] The extreme pornography law that criminalises the possession of images of bestiality, however, goes much broader than this by including intercourse and oral sex with an animal that is dead or alive.[43] There are, of course, sound *moral* and *ethical* reasons for condemning images of sexual abuse of animals. It appears, however, that the justification for the criminalisation is exactly that – morality and ethics-based. If it were premised on prevention of harm to the animal and animal welfare generally, the honest approach should be to ban the causing of injury to animals as a whole (which should in theory also extend to slaughtering and consuming them). If, for the sake of argument, the rationale of the law is to prevent the 'harm' caused to humans by possessing the images, the anomaly between the breadth of both offences of possession and the physical activity somehow seems to indicate that harm will be caused by possessing an image of a person having oral sex with an animal, whereas there is no harm in the actual act of performing oral sex with the animal itself. Similarly, it also conveys the impression that engaging in physical intercourse with a dead animal is somehow harmless and not unlawful, whilst possessing an image of such an act will amount to a criminal offence (albeit it is conceded that it may be an unintended consequence of a poorly thought-out law).

Similar absurdity can be seen with the provision that criminalises images of necrophilia.[44] The SOA 2003 criminalises the 'sexual penetration of a corpse',[45] whilst the extreme pornography law criminalises (images of) a much broader 'sexual interference with a human corpse'. It should be noted that in relation to extreme pornography there is no requirement that the image depicted be a real corpse, as the law requires it only to be 'realistic'. Therefore, it is entirely likely that the 'corpse' depicted is actually a real living actor, and not necessarily a dead person.

If production of the material only involved legally permissible consensual harm (or no actual harm, as would be the case with simulated images), a simple possession offence clearly does not address any 'direct harm' in a legal sense for none was caused in the first place. As seen from the discussion above, the law also encompasses depictions of activities that are not unlawful in themselves, which is an odd anomaly and absurdity.

CONSENSUAL HARM NOT PERMITTED BY LAW[46]

If the consensual activities resulted in harm to the participants to a degree that is not permitted by law, for example actual bodily harm, clearly a crime has taken

41 Sexual Offences Act 2003, s 61(1) (SOA 2003).
42 SOA 2003, s 61(2).
43 CJIA 2008, s 63(7)(d).
44 CJIA 2008, s 63(7)(d).
45 SOA 2003, s 70.
46 If the harm caused is above the permissible threshold by law, it would technically be 'non-consensual harm' in a legal sense (as defined in the CJIA 2008), so in this sense the phrase

place during the production of the material. Can a simple possession offence be justified in such circumstances? The difficulty with such a scenario is that the focus of the simple possession offence is on the end users and not those who actually committed the crime by producing the image. The law is simply focusing on the wrong individuals. The criminal acts took place at the *production* stage, which is separate from *possession* (unless the producer and the possessor is the same person), and therefore the appropriate remedy lies within existing criminal law, such as the law of battery or assault. It can, of course, be argued that this is not feasible where the perpetrators are based abroad, but this does not provide a legal justification for punishing the possessors of the image in the home jurisdiction merely because they are within easy reach of the law.

In fact, matters become rather complicated when the content is produced abroad. For example, let us assume that an extreme pornographic video is created in Freeland. In the process of making the video, if actual harm was caused to participants and the harm was within permissible limits according to the law of Freeland (assuming that the threshold of 'impermissible harm' is higher than in the UK), what purpose does a possession offence of a foreign country (in this case, the UK) really serve? In this case no criminal activity has taken place according to the law of Freeland such as to call for legal intervention. In the event that the harm caused exceeds legally permissible limits according to local laws, there is little UK law can do in terms of punishing those who perpetrated the harm. In such a situation it will usually be the local courts where the criminal activity occurred that will have jurisdiction. It will be a matter for the criminal justice system of Freeland to intervene and punish those who broke the law within their geographical boundaries; a simple possession offence based in another jurisdiction is unlikely to have any impact on addressing the (separate) crime committed during the production stage.

One of the aims of punishment in criminal law is the deterrence it offers to other members of society: the hypothesis being, sanctions deter future offenders from committing a crime.[47] As an example, strict penalties for drink driving would deter people from driving after consuming alcohol as the unpleasant experience of the implications of being caught, such as criminal prosecution or the possibility of the driving license being taken away, would be greater than the pleasure of drinking itself. The law acts as a general deterrence in this case, thereby reducing the recidivism of convicted offenders, as well as discouraging future offenders who might otherwise engage in such practices. In terms of extreme pornography, whilst it is possible that the simple possession offence

'consensual harm not permitted by law' is an oxymoron. However, it is pertinent to adopt this classification in order to examine those situations where there is the fact of consent, but nevertheless the degree of harm would exceed the threshold of what is legally permissible rendering any consent provided irrelevant.

47 The deterrence hypothesis remains the foundation of many criminal justice policies in Western criminal law and criminal justice systems. See generally, Jeremy Bentham, *An Introduction to the Principles of Morals and Legislation* (Macmillan 1948).

could act as a deterrent to those based in the UK against *accessing* such material, does it serve any real deterrence in terms of *producing or participating* in extreme pornography, and thereby prevent direct harm to participants?[48] The answer is likely to be no. As noted earlier, if the harm caused was beyond what is permissible by law it would amount to a criminal act, but then this would be something for existing criminal law (for example, assault occasioning actual bodily harm) to deal with. A possession offence that targets the viewers of the recording would be of no assistance for this purpose. Therefore, it is flawed to assume that a law that criminalises the *possession* of extreme pornography would deter people from the *production* of extreme pornography and therefore minimise direct harm. It would be the relevant provisions within existing criminal law that might deter future offenders, not a content-focused simple possession offence that targets end users.

Non-consensual harm

If the direct harm caused to the participants during production was non-consensual, it will in all likelihood constitute a criminal act. The question, again, is whether a simple possession offence can punish the perpetrators in this situation. As discussed above in relation to consensual harm not permitted by law, there is little a possession offence would achieve in this situation as it focuses only on the end users and not the perpetrators who committed criminal activity during production. Similarly, in terms of deterrence, legislation specifically targeting the consumer of content does not serve any purpose in deterring people from producing the material in question – it is something for existing criminal law to address. It should be borne in mind that the harm caused during production would essentially be the result of a *contact offence*, whereas a simple possession offence is primarily a *content offence*. The former would be the offences of assault occasioning actual bodily harm, unlawful wounding, rape, or in the worst cases in snuff videos, murder. A simple possession offence does not serve to address any of these crimes, and therefore does not really have any purpose in addressing the harm caused to participants of the image as a result of non-consensual criminal activity.

It will be remembered from the discussion on child pornography in Chapter 3 that the possibility of direct psychological harm to the child featured in the material could justify a possession offence. I mentioned earlier that extreme pornography is fundamentally different from child pornography because of the capacity of adults to consent in participating in the material. However, if extreme pornographic material is produced without the consent of the participants, there is the possibility that psychological harm can also be caused to the adult participants due to the existence/availability of the material on the internet. Might this justify criminalising possession? Whilst in principle it should offer a

48 It is, however, theoretically possible to argue that those who have produced it will also be in possession in the context of a digital image.

legitimate basis for criminalisation along the lines of child pornography laws, it needs to be balanced against the rights of individuals to reasonably foresee the consequences of their actions. It is not easily determinable by the average end user whether consent was not provided, or whether the scene was purely acted out. In fact, it was acknowledged in the consultation document itself that it would be onerous for the prosecution to establish that the activities depicted in the material actually occurred (rather than staged or digitally enhanced), which is the reason the term 'realistic' was incorporated to the wording of the section in the context of what constitutes an extreme pornographic 'image'. This is not an issue for child pornography as no child can legally give consent, but given that the participants of extreme pornography are adults, lack of consent is only a possibility (however remote) and not a certainty as with child pornography. In addition, the inclusion of 'realistic' in the wording of the offence would mean that all that is required is that a reasonable person looking at the image should think that the person or animal depicted is real. This implies that it is not just the images that caused actual harm to people of animals that are brought within the remit of the law, but simulated images and scenes (that resulted in no harm) as long as they appear realistic (and give the impression that harm was caused) will also be covered. It would be unreasonable and disproportionate to burden the end user consumer of content with criminal liability for content that may have been produced without consent, which he would have no reasonable means of knowing.

It should be clear from the discussion so far that a simple possession offence for extreme pornography does not address the direct harm caused to participants, regardless of whether or not consent was provided. A possession offence could, however, still have a legitimate reason to exist if it can address any indirect harm stemming from possession. The following section examines whether the prevention of indirect harm could offer a justification for criminalising the simple possession of extreme pornography.

Indirect harm

Indirect harm refers broadly to the harm that might be caused to the viewer as well as to the wider society as a result of viewing or possessing extreme pornography. There is no conclusive evidence available that 'extreme pornography' causes harm to viewers, regardless of any actual direct harm caused to participants during its creation. This is acknowledged in the consultation document that sought to set out the case for legislation: 'We do not yet have sufficient evidence from which to draw any definite conclusions as to the likely long term impact of this kind of material on individuals generally, or on those who may already be predisposed to violent or aberrant sexual behaviour.'[49] The literature and debates on the impact of pornography on viewers, including violent pornography, pre-dates the internet.

49 Home Office/Scottish Executive Consultation (n 5), 1–2.

Whilst there are some studies that suggest a correlation between consuming violent pornography and sexual aggression,[50] the literature is highly inconsistent and reveals major inconsistencies, making it difficult to draw any definitive conclusions regarding harm.[51] From a legal perspective, this would mean that it would be difficult to suggest a causal link between consumption of extreme pornography and harmful behaviour, which renders the desirability of a possession offence questionable. In light of this, criminalising conduct for the purpose of harm prevention, and the limits of the law in this context, merit further consideration.

John Stuart Mill's theory that 'the only purpose for which power can be rightfully exercised over any member of a civilised community, against his will, is to prevent harm to others' was referred to briefly in the discussion on possession offences for child pornography.[52] It is pertinent to return to the harm principle in greater detail in the context of extreme pornography. Whilst there is a fair amount of academic discourse surrounding Millian theory, Joel Feinberg's exposition of the harm principle is particularly useful for our discussion here. Feinberg argues that the criminal law can only be legitimately applied to conduct that: (1) causes harm, or (2) causes profound offence.[53] He interprets 'harm' for this purpose as 'those states of set-back interest that are the consequence of wrongful acts or omissions by others'.[54] Not all harms caused by wrongful conduct call for criminal punishment. Feinberg goes further to argue that even the harmfulness of conduct is not sufficient for its criminalisation. Strictly speaking, criminalisation itself causes harm to the criminal, for instance the deprivation of liberty by imprisonment is harmful to the individual himself, which needs to be balanced with the harm caused by the conduct that has been criminalised. It can be justified only if the latter outweighs the harm caused to the offender by criminalising the conduct.[55]

In the context of extreme pornography, it is difficult to readily accept that the harm caused by possession would be greater than the harm caused by its criminalisation. The law is entitled to prevent certain types of conduct that cause harm to the self; prohibition of certain drugs offers a good example for

50 See for example, Scot B. Boeringer, 'Pornography and Sexual Aggression: Associations of Violent and Nonviolent Depictions with Rape and Rape Proclivity' (1994) 15(3) *Deviant Behaviour* 289–304; Neil M. Malamuth, Tamara Addison and Mary Koss, 'Pornography and Sexual Aggression: Are there Reliable Effects and can we Understand Them?' (2000) 11(1) *Annual Review of Sex Research* 26-91.

51 See Robert Bauserman, 'Sexual Aggression and Pornography: A Review of Correlational Research' (1996) 18(4) *Basic and Applied Social Psychology* 405–427; William A. Fisher and Guy Grenier, 'Violent Pornography, Antiwoman Thoughts, and Antiwoman Acts: In Search of Reliable Effects' (1994) 31(1) *The Journal of Sex Research* 23–38. Also see Catherine Itzin, Ann Taket and Liz Kelly, *The evidence of harm to adults relating to exposure to extreme pornographic material: a rapid evidence assessment (REA)*, Ministry of Justice: London (2006).

52 John Stuart Mill, *On Liberty and the Subjugation of Women* (Penguin 2006).

53 See Joel Feinberg, *The Moral Limits of Criminal Law: i: Harm to Others* (OUP 1984), and Feinberg, *The Moral Limits of Criminal Law: iv: Harmless Wrongdoing* (OUP 1988).

54 Joel Feinberg, *The Moral Limits of Criminal Law i* (1984).

55 Ibid, 217.

this. However, there are many facets of life where the law permits self-imposed harm. Consumption of tobacco is an example. There is well-documented scientific evidence of the dangers of smoking and the actual physical harm it can cause to the human body. It is also well established that secondary or passive smoking can harm others around the smoker. In spite of such clear and scientific evidence of harm, it is not a criminal offence (yet) to smoke on private premises. In contrast, there is no conclusive scientific evidence that supports the position that extreme pornography can harm the possessor or that it could turn a right-thinking member of society into a dangerous person who would harm others. The harm that would be caused as a result of criminalisation, i.e., deprivation of liberty, in all probability would therefore be much greater than the harm stemming from possession. In practice, prosecuting someone for the alleged possession of extreme pornography could in itself amount to a form of punishment. The humiliation and trauma of a public trial, often accompanied by media publicity, could have sufficient punitive and harmful effect in itself, even if the jury ultimately reach a 'not-guilty' verdict. For instance, the case of Simon Walsh, and the later 'tiger porn' case in the UK, both received a fair amount of attention from the media and suffered personal and professional setbacks as a result.[56] These cases are considered in more detail later in the chapter. To deprive someone of his/her individual liberties, however temporarily, and prosecute them at the taxpayer's expense ought to be supported with clear and credible justifications. If the law criminalises conduct on the basis of harm prevention, the precise nature of such harm should be clearly identified and established, failing which the law risks losing its legitimacy.

At this point, it is perhaps also worth noting the opposing arguments in the context of harm caused by extreme pornography. Hornle, for instance, analyses the harm principle and its exposition by John Stuart Mill, H.L.A. Hart, and Joel Feinberg and contends that if grievous or actual bodily harm was caused to the participants of extreme pornography, then the 'harm to bodily integrity justifies the prohibition'.[57] Whilst I fully accept that the law should not encourage harm to the person, the view that the extreme pornography legislation is an appropriate legal response is misguided. This is not to suggest that the law should

56 See for example Paul Peachy, 'Six months on bail – for being sent spoof video of a "tiger" having sex, that was really a man in a tiger suit', *The Independent*, 26 Oct 2014, available at http://www.independent.co.uk/life-style/gadgets-and-tech/six-months-on-bail-for-being-sent-spoof-video-of-a-tiger-having-sex-that-was-really-a-man-in-a-tiger-9819776.html, accessed 22 July 2018; Nick Cohen, 'Simon Walsh: the vindictive persecution of an innocent man', *The Guardian*, 12 August 2012, available at https://www.theguardian.com/commentisfree/2012/aug/12/nick-cohen-simon-walsh-cps-pornography-prosecution, accessed 22 July 2018.

57 Julia Hornle, 'Countering the Dangers of Online Pornography: Shrewd Regulation of Lewd Content' (2011) 2(1) *European Journal of Law and Technology*, citing John Stuart Mill 'On Liberty' in John Stuart Mill, *Utilitarianism, On Liberty, Considerations on Representative Government* (Orion 1993); H.L.A. Hart, *Law, Liberty and Morality* (OUP 1963); J. Feinberg *The Moral Limits of the Criminal Law: Harm to Others* (OUP 1984).

de-criminalise inflicting actual or grievous bodily harm, but, as noted earlier, the appropriate remedy for that lies elsewhere – in existing criminal law such as the law relating to assault and battery which can be applied to prosecute those who committed the crime, i.e., the individuals who were actually involved in creating the content. It is unfathomable, at least from the perspective of prevention of direct harm to participants, that the law would penalise the end user who merely viewed the material but had no part in its production. It could, of course, be argued that it is the demand for such material that caused the harm in the first instance and therefore the viewer is in theory an 'accomplice' for the crime. This argument, however, is far-fetched for non-child pornographic content because that then leads to a slippery slope and there are many attributes of the internet which would make everyone an accomplice to a crime committed somewhere merely by watching it. An analogy could be drawn to the countless videos available on YouTube that depict violence, including that leading to death and serious injury. For instance, a video that captures the brutal assault and killing of a teenager by burning her to death in Guatemala by a violent mob was viewed nearly 250,000 times within a month (as at 2 July 2015). There is no doubt that actual harm leading to the death of a person was caused in this instance, and the title of the video very clearly warns the viewers about the content they are about to see – 'VIDEO!!! Shocking moment girl, 16, is surrounded and beaten by mob that burned her to death'. Therefore, it is unlikely that viewers may have viewed the whole video by accident; in most cases they will have made a conscious choice to watch it. If the argument that the possession of content depicting actual harm should be criminalised, there is a stronger case for punishing the viewers of this video. It could be argued that this particular video was not created or uploaded to cater to consumer demand as would be the case with pornography. However, it is also the case that by watching it the viewers are clearly meeting the intended purpose of the person who made it available in the first instance – to share the humiliation and brutality of the attack on an unarmed girl by a violent mob. Further analogies can be drawn by a myriad of other images and videos available on the internet – for instance, the brutal beheadings of innocent men and women by terrorists and radical extremists are available on the open internet and are viewed by a number of people. There is a stronger case to criminalise accessing such material as it is arguable that the organisations that shared the video get more publicity from such viewing, which could potentially encourage more extremists to follow suit and harm more people. In spite of such clearer instances of actual harm, sometimes resulting in death of the persons featured in the material, the law has not always responded by introducing possession offences for such material. The only inference one feels able to draw from the different standards that apply to violent material generally, on the internet on the one hand and extreme pornography on the other, is that the real reason for criminalising the latter is not based on harm prevention, but instead stems from notions of puritan morality and a negative attitude towards pornography generally.

Other commentators point to the wider 'cultural harm' inherent in extreme pornography – McGlynn and Rackley argue that 'extreme pornography may contribute to a cultural context in which violent pornography is encouraged or legitimated', which they refer to as a form of 'cultural harm'.[58] This is different from the notion of a direct link between extreme pornography and committing sexual violence; it refers to the possibility that extreme pornography may encourage an interest in violent or aberrant sexual activities, thereby contributing to 'a climate in which sexual violence is not taken seriously'.[59] They argue that it is cultural harm such as this, indirectly caused by extreme pornography, that the law should seek to reduce. There are genuine concerns that such material would normalise violent sexual behaviour and rape culture, and generally contribute to distorting the perception of healthy sexual relationships, especially among young people. There is merit in this argument and nobody can dispute that the law has to step in to address harms that encourage violence against women or that foster inequality and discrimination. It is submitted, however, that criminalising possession will not achieve this objective. The risk of any 'cultural harm' arises when there is widespread availability of the material on a scale that can influence the norms of cyberspace users. If extreme pornography poses such a risk, it is the distribution and availability of such material that should be regulated in order to have any meaningful effect on minimising the risk of social conditioning leading to cultural harm. Targeting a handful of individual end users for possession is unlikely to make a difference at a wider societal/cultural level.

It should also be noted that law is not the only, and sometimes not an appropriate, tool to regulate behaviour in cyberspace. There are other more effective ways to influence norms in cyberspace – education being one of them. Educating children and young people about sex and healthy relationships in the context of their risk of exposure to inappropriate internet content will go a long way to reduce risk and harm. Law, of course, has a purpose here too –requiring internet safety and sex education as part of the compulsory curriculum for all children would be a good start.

Morality, disgust and offence

It should be clear from the discussion so far that the prevention of harm cannot offer a justifiable basis for criminalising the simple possession of extreme pornography. We need to examine other possible justifications in order to evaluate whether a possession offence is a proportionate and appropriate response in light of the challenges presented by the internet.

Whilst harm prevention was a clear objective of the original proposal for the law, the final text of the legislation actually points to notions of morality and

58 Clare McGlynn and Erika Rackley, 'Criminalising Extreme Pornography: A Lost Opportunity' (2009) 4 *Criminal Law Review* 245 at 258.

59 Ibid.

disgust as key driving forces behind the law. The wording of the statute, which requires that the image must be 'grossly offensive, disgusting or otherwise of an obscene character', suggests that morality and disgust are at the heart of the justification for the law.[60] The practical effect of the inclusion of these terms is that it provides an explicit link to the existing provisions under the Obscene Publications Act 1959, in other words only material that would be deemed as 'obscene' under the Obscene Publications Act 1959 would be covered by the new legislation. McGlynn and Rackley call this a 'lost opportunity' to prevent the 'valorisation and legitimisation of cultural harms, particularly to women' and argue that the Government eventually gave in to the pressure from libertarian activists.[61] They argue that it introduced the lack of clarity associated with the traditional interpretation of 'obscene' to the extreme pornography offence, as well as bringing in even less clarity in terms of the likely interpretation of broader terms such as 'disgusting' and 'grossly offensive'.[62]

The debates in Parliament during the legislative process also point to morality as being the main justification for the legislation. Johnson uses the example of Lord Hunt's speech during the final reading of the Bill to emphasise that the rationale for the proposed offence was primarily based on morality and disgust:[63] for example, during the final reading of the Bill in the House of Lords, in response to the concerns raised by peers, particularly Lord Faulkner and Lord McIntosh, regarding the proportionality of the offence in light of the lack of causal link from the Rapid Evidence Assessment, and the duty of the House to 'work hard to preserve the human right to do what one wishes in one's own home that is not a threat to anyone else in the outside environment'[64] the then Minister of Justice Lord Hunt stated:

> 'I actually felt very sick, because they were pretty disgusting images, and I frankly find it horrific that they are available and that people can see them. I am sorry, but I do not take this very liberal approach of "If it does no harm to the people taking part, why should we worry about it?" I do worry about it, and about the access that people have to that kind of disgusting material ...We are targeting that material not on account of offences which may or may not have been committed in the production of the material, but because the material itself, which depicts extreme violence and often appears to be non-consensual, is to be deplored ... It is appalling that this material is available and we have to do something about it.'[65]

60 CJIA 2008, s 63(6)(b).

61 McGlynn and Rackley (n 58).

62 Clare McGlynn and Erika Rakley, 'Striking a Balance: Arguments for the Criminal Regulation of Extreme Pornography' (2007) *Criminal Law Review* 677–680.

63 See Paul Johnson, 'Law, Morality and Disgust: The Regulation of "Extreme Pornography" in England and Wales' (2010) 19(2) *Social & Legal Studies* 147–163.

64 *Per* Lord Cobbold, *HL Debates*, 21 April 2008, Col 1355.

65 *HL Debates*, 21 April 2008, Cols 1358–1359.

As Johnson points out, it is clear from this passage that it is not the harm caused to the participants that was the main concern of Lord Hunt, for his justification for the law lies on notions of the protection of morals[66] (although, as noted earlier, one of the main justifications for the proposed law as per the public consultation paper was to prevent the direct harm to participants).

It needs to be examined whether the concept of disgust, offensiveness, and more generally a morality based approach might provide the basis for criminalising the possession of extreme pornography. Is the possession of extreme pornography so 'disgusting' that an individual's private consumption of such material be criminalised? If the knowledge of someone viewing extreme pornography within the privacy of their home causes disgust or offence to some members of the public, does that justify its criminalisation? Criminalising conduct that causes no harm purely on the basis of morality has already been the subject of discussion by eminent jurists, and it is pertinent to revisit some of these debates for the purpose of our analysis. It will be clear from the discussion below that morality and disgust cannot offer a legitimate basis for criminalising the possession of extreme pornography.

It is now well known that Lord Devlin was not quite convinced about the boundaries between public and private morality for the purpose of legal intervention.[67] He argued that moral standards that the majority places beyond toleration is an important aspect of what bonds society together, integral to its very existence, and 'the law can be used to preserve morality in the same way it uses it to safeguard anything else if it is essential to its existence'.[68] Lord Devlin was not suggesting that the law should intervene on every occasion of immorality, and argued that there 'must be toleration of the maximum individual freedom that is consistent with the integrity of society'. This would mean that there needs to be a balancing act, where legal intervention will be justified when private conduct gives rise to a general public feeling of 'intolerance, indignation and disgust'.[69] If certain conduct is generally regarded as abominable, the law can legitimately intervene, even if carried out in private. But how is 'general public feeling' to be ascertained?

66 See Johnson (n 63), 151. McGlynn and Rackley (n 58) also tend to agree with this and suggest that the Government came under pressure from pro-liberty/privacy activists and 'lost sight of the nature of the harm it was seeking to legislate against and reverted to the weakest possible justification for action, disgust'.

67 See Patrick Devlin, *The Enforcement of Morals* (OUP 1965). Lord Devlin's lectures followed the Wolfenden report that decriminalised homosexuality in England and Wales. The Report recommended that, where individuals engaged in sexual activities with full and informed consent, the state had no business to interfere and regulate matters of private sexuality. Lord Devlin argued that the law can legitimately intervene where acts, even if carried out in private, cause disgust to right-minded members of the society.

68 Ibid,11.

69 Ibid,17.

'Disgust' has to be more than mere dislike – it should amount to a feeling that is more profound and sincerely expressed by society.[70] In ascertaining disgust Lord Devlin relies on the judgement of the right-minded, reasonable man – the individual in the jury box, and not necessarily the (higher thinking, learned) 'rational man'. So, if the vast majority of right-minded men are genuinely disgusted by certain conduct and it is so profound that it threatens the very moral fabric of society, it can be criminalised regardless of its being carried out in private. This would then be consistent with the 'democratic principles' within which Lord Devlin permitted any legal intervention in order to protect morality.

Lord Devlin's arguments were received with a fair amount of criticism from other distinguished jurists such as Hart, Dworkin and Wollheim.[71] Nevertheless, even if, for the sake of argument, we accept Devlin's position criminalising private conduct on the basis of the wider public morality, it is fraught with difficulties in relation to extreme pornography. The breadth of the legislation is such that it may not actually cause 'disgust' in the sense of what Devlin envisaged. Parliamentary debates on the legislation offers a good example. A number of lawmakers argued against criminalising the possession of extreme pornography. Of course, the view of the then Justice Minister and other lawmakers who were in favour of the legislation logically represented the view of a section of our society – after all, they are representatives of the people (although some of the debates referred to here actually took place in the House of Lords, which is not elected), but equally a number of lawmakers also opposed the legislation on the ground that it was too broad and disproportionate. Eventually, the majority view prevailed – as happens in parliamentary democracies – and resulted in legislation. But Lord Devlin's idea of disgust is not that of a simple majority– it has to be what the society *generally as a whole* would find disgusting.[72] In other words, the average right-thinking member of society must be 'disgusted' – it would not suffice that 55 per cent of society would find something disgusting as opposed to the 45 per cent who would not, something that works perfectly well in Parliament (through elected representatives of society) for law-making purposes. Devlin's definition of disgust requires a much broader consensus among members of society than was apparent from the different stages of the law-making process ranging from the consultation responses to the deliberations in Parliament. In addition, there are also lessons to be learnt from how the law has operated in practice (discussed later in the chapter), in terms of how perceptions

70 Dworkin interprets this as nothing more than 'passionate public disapproval'. See, Ronald M Dworkin, 'Lord Devlin and the Enforcement of Morals', *Faculty Scholarship Series* Paper 3611, available at http://digitalcommons.law.yale.edu/fss_papers/3611, accessed 23 July 2018.

71 See H.L.A. Hart, 'Law' (1963) *Liberty and Morality* 51; Dworkin (n 70); Richard Wollheim, 'Crime, Sin and Mr Justice Devlin' (1959) *Encounter* (November) 34–40.

72 Dworkin cautions against interpreting Lord Devlin's argument as 'depending upon any assumption that when the vast bulk of the community thinks a practice is immoral they are likely right'. See Dworkin (n 70), 990.

of immorality differed between the prosecutors and the jury. Proponents of the extreme pornography law might be inclined to rely on Lord Devlin's stance to justify a possession offence, but it should be clear by now that the law falls short of the restraints set by Lord Devlin for legal intervention.[73]

It should be noted that Lord Devlin's argument, of course, was in the context of the decriminalisation of homosexuality following the Wolfenden Report,[74] where he criticised the principles upon which the report drew its conclusions (and not the Report as a whole). A discourse surrounding the morality of homosexuality would be even more controversial now, in light of the changes in attitudes and legal recognition of same-sex relationships in the UK and elsewhere. With the benefit of hindsight, it shows how fluid and flexible notions of morality are within the same society – it is something that continuously evolves. Law, on the contrary, is slow to change and therefore criminalising conduct on the basis of *existing* perceptions of morality carries an element of risk, and this is particularly so for matters of sexual preferences and pornography.

Feinberg also generally rejects the sufficiency of immorality for criminal punishment. He argued that if immoral conduct causes no harm to others, it may not be legitimately punished through criminal law.[75] Feinberg adopts a similar position where harm is caused, but when that harm is too small to justify the harms caused by criminal punishment.[76] It is arguable that possession could harm the individual possessor's own moral character, but its criminalisation on this basis would amount to moral paternalism, something Feinberg rejects.[77]

Profound offence

Feinberg, however, examines a category of conduct pertinent to our discussion, which he considers to be within the purview of the legitimate authority of the criminal law – conduct that causes profound offence to others.[78] He separates this category from 'harm' and concludes that offence, no matter how serious, is outside the remit of harm as defined in his work, *Harm to Others.*[79] This is not suggesting that conduct that causes profound offence cannot be criminalised – in fact, Feinberg argues that it can legitimately be criminalised (the Offence Principle).[80] However, Feinberg imposes a major restriction on the manner in

73 Johnson undertakes a sophisticated exposition of Lord Devlin's notion of disgust in the context of extreme pornography and reaches a different conclusion. It just shows how polarised views are on morality as the basis of regulation. See Paul Johnson (n 63).

74 Home Office/Scottish Home Department, *Report of the Committee on Homosexual Offences and Prostitution* (Cmnd 247, 1957).

75 Joel Feinberg, *The Moral Limits of Criminal Law: iv: Harmless Wrongdoing* (OUP 1988).

76 Ibid.

77 Ibid, 133–140.

78 Joel Feinberg, *The Moral Limits of Criminal Law: ii Offense to Others* (OUP 1985).

79 Joel Feinberg, *The Moral Limits of Criminal Law: i: Harm to Others* (OUP 1984).

80 Ibid, 1.

which the Offence Principle can be construed – it should apply only to conduct that occurs in public. Conduct that occurs in private, no matter how offensive once it comes to light, cannot be criminalised, for doing so would be analogous to legal moralism, which he vehemently opposed.[81] Applying the Offence Principle to extreme pornography, viewing or possessing it within the privacy of one's home, which amounts to conduct that is carried out in private, cannot be criminalised. It would not suffice, for the purpose of criminalisation, that the knowledge of someone possessing extreme pornography causes profound offence to another person. So, B taking (profound) offence by coming to know that A has viewed extreme pornography in private will not be sufficient justification for prohibiting A from viewing it in private. There are many facets of life that offend some people whilst being perfectly acceptable to others. Let us take the example of homosexuality. Homosexuality, whilst becoming more acceptable today than in the past, continues to offend some people, however subjectively. Therefore, would A becoming 'profoundly offended' upon hearing that two homosexuals B and C engaged in sexual acts in private justify its criminalisation? Logic (and thankfully current law) dictates otherwise. It is important to remember that the boundaries drawn here are with respect to conduct carried out in private, i.e., away from public eyes. Law places certain restrictions on the same conduct carried out in public. So engaging in sexual acts in public could be criminalised and is in fact criminalised in many jurisdictions on the basis of preventing offence to the public (this is not confined to homosexual conduct, but also applies to heterosexual acts). Sexual acts between two consenting adult homosexuals carried out within the confines of one's home cannot be criminalised, no matter how much the knowledge of such conduct causes offence to someone who strongly disapproves of homosexuality. It is difficult to see why extreme pornography should merit a different treatment. Of course, if there were conclusive evidence available of harm stemming from the consumption of extreme pornography it would be an entirely different matter. As long as such evidence remains inconclusive, criminalising simple possession on the basis of offence to others, however profound, cannot offer sufficient justification. It is safe to reach the conclusion that a possession offence for extreme pornography does not meet the standard postulated by Feinberg for criminalising conduct on the basis of causing profound offence to others.

Lack of clarity

The adoption of a morality-based obscenity standard for criminalising possession of extreme pornography is problematic and suffers from an inherent lack of clarity. McGlynn and Rackley voice concerns that the broad definition of

81 For an excellent critique on Feinberg's work in this context, see Larry Alexander, 'The Philosophy of Criminal Law', in Jules Coleman and Scott Shapiro (eds), *The Oxford Handbook of Jurisprudence & Philosophy of Law* (OUP 2002).

'obscenity' under OPA 1959[82] and its 'moralistic nature' in light of its focus on depraving and corrupting the consumers, with no requirement to demonstrate harm, has meant that the offence is 'opaque' in nature and offers no clarity to anyone.[83] In addition, due to the reliance on the notions of disgust and offence, it is possible that obscenity prosecutions can result in situations where images that depict activities that are not unlawful in themselves can attract the offence, which 'raises serious issues of clarity and coherence' as well as raising the question 'where is the harm?' Therefore, the law simply imposes what they call 'conservative and conventional views of appropriate sexuality'.[84] McGlynn and Rackley concede that this amounts to an 'offense based' charge, which provides insufficient basis for a criminal possession offence.

Not all commentators agree. Johnson argues that, with all its flaws, the 'morality test' has a 'delimiting' effect on the scope of the law owing to the fact that jurors may reject prosecutions 'in favour of tolerance and the respect for private life' and the extreme pornography offence will benefit from the 'safeguard of ongoing interpretation and assessment', as is the case with the Obscene Publications Act 1959.[85] Whilst the argument that the test under traditional obscenity law offers a degree of flexibility that is capable of accommodating the changing norms and moral standards is relatively acceptable for laws that focused on the publication and distribution of material, it is in fact counterproductive for extreme pornography law – especially in view of the intrusive nature of the offence which targets individuals. People need clarity regarding the law and reasonable foreseeability of actions in terms of behaviour that would be deemed criminal. Johnson concedes that the moral evaluation of extreme pornography will require consumers of content (rather than just courts) to judge it against notions of offence, obscenity and disgust – assessed against the standards of others. This imposes an impermissible burden on end users who have no definitive way of knowing whether the material will attract the offence. Apart from the vagueness inherent in standards of obscenity, disgust and offensiveness, other provisions of the statute, for example what amounts to possession, serious injury, etc., also do not offer certainty to the individual. In addition, as Johnson points out, the requirement for the consumer to judge content against the

82 Section 1 of the Obscene Publications Act 1959 defines obscenity as 'an article shall be deemed to be obscene if its effect or (where the article comprises two or more distinct items) the effect of any one of its items is, if taken as a whole, such as to tend to deprave and corrupt persons who are likely, having regard to all circumstances, to read, see or hear the matter contained or embodied in it'.

83 McGlynn and Rackley (n 58). See also, for a discussion on the application of the Obscene Publications Act, Susan S.M. Edwards, 'On the Contemporary Application of the Obscene Publications Act 1959'[1998] *Criminal Law Review* 843.

84 See McGlynn and Rackley (n 58). For a different perspective see, Eleanor Wilkinson, ''Extreme Pornography' and the Contested Spaces of Virtual Citizenship' (2011) 12(5) *Social and Cultural Geography* 493, 498.

85 Paul Johnson, 'Law, Morality and Disgust: The Regulation of "Extreme Pornography" in England and Wales' (2010) 19(2) *Social and Legal Studies* 147, 156.

standards of others could theoretically amount to the imposition of public morality upon matters that fall within the private sphere, and therefore is contrary to the right of moral independence. However, he makes an interesting argument that this would not be problematic in the context of the internet, claiming that the very notion of public and private spheres, the 'Wolfenden distinction', is irrelevant to the internet: 'The private possession of extreme pornography is only theoretically private since the procurement of images relies on forms of social interaction afforded by the internet.'[86] This has the implication, that the 'Hartian claim that sexual behaviours that take place "behind closed doors" are beyond the law' does not really apply to the internet owing to the 'social interaction' offered by internet, which means the individual no longer has to leave his/her home (and venture into public spaces) to acquire the material (that would be illegal to publish or distribute, but under traditional law not illegal to possess). This is, however, a fundamentally flawed interpretation of the so-called public and private spheres of the internet and fails to appreciate the different ways of accessing pornography on the internet. There is admittedly some form of social interaction that takes place on peer-to-peer websites, but to access content from many mainstream websites that offer 'free' content hardly requires any form of 'social interaction'. People could simply choose to remain anonymous and browse content using 'InPrivate browsing' or going 'Incognito'.[87] This is not to say that the user cannot ever be tracked down, but that would require effort and assistance of the ISP – which is not quite the 'social interaction' envisaged by the author. In the majority of cases possession can, and in most cases will, very much remain a private act (except in cases where the material is made available for distribution, for example through a peer-to-peer network, which is obviously a matter of 'distribution' rather than simple possession).

Returning to the issue of lack of clarity for the consumer, the 'safeguard' of the jurors rejecting prosecutions by finding the material to be not illegal does not go far enough in mitigating the harshness of the extreme pornography law. The trial of Simon Walsh in the UK is pertinent here.[88] Walsh was charged under section 63 CJIA 2008, on five counts of possessing extreme pornographic images which included images of anal fisting (a sexual practice which is not illegal *per se*), and urethral sounding. The prosecution argued that anal fisting was likely to cause serious injury to a person's anus, and that urethral sounding, where a rod-like instrument is inserted into through the penis into the urethra, was likely to cause serious injury to a person's genitals. He was also charged with one count of possessing what was thought to be an indecent image of a child, which was sent to him unsolicited and contested by the defence as an image of someone in his 20s rather than a child. The jury unanimously reached a 'not-guilty' verdict and cleared Walsh on all counts in

86 Ibid.

87 Offered by Internet Explorer and Google Chrome browsers respectively.

88 *R v Walsh* (12 August 2012) Kingston Crown Court (unreported).

Kingston Crown Court, which closed the matter from a legal perspective, but the whole escapade cost Walsh a great deal in terms of his job, reputation and professional standing as a barrister.[89]

There are also other cases where the jury and prosecutors disagreed on the 'obscenity' of the material in question. *R v Peacock* is a good example, in which a man was prosecuted on six counts of obscene publication under the Obscene Publications Act 1959.[90] The material in *Peacock* also featured fisting, urination and whipping, which the prosecution argued amounted to obscenity under the Act. The jury, however, unanimously found him not guilty on all counts. Peacock pleaded not guilty in this case – apparently a first for the kind of gay pornography he published – and eventually won.[91] Whilst *Peacock* was not based on possessing the material under the extreme pornography legislation, in principle the case demonstrates that distorted notions of obscenity and the ambiguity surrounding the law can lead to undesirable results. From the perspective of the accused, it led to a torturous experience of being prosecuted, essentially for their sexual preferences. Some of the acts that form the basis for such prosecutions, such as fisting and urethral sounding, are not illegal as such. It may be outside what many would regard as the 'norm', but nevertheless legal to perform. It is clear that the driving force behind the decision to prosecute was guided by moralistic notions, i.e., to prevent people from becoming 'depraved and corrupted'.[92] Whilst the eventual outcome was the right one in both cases, it did not spare the men the agony and humiliation of a public trial. Walsh is a barrister and an Oxford-educated man, evidently with a strong resolve, so he decided to fight the case and prove his innocence, but it clearly was not an easy ordeal for him, and many people do not have his privileges in terms of access to legal representation.

There is a significant element of subjectivity, and associated uncertainty, involved in jury decisions involving pornographic material. For a case of murder or rape, the fundamental duty of the jury is to reach a verdict as to whether the person accused has committed the crime (or not) in light of the evidence presented before it: there is no element of (moral) subjectivity involved in its decision. Put simplistically, it is ultimately a yes or no decision – i.e., whether it is proven beyond reasonable doubt that the accused has committed the crime. In

89 There is academic criticism of the Simon Walsh case as demonstrating a classic example of misusing the law (and something that highlights the deficiency within the law itself). See McGlynn and Rackley, 'Prosecuting the Possession of Extreme Pornography: A Misunderstood and Misused Law' (2013) 5 *Criminal Law Review* 400–405.

90 See *R v Peacock* (2012) Southwark Crown Court, unreported. Whilst this case was not based on extreme pornography, it shows how the perceptions of 'obscenity' can differ between prosecutors and the jury and demonstrated the challenges of obscenity prosecutions generally.

91 See Nichi Hodgson, 'Michael Peacock's Acquittal is a Victory for Sexual Freedom', *The Guardian*, London, 6 January 2012, available at http://www.theguardian.com/commentisfree/libertycentral/2012/jan/06/michael-peacock-obscenity-trial, accessed 23 July 2018.

92 For a good discussion on *R v Peacock*, see S Beresford, 'Obscene performative pornography: *R v Peacock* (2012) and the Legal Construction of Same-sex and Gendered Identities in the United Kingdom' (2014) 1(4) *Porn Studies* 378–390.

extreme pornography cases, however, the jury has to make essentially two decisions: first, whether the accused was actually in 'possession' of the material at the relevant time – whilst the legislation does not specifically define 'possession', case law relating to child pornography legislation would be of assistance.[93] In addition, the jury must also make a decision which involves a hugely subjective element regarding the obscene nature of the images in question. Whilst juries are theoretically representative of society, it cannot be ignored that societal values and norms are not uniform across the country. For instance, it is perfectly possible that cosmopolitan cities such as London would generally hold more liberal standards compared to Lincoln, a small city in the East Midlands of the UK. This could, in theory, mean that jurors comprising members of society from London may be less likely to find material to be obscene compared to their counterparts in a more conservative part of the country. This is, of course, a hypothetical comparison as it is extremely difficult to measure contemporary standards across the country and contextualise this with jury decisions. In addition, the members of the jury are usually directed by the judge to set aside their individual subjective moral perception while considering a case and factor in the standards prevalent in the wider society. However, it is also the case that there are concerns about the risk of jury 'bias' that reflect heteronormative and patriarchal morality, which may be disadvantageous to sexual minorities such as homosexuals and those who lead alternative sexual lifestyles.[94] Research on this is far from conclusive, and no safe conclusions can be drawn either way. What remains clear, however, is that jury (or the Magistrates') decisions nevertheless carry a certain element of subjectivity in determining whether the material in question falls within or outside the obscenity threshold, which adds to the lack of clarity that the law offers to consumers of pornography.

It should be clear from the discussion so far that a morality-based standard of obscenity and disgust is problematic and inappropriate for criminalising the possession of extreme pornography. Criminalising simple possession also has an impact on individual rights, some of which have already been touched upon in the discussion so far. It is pertinent here to briefly examine the law, specifically in light of its potential interference with fundamental rights.

Individual freedoms

Criminalising the possession of adult pornography also interferes with individual freedoms: from an ECHR perspective, particularly the right to freedom of expression[95] and the right to respect for one's private life.[96] By prohibiting the

93 *R v Porter* [2007] 2 All ER 625, discussed in Chapter 3, where the court adopted a test based on 'custody and control' of the material. See also *R v Leonard* [2012] All ER (D) 235 (Jul).

94 See for example Carl F Sytchin, *Law's Desire: Sexuality and the Limits of Justice* (Routledge 1995).

95 European Convention on Human Rights, Art 10(1).

96 Ibid, Art 8(1).

private consumption of extreme pornography, there is a clear implication for the right to respect for private life (consumption of pornography being an aspect of this) as well as the right to freedom of expression, which includes the right to receive information. In the consultation paper, whilst acknowledging that the law will 'impact upon the freedom of individuals to view what they wish in the privacy of their homes', the Government justified it by stating that the 'target of the new offence is at the very extreme end of the spectrum' that most people would 'abhorrent' and that 'there will be no restriction on political expression or public interest matters, or on artistic expression'.[97] Of course, neither of the rights is absolute, and states are allowed to restrict these rights where such regulation is 'in accordance with the law' or 'prescribed by law', and is 'necessary in a democratic society' for the purposes of a legitimate aim, which in this case would be the 'protection of health or morals'.[98]

'In accordance with the law' and 'prescribed by law' essentially require the state to ensure that the restriction is enshrined in law, and that the regulation is sufficiently clear and precise so as to allow individuals to reasonably foresee the consequences of their conduct.[99] The lack of clarity of the law, for instance what constitutes 'serious injury', has been discussed earlier and will not be repeated here. Owing to the inherent subjectivity of the offence, the law provides no clarity to individuals to foresee the consequences of their action.

In relation to necessity, the ECtHR defined the test for 'necessary in a democratic society' in *Sunday Times v United Kingdom*[100] as constituting 'whether the "interference" complained of corresponded to a "pressing social need", whether it was "proportionate to the legitimate aim pursued", whether the reasons given by the national authorities to justify it are "relevant and sufficient under Article 10(2)"'.[101] The 'pressing social need' implies that the aims pursued by the restriction of the fundamental rights are not just legitimate, but should also be 'pressing'. The restrictions imposed must also be proportionate to the aims pursued.[102] The consultation paper identified three areas of concern that rendered the law necessary – inability to regulate supply of the material on the internet, protection of participants featured in the material from harm, and protection of children from exposure to the material. The efficacy of a possession offence to have any meaningful impact on demand, and thereby

97 Home Office/Scottish Executive Consultation (n5), para 57.
98 European Convention on Human Rights, Arts 8(2) and 10(2).
99 For an excellent critique on these aspects, see the opinion of Rabinder Singh QC, included in the memorandum submitted by Backlash to the Criminal Justice and Immigration Bill Committee. See https://publications.parliament.uk/pa/cm200607/cmpublic/criminal/memos/ucm40502.htm, accessed 23 July 2018.
100 (1979) 2 EHRR 245.
101 Ibid, para 62.
102 For a critical analysis of the necessity test of the ECtHR, see Janneke Gerards, 'How to Improve the Necessity Test of the European Court of Human Rights' (2013) 11(2) *International Journal of Constitutional Law* 466–490.

destructing supply, is questionable, as discussed earlier. The relevance of a possession offence in terms of prevention of harm to the participants of extreme pornography has also been analysed in some detail. It is unquestionable that protection of children is a compelling interest for states and in this sense it is a necessary objective: whether a possession offence achieves this is, however, questionable. If the law were capable of addressing the availability of the material by reducing demand, this would of course logically reduce the scale of children's exposure to the material. However, as pointed out earlier, a possession offence in the UK is unlikely to have any impact on the trade or supply given that very little of such material is produced in the UK. The state's interest in preventing children's exposure to inappropriate content is not limited to extreme pornography, but applies to a broader set of material, including pornography that is lawful for adults to consume. In addition, children are unlikely to be active consumers or seekers of extreme pornography. Criminalising its simple possession is therefore unlikely to prevent children's exposure to extreme pornography: any regulation that attempts to protect children in this context should focus on the distribution and supply of the material, for example by requiring providers to institute age verification mechanisms and requiring ISPs to implement them. This is very much the crux of the new Digital Economy Act 2017 in the UK, and might well be a more workable and effective solution for regulating extreme pornography, which is considered in more detail below.

Criminalising the possession of extreme pornography appears to be a disproportionate interference with individual freedoms. The restriction on individual rights does not strike a fair balance with the aims pursued in that the reasons given by the Government for the law are insufficient to justify the interference with fundamental rights. As Rabinder Singh QC (now Singh J) neatly summarises it,

> '[A] prosecution or the threat of a prosecution, with the potential penalty of three years imprisonment, for looking at adult pornography in private is a very serious interference in an individual's right to respect for an intimate aspect of their private life under Article 8 and their freedom of expression under Article 10. It requires a powerful justification. Its justification must be stronger than that required to regulate the publication and distribution of pornography by commercial operators because the interference in the rights of the individual are so much more serious.[103]

The Government was confident that the law will be compatible with Articles 8 and 10 of the European Convention on Human Rights and that the Strasbourg court will not find it otherwise should it be raised.[104] Whilst the law is seemingly in disharmony with individual freedoms envisaged by the Convention, the Government may actually be right in that, should a case progress to Strasbourg,

103 Rabinder Singh QC (n 99).
104 Home Office/Scottish Executive Consultation (n 5), 57.

that court may not find it incompatible. This is, however, not likely to be based on the merits of the substantive law itself, but on the basis of the UK's 'margin of appreciation' as a Contracting State within the framework of the Convention. Whilst Article 10(1) of the ECHR provides that states can restrict freedom of expression for the protection of morals, it is recognised that individual states are in the best position to assess the moral outlook and standards of their own country.[105] A law that seeks to restrict freedom of expression on the basis of 'protection of morals' will fall squarely within the rather wide 'margin of appreciation' of Contracting States.[106] No complaint to the court has in fact been successful in relation to adult pornography and freedom of expression under Article 10.[107] Examples include the earlier landmark case of *Handyside v UK*,[108] and the more recent (and internet specific) case of *Perrin v UK*.[109] The only cases that had some success were where the work involved elements of political or artistic freedom and expression.[110] These are, however, specifically exempt categories in the offence and are therefore not likely to be prosecuted in any case. It remains to be seen how the ECtHR will actually answer the question of compatibility should the Court have the opportunity to consider a legal challenge to the extreme pornography law. Nonetheless, it does not take away the need for the UK Government to do some self-introspection in light of the prevailing norms of our own country, and to reconsider the possession offence in light of its disproportionate impact on individual freedoms. Diverting the focus of the law back to controlling its publication and distribution, rather than targeting end users, would be a much more proportionate approach, and would render the law more legitimate and worthy of respect.

Power imbalance: the state versus the individual

I have argued that criminalising the simple possession of extreme pornography puts individuals in a more vulnerable position than they were previously in relation to traditional obscenity laws which focused on the publisher or distributor, which also restricts their ability to be involved in open and constructive dialogue with the state.[111]

This power imbalance between the state and the individual is significant for extreme pornography. Law, as a tool of control of human behaviour, undoubtedly has the potential for abuse, which is the reason it is generally subject to

105 *Handyside v United Kingdom*, App. No. 5493/72 (ECtHR, 7 December 1976), para.48.
106 Ibid.
107 Paul Johnson (n 63), 316.
108 *Handyside v the United Kingdom* (n 105).
109 *Perrin v the United Kingdom*, App. No. 5446/03, (ECtHR, 18 October2005).
110 Paul Johnson (n 63).
111 See Abhilash Nair and James Griffin, 'Regulation of Extreme Pornography: Purposive Teleology (in)action' (2013) 22(4) *International Journal of Law and Information Technology* 329–353.

scrutiny at many levels in modern democracies. Traditionally, potential abuse of power (through laws and rules) is countered by a balance between the different wings of the governmental machinery – the executive, legislature and judiciary. Courts interpret the law and ensure that it complies with the constitutional law of the land and other supranational obligations – for example, compliance with EU law from the context of the UK. It is not unusual for the validity of national laws to be challenged in national courts. Legal challenges, however, are expensive processes and are often beyond the means of the average individual. In terms of pornography, its producers and distributors, typically companies and businesses, generally tend to be in a better position than the average individual user when it comes to legal and financial resources to challenge the validity of the law, for example by applying for judicial review. A good example to illustrate this would be the judicial review application brought against the Digital Economy Act 2010 by two of the largest ISPs in the UK.[112] Whilst the final outcome of the judicial review application was not favourable to the ISPs, the legal challenge generated substantial political and academic debate, which informed subsequent policy. The fact that the applicants were corporations meant that there was access to the legal and financial resources needed to meet the considerable costs involved in bringing a legal challenge. In contrast, the average individual user will not usually have the financial means or legal resources necessary to contest the validity of a law in courts. This would mean that the individual would either accept the law regardless of what he thinks about it, or simply carry on with his activities in cyberspace, in total disregard of the law. Both create problems for the legitimacy of the law, as I shall set out below.

Accepting the law as is, without protest

It could be argued that individuals are required to obey the laws applicable to their geographical location. Some people may find certain laws to be harsh or unacceptable, and the lack of resources to contest what they consider to be 'bad laws' in courts is not specific to pornography. For instance, there may be many who think copyright laws are too harsh and that they favour big corporations, but the legal and financial hurdles involved in challenging the law in the courts pose a barrier to the average individual. The same can be said about many other areas of law. Pornography, however, is particularly problematic – not just because the criminal law is invoked in its regulation rather than civil penalties, which could lead to serious consequences including deprivation of liberty in cases of imprisonment, but also due to its relationship with innate human needs and sexual autonomy. Firstly, viewing pornography is essentially a private act. Owing to the very nature of the topic, it would be beyond the average individual to come out in the open and challenge the harshness of a law that

112 *R (British Telecommunications Plc) v BPI (British Recorded Music Industry) Ltd* [2012] EWCA Civ 232.

restricts their ability to view certain categories of pornography without revealing very personal, and what should remain private, sexual preferences. Courts have previously intervened to protect the interests of individual consumers, albeit in the context of copyright infringement. For example, in *Golden Eye (International) Ltd and others v Telefonica UK Ltd*,[113] Golden Eye applied for an order that Telefonica (an ISP) disclose personal information of the suspected infringers of their copyright.[114] It was Golden Eye's intention to send letters of claim to the alleged infringers, after obtaining their details subsequent to the court order, asking for £700 in settlement in order to avoid litigation. Whilst *Telefonica* was willing to consent to the order, the court was concerned that the individual consumers might not have a practical means of opposing the order, and therefore appointed Consumer Focus, a statutory organisation, to represent their interests. The High Court granted the relief sought, but subject to a number of reservations. In particular, the court ensured that the letter of claim was appropriately framed to safeguard the interests of the consumers. In doing so, the court recognised the embarrassment and distress stemming from allegations of involvement in file-sharing of pornography, which puts the individual in a really vulnerable position even if innocent.[115] Golden Eye had proposed to undertake not to disclose recipients' names to the public until they formally became defendants to the proceedings, but the court held that it still had the potential to cause 'unnecessary distress because it could be read as an implicit threat of publicity once proceedings have been commenced'. The prospect of such publicity would form the very basis for many individuals choosing to pay a settlement, which in many cases was disproportionate. Whilst *Golden Eye* was very much a copyright case that was trying to balance the rights of the commercial right-holders' interest with those of the consumers, the court endeavoured to safeguard the privacy of those consumers by not allowing the claimants to exploit their vulnerability associated with the pornographic nature of the subject matter. One should not lose sight of the fact that this dispute was essentially between two private parties, albeit one of them was much more powerful than the other. As for the extreme pornography law, the powerful party is the state. The state is in a far superior position against the individual, and if it chooses to impose a law people would be reluctant to

113 *Golden Eye (International) Ltd and others v Telefonica UK Ltd, Consumer Focus intervening* [2012] EWHC 723 (Ch).

114 In the UK, these court orders are referred to as 'Norwich Pharmacal' orders, named after the first case in which such a request was granted.

115 Mr Justice Arnold, at para 123: 'Although it is not normally the role of the courts to supervise pre-action correspondence, the draft order requires the letter of claim to be in the form set out in Schedule 2 and which I have reproduced above ... the court needs to consider the impact of the letter of claim upon ordinary consumers who may not have access to specialised legal advice, who may be innocent of what is alleged against them and who may be embarrassed and/or distressed by being alleged to have been involved in filesharing involving pornography.'

challenge it for the same reasons as in *Golden Eye*. This would practically mean that some people would simply obey the law for fear of getting caught and the embarrassment that would follow. A law that commands obedience purely out of fear may be one that the state would regard as 'successful', but it is not necessarily 'good law'. It may command obedience, but not the respect of cyberspace users. As Reed argues persuasively in his book, laws that cyberspace users consider to be not respect-worthy or meaningful are bound to fail.[116] For those who continue viewing and getting caught, it would mean more guilty pleas so as to avoid a public trial regardless of the merits of the case or possibility of acquittal.

Apart from the potential reluctance of individuals to contest the validity of the law itself, it appears that there is a lack of sufficient expertise among lawyers themselves regarding the extreme pornography law – something evidenced from the fact that a significant number of prosecutions on the basis of extreme pornography result in a guilty plea as 'advised' by their lawyers. The so called 'tiger-porn' case in the UK offers a good example – Andrew Holland was charged with possessing two clips of extreme pornography on his computer, despite his protestation that it had been sent to him unsolicited as a joke and that he had no interest in such material.[117] One of the clips was alleged to have been involving a woman having sex with a tiger, which turned out to be a parody video featuring a man in a tiger suit rather than an actual tiger. Rather embarrassingly for the prosecution, this was discovered only when the judge ordered the video to be played in court with the sound on, and upon realising their mistake the prosecution dropped the charge. On the other alleged 'extreme pornographic clip', the initial legal advice Holland received from his lawyers was apparently to plead guilty, which he followed, but upon finding out that it could lead to a prison sentence he eventually got in touch with a specialist lawyer who advised him that there were grounds for pleading not guilty. Accordingly, he moved court to vacate his original plea, and in a rather dramatic turn of events the prosecution eventually dropped that charge too by declining to provide evidence.[118] The entire saga lasted for almost a year, which predictably subjected the accused to ridicule and, also predictably, a fair amount of stress. Holland had the opportunity to seek specialist advice – which many others may not be able to access.

The impact of a prosecution for extreme pornography on an individual can only be imagined – their private lives are exposed to the full glare of the media and the goriest details of their sexual preferences and choices will be dissected in court. The practical consequence is that the accused is often presumed guilty even before guilt is established, contrary to the principle of presumption of

116 See Reed (n 26).

117 *R v Holland* [2010] Unreported.

118 See Jane Fae, 'Extreme Porn Law on the Ropes', *The Register*, 6 August 2010, available at http://www.theregister.co.uk/2010/08/06/tiger_freed/

innocence until proven guilty. It is often the prospect of this unwelcoming and intrusive public trial that leads many to enter a guilty plea in the first instance so as to avoid the trauma of a prosecution and negative publicity that may follow.

The possibility of such misuse of the law, however unintended, is another reason why such laws need to be treated with caution. Criminalising the simple possession of extreme pornography provides the state with a rather unfettered right to intrude into the private, sexual life of individuals, which can have particularly harsh consequences. The individual end user is vulnerable and weak – of course, this is an argument that could also be made for prosecutions for other offences, and therefore this is not suggesting that the state should never prosecute the relatively weak individual. However, as noted earlier, there is no credible evidence of a possession offence for extreme pornography preventing harm – neither direct harm nor indirect harm – and the problems with respect to relying on notions of morality, disgust and offence have also been examined in some detail. The law serves no real purpose, nor does it offer any clarity – assisting neither law enforcement with interpreting the law nor the general public as to what exactly constitutes 'extreme pornography' in order to reasonably foresee the consequences of their actions as being criminal or legitimate. For those who simply choose to comply with the law without protest, this would mean that a wider category of material will be excluded from the remit of their consumption in order to avoid risking breaking the law.

People disregarding the law

People disregarding the law and carrying on with the activities proscribed by the legislation is also problematic for the validity of the law in cyberspace. Reed argues that this will inevitably have the effect of the law losing its legitimacy.[119] Extreme pornography law is particularly vulnerable to this risk. Pornography is a form of expression – something which is well settled in free speech jurisprudence, although obscenity does not merit the protection of free expression. The sheer volume and demand for pornography on the internet is indicative of its normative value in cyberspace. Whilst most 'extreme pornography' is not reflective of the sexual preferences and activities of the majority, it would nevertheless be representative of the sexual preferences and sexuality of a section of the society. To take an example, communities practising bondage, discipline, sadism and masochism (BDSM) form a minority group: BDSM is perhaps not part of 'mainstream' sexuality, but nonetheless is not unlawful (nor should it be) as long as the practices within the community are within legally permissible bounds under established criminal law. Pornography depicting the same BDSM practices, however, are likely to attract the extreme pornography offence; and if someone who practises such activity as part of their sexual lifestyle is interested in that

119 Reed (n 26).

genre of pornography he/she is likely to carry on watching it regardless of the proscription by the state. This could possibly be due to the status of pornography itself in relation to human emotion and desire. Pornography is not generally sought as an intellectual pursuit, nor is it mere passive information in the context of expression; it could be argued that pornography is consumed in order to satiate a need, something akin to a 'higher level' need that is interlinked to one's sexual desires and sexuality. Pornography in this sense perhaps classes as information with which an individual can communicate emotionally.[120] To ban the private consumption of adult pornography in this sense is not just a matter of restricting 'speech'; it arguably has implications for individual autonomy and what Dworkin calls an interference with the right to moral independence.[121] It would be unacceptable to prohibit consenting adults' right to view pornography in private because the social majority or state officials consider pornography to be immoral or offensive. This is also in line with Mill's thinking, that legal moralism will lead to 'tyranny of the majority'.[122]

It could be argued that the same logic should apply to other forms of illegal pornography – for example, a paedophile is likely to be interested in child pornography and is therefore also likely to disregard child pornography legislation and carry on consuming it anyway. However, what renders child pornography different is the fact that the underlying activity that forms the subject matter of child pornography is always a criminal act, and involves *harm* to children. As discussed earlier, 'extreme pornography' may well be lawful to perform, or may be simply staged or digitally enhanced, and therefore merits an entirely different treatment from child pornography.

Copyright law in the context of online infringement of copyrighted works offers a good example for the apparent disregard of the law by those who are theoretically bound by it. For instance, private home copying of copyrighted works has been technically a breach of copyright law in the United Kingdom. However, private copying has been commonplace in the UK (and elsewhere) regardless of the law, and the UK Government even attempted to introduce a new exception to permit acts of private copying into UK law,[123] which was subsequently quashed by the High Court following judicial review.[124] In spite of the law clearly prohibiting private copying, it is estimated that about 18 per cent of UK internet users aged 12 and above (this would amount to

120 See Immanuel Kant, *Lectures on Ethics* (L Infield tr, Methuen 1930) 163.

121 Ronald M. Dworkin, 'Do We Have a Right to Pornography?' in *A Matter of Principle* (Harvard University Press 1985) Ch 17.

122 John Stuart Mill, 'On Liberty' in *Three Essays* (OUP 1975).

123 The Copyright and Rights in Performances (Personal Copies for Private Use) Regulations 2014.

124 *British Academy of Songwriters, Composers and Authors Musicians' Union, R (on the application of) v Secretary of State for Business, Innovation and* [2015] EWHC 2041 (Admin) (17 July 2015).

approximately 7.8 million users) consume at least one item of online content illegally.[125] Clearly, not even a fraction of such cases are pursued or actions brought, and the sheer number of people who disregard the law and carry on with their activities demonstrates that the law does not really command the respect of the people. The number of prosecutions for extreme pornography has also been relatively low. In fact, the Association of Chief Police Officers stated at the time the law came into force that extreme pornography will not be actively sought and will be prosecuted only when found.[126] This leaves one to ponder: why enact a law in the first place with criminal sanctions when there is apparently no resolve to enforce it? There are, of course, practical reasons for this position – probably the lack of resources needed to police and actively seek extreme pornography could be the main factor and more serious offences, such as child pornography, are being prioritised in allocating resources. The low risk stemming from possessing extreme pornography means that individuals may decide to disregard the law and carry on consuming extreme pornography. In addition, possession of extreme pornography is not unlawful in other influential jurisdictions such as the United States and most European countries. It is unlikely that the law will have much normative force in cyberspace, and is therefore likely to be disregarded by those who have a genuine, keen interest in such material.[127] As Reed argues, a law that is not enforceable, or not enforced, risks losing its legitimacy in cyberspace.[128] There is nothing to suggest that the possession offence for extreme pornography would be an exception.

Taking the burden away from the consumer

The criminalisation of simple possession of adult extreme pornography is a classic example of bad law-making in cyberspace. Possession offences existed long before the extreme pornography laws to combat child pornography, and given the clear illegality and harm caused by child pornography it was the right approach. Extending the same regulatory approach to adult (extreme) pornography by criminalising private consumption is fraught with difficulties. Criminalising conduct carried out in private which causes no harm to others is not desirable in a democratic society – a position which draws support from leading philosophers and scholars such as Mill and Feinberg. The inherent lack of clarity and vagueness currently found in the law has the effect that people are left in the dark regarding

125 See Euan Mackay (Kantar Media), Report to the Intellectual Property Office, *Online Copyright Infringement Tracker, Wave 5 (March 2015-May2015), Overview and Key Findings*, The Intellectual Property Office, Newport, July 2015.

126 See Rachel Williams, 'Police will not Target Offenders Against Law on Violent Porn', *The Guardian*, 26 January 2009, available at https://www.theguardian.com/politics/2009/jan/26/police-offenders-law-violent-porn, accessed 23 July 2018.

127 See Reed (n 26), for a detailed analysis of the interaction between the law and its normative value in cyberspace.

128 Ibid.

what is permissible and impermissible content. Morality-based standards of obscenity do not offer sufficient grounds for targeting an individual's private consumption of extreme pornography. It also imposes an impermissible intrusion into people's fundamental freedoms – in particular the right to respect for private life and freedom of expression. All these factors have one combined effect: the law is meaningless and focuses on the wrong individuals.

So what is the solution to the extreme pornography problem? States do have the right to regulate content that is deemed unlawful – in this case 'obscene' as measured by the relevant society's local community standards. The problem, therefore, is not that extreme pornography has been regulated: quite the contrary. Pornography that is violent, cruel and degrading or content that is produced as a result of unlawful activities should really have no place in a civilised society, and therefore it is not my contention that such material should be left entirely unregulated. I am a firm believer in the principle that what is illegal offline should be illegal online, and pornography should be no exception. Extreme pornography is something that would be subject to traditional regulation in the UK, albeit that under the Obscene Publications Acts of 1959 and 1964 the focus of regulation would have been on the publisher and distributor rather than end users. The challenges posed by the internet meant that the state lost its ability to regulate extreme pornography at the point of supply. States have an inherent tendency to retain control over content disseminated within their territories, and inability to do this is perceived as a threat to their very sovereignty.[129] The inefficacy of transposing traditional rules to the internet to maintain such controls have prompted states to adapt regulatory models that are workable for the internet. For child pornography, this included robust substantive laws including possession offences combined with a self-regulatory framework. The relative success of child pornography laws must have influenced the Government's decision to criminalise extreme pornography as 'illegal content' along the lines of child pornography. It led to a similar regulatory response of criminalising simple possession combined with tasking the Internet Watch Foundation (IWF) to assess and block the material – similar to child pornography.[130] The initial remit of the IWF in relation to extreme pornography was, however, limited to content hosted in the UK. This was not surprising – there are no similar offences in most of the other jurisdictions and therefore international cooperation will not be available to take down content hosted abroad. Extending the regulatory model used for child pornography to adult pornography, even in its extreme form, is highly problematic. It is reminiscent of the concerns raised by some commentators of the 'mission creep'

129 See Henry H. Perritt Jr, 'The Internet as a Threat to Sovereignty? Thoughts on the Internet's Role in Strengthening National and Global Governance' (1998) 5(2) *Indiana Journal of Global Legal Studies* 4.

130 Extreme pornography hosted in the UK was part of the remit of the IWF until early 2017, but this is no longer the case.

of child pornography laws to other areas.[131] This is not only problematic for extreme pornography, but it also serves to undermine the legitimacy of the child pornography laws.

Successful and effective regulation in cyberspace can be achieved only by the law focusing on the right individuals, and as far as extreme pornography is concerned the current focus on end users is fundamentally flawed. The focus of the law should, in turn, revert to the publisher and distributor who are in a better position to actually control the publication and distribution of extreme pornography. They are also in a stronger position to challenge when the law over-steps its mark, unlike the relatively weaker individuals. The recent enactment of the Digital Economy Act 2017, which envisages an 'age verification regulator' with the remit to address extreme pornography on the internet, may just achieve this objective of shifting the focus of the law back to the publishers and distributors. The merits and demerits of online age verification, and how extreme pornography can be regulated under the new regime, are considered in further detail in Chapter 7. The Digital Economy Act 2017 envisages that all pornography providers, regardless of where they originate from, ensure that appropriate age verification mechanisms are in place so that children cannot access content intended for adults. As an age verification regulator, British Board of Film Classification (BBFC) will undertake the job of ensuring compliance, which includes requiring ISPs to block access to websites that do not comply with the new law. The regulator's remit also includes requiring internet service providers to block access to websites that contain extreme pornography.[132] It remains to be seen how effective or practical this would be, but it would be a much more efficient and less intrusive way of regulating extreme pornography than the current system. The Digital Economy Act 2017 as currently envisaged requires the age verification regulator to perform a content assessment role for the purpose of identifying extreme pornography, the problematic aspects of which are set out in the next chapter as part of the discussion on mandatory age verification. Nevertheless, the age verification regulator has a pertinent role to play in regulating extreme pornography and the new law presents a golden opportunity in this regard to control it at the point of supply rather than consumption. The regulator can identify potentially illegal content in this respect, and ideally with judicial oversight can secure the blocking or removal of extreme pornography with the assistance of ISPs. This way the law can remove the onerous and disproportionate burden from the end users and reinstate its focus on those parties who should be held accountable – Digital Economy Act 2017 has, if anything, made the possession offence for extreme pornography all the more indefensible.

131 See TJ McIntyre, 'Child Abuse Images and Cleanfeeds: Assessing Internet Blocking Systems', in Ian Brown (Ed.) *Research Handbook on Governance of the Internet* (Edward Elgar 2013), 292.

132 Digital Economy Act 2017, s 23.

PART III

7 Adult pornography

Introduction

The discussion in the previous chapters examined certain specific types of illegal pornography, albeit with varying degrees of 'illegality' depending upon the nature and form of the content and the jurisdiction involved. The focus of this chapter is on the more 'mainstream' adult pornography, which is controversial and rather complex from a regulatory perspective. 'Adult pornography' examined here does not include the more serious types of obscene material classed as 'extreme pornography' discussed in the previous chapter. The discussion covers pornography which could range from soft erotica to 'hardcore' adult pornography, which could also include material that may be classed as 'obscene' under relevant laws such as the Obscene Publications Act 1959 of the UK and therefore illegal to publish or distribute, but lawful to possess for private consumption.[1] The type of content covered here is therefore not illegal for adults to consume, although it may be inappropriate or probably harmful for children to view. This is to be distinguished from 'child pornography', in that it is not the harm inherent in the creation of the images *per se* which is the focus of the discussion, but the possible *effect* of such images on others, particularly children, and the legal issues involved in regulating content on that basis.

The regulation of adult pornography is arguably the most complex of all forms of content regulation in cyberspace, for a number of reasons. Regulating adult pornography creates significant conflict with protected freedom of expression guaranteed under various national constitutions and international instruments. In the context of the internet, this is exacerbated by the different thresholds as to what is acceptable in terms of obscene, indecent and permissible pornography in different societies. It should also be noted that 'societies' as understood in the physical world are becoming less relevant on the internet, which complicates the

1 The illegal pornography analysed in previous chapters, i.e. child pornography and extreme pornography, will almost certainly be deemed as 'obscene' under the Obscene Publications Act 1959. The discussion here excludes these specific categories and focuses on the 'less serious' material that may or may not be classed as 'obscene', as the test for obscenity is dependent on the likely recipient of the material in question.

issue further, as values and norms on the internet are changing rapidly owing to the global, inter-cultural interactions that take place in cyberspace. People's perception as to what is acceptable content in the context of pornography and obscenity changes with time, and it is perhaps fair to suggest that the internet may have accelerated this process due to the large scale and real-time cultural and social interaction that takes place in virtual communities globally. The law has often struggled to cope with the pace of changing technology, as well as with the evolving norms in cyberspace, rendering some of the laws pertaining to obscenity and indecency outdated, or simply inappropriate for the internet.

As stated briefly in Chapter 1, various justifications have been advanced generally for the regulation of pornography in the offline world, including feminist perspectives on pornography that argue for stricter regulation on the basis that pornography objectifies, and is degrading to, women.[2] Notwithstanding these viewpoints, an examination of existing laws indicates that regulation has been influenced by notions of morality, i.e., the assumption that obscene pornography can corrupt the minds of vulnerable individuals. The 'deprave and corrupt' test found in section 1 of the Obscene Publications Act 1959 in the UK and the *Miller* test of 'appealing to the prurient interest' in the US[3] are good examples of judging unacceptable pornography, legally referred to as 'obscene' or 'indecent' material, through a moral lens. The problem generally with morality-based regulation of pornography has been discussed in Chapter 6, and will not be repeated here. It is, however, the case that there is little consensus within and between jurisdictions regarding morality-based regulation of adult pornography owing to its inherent subjectivity. The law has traditionally focused on the image, i.e., whether the material is obscene or indecent, for regulating adult pornography in the physical world. The concepts of 'obscenity' and 'indecency', in turn, are intrinsically linked to the prevailing moral standards of a relevant community, as the lawfulness of the content is ultimately measured against those standards. This is problematic in terms of the internet as it is a lot more difficult to identify a specific community standard in cyberspace, compared to the offline world.

Furthermore, traditional regulation has focused on controlling the publication and distribution of content rather than criminalising its private consumption. This did not create a lot of challenges for governments in terms of enforcing the law as far as traditional forms of media were concerned: each state could simply enforce its own laws within its geographical boundaries. The internet obviously changed this scenario, as physical borders became insignificant in cyberspace, and the ability of states to exercise control over pornography within their (physical)

2 See for example Andrea Dworkin, *Pornography: Men Possessing Women* (Women's Press 1981); Catherine MacKinnon, 'Pornography as Defamation and Discrimination' (1991) 71 *B.U.L. Review* 793–815; Catherine Itzin, *Pornography: Women, Violence, and Civil Liberties* (OUP 1992); Susanne Kappeler, *The Pornography of Representation* (Polity Press 1986); Susan M. Easton, *The Problem of Pornography: Regulation and the Right to Free Speech* (Routledge 1994).

3 The three-prong test for obscenity was stated in the landmark case of *Miller v California* 413 US 15 (1973), discussed in more detail below.

territories became seriously constrained. Cyberspace offered easy access to content hosted anywhere in the world, making each household with an internet connection a potential 'porn shop', rendering the traditional controls focused on publishers, licensed sex shops, and licensed cinemas practically pointless, especially for preventing children from accessing pornography, as they could simply obtain it on the internet. This has resulted in a peculiar situation where there are strong safeguards to restrict exposure of children to adult content in the offline world, but relatively little control in the online world.

Protecting children from pornography became a matter of importance for governments following rising public concerns on the extent of pornography on the internet.[4] The US Government responded by legislation in 1996 through the Communications Decency Act 1996 (CDA 1996). However, the burden it placed on the right to free speech resulted in the Supreme Court striking down the relevant provisions of the Act as unconstitutional.[5] A subsequent legislative attempt, the Child Online Protection Act 1998 (COPA 1998) suffered the same fate, following a long and protracted litigation. The failure of CDA 1996 and COPA 1998 has had the effect that adult pornography has been left largely unregulated on the internet, not only in the United States, but it also meant that the ability of other countries to regulate was seriously hindered. As a number of pornography websites were hosted in the United States, the laws of other countries were effectively rendered ineffective owing to these laws being largely focused on controlling the publication and distribution of obscene pornography. If a case were to result in successful prosecution in another country, its enforcement in the US would be challenging, and with no real prospect of success if the content in question was within protected speech under the First Amendment.[6] For most countries, this has meant that online adult pornography either remains largely unregulated (in line with the US position), or alternative means had to be found to control access to content from within their territories.

Regulation of adult internet pornography remains a complex task. This chapter sets out the complexities and challenges involved in the regulation of adult pornography on the internet, and analyses the different regulatory initiatives and strategies. I argue that whilst there are different justifications for regulating pornography generally, protecting children from exposure to adult content will provide the sole basis of legitimacy for the regulation of adult pornography on

4 For example, in the 1990s a number of states in Australia introduced legislation aimed at censoring content and restricting access. This was followed by initiatives at Commonwealth level in the Broadcasting Services Amendment (Online Services) Act 1999, which came into force in 2000. It used a classification regime similar to one applied to films and videos to censor content on the internet, and actions were initiated upon complaints received from the public.

5 *Reno v ACLU* 136 L Ed 2d 436 US Supreme Court (1997)

6 *Yahoo!, Inc. v La Ligue Contre Le Racisme et L'Antisémitisme*, 169 F. Supp. 2d 1181, 1194 (N.D. Cal. 2001) provides a good example of the difficulties in enforcing foreign judgments in the US. See n 17, Chapter 2.

the internet. This can be achieved only through purposive and respect-worthy laws that can command the obedience of cyberspace users, for anything less is bound to fail. Cyberspace users are likely to reject any laws that appear to be based on purely moralistic grounds and therefore the existing regulation of adult pornography, focusing on the obscenity and indecency of the material, is highly problematic for transposing to the internet environment. Meaningful regulation will require establishing an enforceable model that balances the right of adults and preserves the best interests of children. The law so far has been image-based, which is intrinsically linked to a community standards-based test. This model cannot be transposed to the internet: effective regulation will require moving the focus of the law away from the image to establishing a model that seeks to restrict children's access to pornography. This will result in the focus of the law eventually shifting to other stakeholders and will witness an increasing level of participation by new stakeholders, including intermediaries and access providers.

The chapter begins with a brief overview of the traditional regulation of adult pornography in the UK and the challenges raised by the internet for the conventional regulatory model. It will then examine the early legislative initiatives in the United States in order to contextualise the complexities of regulating adult pornography on the internet, both for the US as well as other countries. The chapter will thereafter explore alternative regulatory strategies, by referring to relevant initiatives and recent legislation in the United Kingdom. It will be clear by the end of this discussion how states have endeavoured to regain control over the dissemination of pornography within their territories, and continue to do so despite the challenges posed by the internet.

Regulating obscenity: UK

In the UK, which has been a relatively conservative society by Western standards, pornography is something which has been traditionally frowned upon. It was not until the enactment of the Obscene Publications Act 1959 that at least some form of pornography, i.e., content not classed as 'obscene' under the Act, became legally permissible. The early test for obscenity was based on the *Hicklin* test, after the landmark case of *R v Hicklin*,[7] in which Cockburn CJ famously defined the test for obscenity:

> 'The test of obscenity is this, whether the tendency of the matter charged as obscenity is to deprave and corrupt those whose minds are open to such immoral influences, and into whose hands a publication of this sort may fall.'[8]

The test under *Hicklin* was broad enough to encompass a wide range of publications owing to the breadth of its definition. In particular, the inclusion of 'those

7 *R v Hicklin* LR 2 QB 360 (1868).
8 Ibid.

whose minds are open to such immoral influences' would have easily included children, and therefore a publisher would be risking prosecution by publishing anything 'pornographic' which can be read or seen by children. Therefore, the practical effect of *Hicklin* was that publication of pornography within the UK was almost impossible. It was also illegal to import obscene material from abroad due to the Customs Consolidations Act 1876, which also made it difficult to obtain pornography produced abroad in the UK. The net effect was that it was very difficult to publish or obtain any pornography in the UK. *Hicklin* was subject to criticism for a number of reasons. From a criminal law point of view, it was criticised for effectively lacking the requirement of intention necessary for a publisher to be prosecuted under the offence.[9] For instance, it was entirely possible that a publisher did not contemplate the material to fall into the hands of children while publishing, and if it did happen, then the material would be deemed obscene per *Hicklin*.[10] This meant that it was a very risky business to publish sexually explicit material in the UK as there was no guaranteed way of ensuring that children did not obtain it or encounter it accidentally.

The enactment of the Obscene Publications Act 1959 effectively brought statutory certainty to the principle in *Hicklin*, but it also narrowed its scope, resulting in what was to be a slightly less stringent approach to pornography in the UK. Section 1 of the Obscene Publications Act states that an article is deemed to be obscene if:

> its effect or (where the article comprises two or more distinct items) the effect of any one of its items is, if taken as a whole, such as to tend to deprave and corrupt persons who are likely, having regard to all relevant circumstances, to read, see or hear the matter contained or embodied in it.

The removal of the words 'those whose minds are open to such immoral influences' found in *Hicklin* meant that the material could be judged against adults (who are more likely to come across such material) rather than children. In this sense, it is arguable that the practical impact of the law moved away from prevention of harm (or risk of harm) from exposure of pornography to children to one based on generally upholding 'morals' in society. The wording of section 1 offered a degree of flexibility for courts and juries to apply it on a case-by-case basis as it allowed room to accommodate the changing values and norms in society in relation to what is acceptable or obscene at any given time. However, some of the early cases which followed the enactment of the legislation demonstrated the UK's continuing resistance to pornography and tendency to exert strict controls over such content. For example, the very fact that prosecution

9 See, for example, St John Stevas, 'Obscenity and the Law' [1954] *Crim L Rev* 817–821.

10 See J.E. Hall Williams, 'Obscenity in Modern English Law' (Fall 1055) 20 *Law and Contemporary Problems* 630–647.

was brought against D.H. Lawrence's *Lady Chatterley's Lover* in *R v Penguin Books Ltd*[11] demonstrated the lack of tolerance for pornographic content even after the enactment of the Obscene Publications Act 1959. Prosecution was unsuccessful in this case, with the jury finding the publication not obscene – perhaps indicating that society had moved forward in terms of the general acceptance of pornography. Societal attitudes change with time: pornographic material that is considered to be acceptable today may have offended and deemed obscene some time ago. It would be inconceivable today to suggest that prosecution would even be considered for a work similar to *Lady Chatterley's Lover*. Nevertheless, it seems to be the case that law enforcement authorities and prosecutors still tend to assess the prevailing standards of society incorrectly, and are driven by an inherent tendency to apply a 'higher moral standard' on matters pertaining to obscenity. A classic example to illustrate this point might be the prosecution of Simon Walsh,[12] discussed in Chapter 6. Whilst the case involved the alleged possession of extreme pornographic images contrary to section 63 of the Criminal Justice and Immigration Act 2008, readers may remember that a test of 'obscenity' still applies for the offence. Walsh's acquittal prompts one to wonder whether prosecuting authorities are always up to date with their perception of what society considers obscene, for what the prosecutor insisted to be obscene material was adjudged otherwise by a jury of peers.

Obscenity and the internet

Notwithstanding the criticism and some flawed prosecutions, the test under the Obscene Publications Act 1959 generally turned out to be a workable model for traditional forms of media such as print, video and television, although prosecutions have been rare in recent times.[13] Certain changes were made to the Act to accommodate newer methods of 'publication' using new technologies, for example an amendment made by the Criminal Justice and Public Order Act 1994 brought the transmission of electronically stored data within the meaning of 'publication'.[14] Nevertheless, as the focus of the Obscene Publications Act was on the publisher and/or distributor of content, it became questionable whether it was capable of regulating obscenity on the internet. In particular, a pertinent

11 *R v Penguin Books Ltd* [1961] Crim LR 176.

12 Unreported, Kingston Crown Court 2012. See for a critique http://www.backlash-uk.org.uk/wp/?page_id=976, accessed 23 July 2018.

13 See Susan M. Edwards, 'On the Contemporary Application of the Obscene Publications Act 1959'(1988) 12 *Criminal Law Review* 843–853, where the author, by analysing pornography trials in the Crown Courts in England and Wales over a six-month period, concludes that the 'deprave and corrupt test' is an 'inappropriate and blunt measure' to determine whether publishers are guilty of publishing an obscene article, and that the Act is obsolete as far as this offence is concerned.

14 Criminal Justice and Public Order Act 1994, c 33, Sch.9, para 3.

question to be clarified was where exactly does 'publication' take place on the internet when content is published or hosted in a server abroad. This, amongst other issues, was examined in the landmark case of *R v Perrin.*[15]

R v Perrin

The suitability of the obscenity test for the internet was discussed in *R v Perrin*[16] during which the Court of Appeal ruled on matters ranging from jurisdiction to the right to freedom of expression, and revisited a key question of the obscenity test, i.e., the proportion of viewers who were likely to be depraved and corrupted. The case concerned a pornographic website which contained a webpage with sexually explicit material in the form of short preview trailers (so called 'teaser pages') which was available to anyone with internet access. Full access to the website was possible only upon subscribing, which involved providing personal and payment card details. The appeal was from the trial court's conviction of the appellant for publishing an obscene article on the preview page which was accessible to anyone, including children and vulnerable young people (the appellant was acquitted on the other counts relating to the paid subscription pages).[17]

An interesting argument was raised with respect to jurisdiction: the appellant argued, citing the American case of *ACLU v Reno*,[18] that the jury ought to consider where the major steps in relation to publication first took place, and to convict only if satisfied that those steps took place within the jurisdiction of the court. There was no English or European authority to support this argument at the time, and therefore this was an important point for the court to consider. If the court ruled in favour of the appellant on this point, it would effectively mean re-interpreting section 1(3) of the Obscene Publications Act in terms of electronic publication. The court however rejected the argument and noted that by approaching the jurisdiction issue based on *ACLU v Reno* 'would lead to publishers taking their major steps in countries with the most relaxed laws, but such countries might also have little interest in prosecuting, especially if the offensive material was targeted elsewhere'.[19]

It was also argued that the issues raised in relation to the 'contemporary community standards' test of the US (the test is discussed in more detail later in the chapter) are similar to the problems in Europe as 'community standards' are not the same in all Member States. The court rejected this, stating that the US authorities cited were of limited value in light of the 'protection given to free speech under the US Constitution and the different

15 *R v Perrin* [2002] EWCA Crim 747.

16 Ibid.

17 Southwark Crown Court, 16 October 2000.

18 [2000] 217 F.3d 162 at 168–169.

19 Ibid, para 51.

inter-relationship between the states'.[20] On a related note, the appellant also argued that the conviction was in breach of his right under Article 10 of the European Convention on Human Rights, the right to freedom of expression. The court rejected this too, and noted that the restriction on Article 10(1) imposed by the Obscene Publications Act 1959 is one that is prescribed by law and necessary in a democratic society as stipulated by Article 10(2). The court referred to the earlier case of *Handyside v UK*[21] in support of the judgment, which held that Article 10(2) leaves to the Contracting State a margin of appreciation, which is 'given both to the domestic legislator ("prescribed by law") and to the bodies, judicial amongst others, that are called upon to interpret and apply the law in force'.[22] *Handyside* involved the publication of a book, *Little Red School Book*, which was held to be obscene under English law, but was allowed to be published in some other Contracting States. The European Court in *Handyside* had pointed out that each state has its own views as to what was acceptable in terms of protection of morals, and the fact that some states allowed its distribution did not necessarily render the English decision a breach of Article 10. In other words, it could mean that each Contracting State has its own community standards, and that does not entitle someone to publish content which is illegal in the UK from a state where the same material might be acceptable by relying on Article 10.

On the issue of 'publication' itself, the court held that the mere transmission of data constitutes publication, i.e., publication occurs when anyone accesses (downloads) the preview page in this jurisdiction. Following *Perrin* and the earlier case of *R v Waddon*,[23] publication takes place both when the material is uploaded and when it is downloaded, even if the material was uploaded to the website from abroad. The decision in *Perrin* would also therefore mean that an online publisher could not rely on the 'community standards' of another jurisdiction (even within the EU) to avoid liability for publication in the UK.

Perrin was a significant ruling for internet pornography as it dispelled any notion that the internet could be used as an alternative medium for publishing pornographic material which would be illegal in other existing forms of media. *Perrin* also had another implication, at least in theory. As far as internet pornography is concerned, it pretty much reinstated the *Hicklin* standard in that if webpages are not protected with access controls to prevent children accessing them, that would potentially amount to an 'obscene publication'. This is because in practice there was no guaranteed way of ensuring that children did not come across adult content that could be accessed in the UK, and therefore it is arguable that *Perrin* brought back the broader standard of obscenity that was prevalent

20 *R v Perrin* (n 15), para 50.
21 [1979 to 1980] 1 EHRR 737.
22 Ibid, para 48.
23 *R v Waddon* 6 April 2000, unreported. The Court of Appeal held that material hosted on US websites could come under UK jurisdiction when downloaded in this country.

under the old regime. In this sense one could say that the breadth of the Obscene Publications Act 1959 suddenly expanded to the old *Hicklin* test in terms of internet pornography.

Whilst therefore it appears as though *Perrin* reiterated the UK's authority over the publication of pornography within its territorial limits, practical difficulties in enforcing the law if the publisher was based abroad remained as complex as before. For example, even if a court found that the publication constituted an offence under UK law, there are numerous constraints in identifying a publisher based abroad and extraditing (if at all possible) them to the UK for trial. Firstly, there is the issue of identifying the publisher. Unless it is a commercial website with the details of the publisher or company registration information available on the website itself, it will normally be possible to identify the publisher only by contacting the internet service provider to obtain identifying information. As ISPs would usually be subject to their own privacy policies that undertake not to disclose information revealing their users' identities, this would normally involve a search warrant, or in civil proceedings would require applying for a court order to require the ISP to reveal the identifying information, which can be time-consuming and expensive. Assuming a court order is obtained, there is no guarantee that the ISP will be able to track down the publisher, or that it can be proved exactly who uploaded the material from a particular IP address.[24] Further investigation will be required to ascertain the identity of the individual, which would involve a police investigation. If the material in question is not illegal in the host country, it will be inconceivable to expect any meaningful cooperation from their courts or policing authorities. In the event that extradition is not necessary and a successful prosecution is possible against a foreign publisher, enforcement of the judgment in the publisher's country also can prove challenging. A good example of the difficulties in enforcing judgments extra-territorially is *Yahoo! v LICRA*, in which enforcing a French court order in California proved problematic owling to the breadth of the First Amendment protection available in the US.[25]

The fact that a large number of pornographic websites are hosted in the US has made it particularly challenging, cumbersome, and impractical for the UK to meaningfully regulate adult pornography on the internet, in spite of the ruling in *Perrin*. It is pertinent at this point to examine in further detail the legislative initiatives and the current position in the US in order to appreciate and contextualise the complexities of regulating adult pornography on the internet.

24 ISPs can match up the IP address to the customer to whom the address is allocated. This is by no means fool proof as it is entirely possible that multiple users use the same IP address to access the internet (for example, a large household, or unauthorised wi-fi access on unsecured connections, etc.).

25 *Yahoo!, Inc. v La Ligue Contre Le Racisme et L'Antisémitisme*, 169 F. Supp. 2d 1181, 1194 (N.D. Cal. 2001). See Chapter 2 (n 17).

US: pioneer and the problem

The United States was one of the first liberal democracies in the world to enact legislation to address adult pornography on the internet. Whilst pioneers in this respect, it is ironic that the status quo in the United States is also part of the problem for the current state of regulation of adult pornography on the internet.

The US, when compared to the UK, has traditionally had a more relaxed approach to pornography generally, mainly due to the broader protection of free speech afforded under the First Amendment to the US Constitution. Whilst pornography *per se* is not outside protected free speech, it is well established that obscenity is not protected under the First Amendment: it was held in *Roth v United States*[26] that sexually explicit material will be protected by the First Amendment unless it is deemed to be *obscene*. The current US standard of obscenity was laid down in *Miller v California*,[27] which formulated a three-prong test for judging obscenity:

1. whether the average person, applying contemporary community standards would find that the work, taken as a whole, appeals to the prurient interest [Roth, *supra*, at 489]
2. whether the work depicts or describes, in a patently offensive way, sexual conduct specifically defined by the applicable state law, and
3. whether the work, taken as a whole, lacks serious literary, artistic, political, or scientific value.

Overall, the effect of *Miller* was that obscenity was left outside the purview of protected speech, and the test for obscenity itself was left to the law of individual states, either written or construed.[28] The jury may measure the factual issues of prurient appeal and patent offensiveness by the standard that prevails in the forum community, and need not employ a 'national uniform standard'. The 'contemporary community standards' test would mean that the material can be assessed in light of the prevailing norms and standards of the relevant society where the material is published. Therefore, it is perfectly possible that the same content which is deemed acceptable in a more liberal state, such as New York, might be deemed obscene in the more conservative society of the state of Tennessee. The court essentially recognised in *Miller* that the US as a nation is too big and diverse to reasonably expect a uniform community standard for all 50 states and, therefore, to expect that material found tolerable in more liberal societies will be regarded similarly in relatively conservative societies.

26 *Roth v United States* 354 US 476.
27 *Miller v California* 413 US 15 (1973).
28 Ibid, 27.

As convincingly argued by Hertz-Bunzl, the application of contemporary community standards in *Miller* is 'particularly unique in American jurisprudence' because of the rather geographical location-based treatment accorded to what is essentially a constitutional right, which in most cases remains the same across the country.[29] The third prong of the test acts essentially as a defence for certain types of content which has a legitimate reason to exist other than solely for sexual gratification. In terms of the standard to judge this aspect, it was clarified subsequently in *Pope v Illinois*[30] that the test for literary, artistic, political or scientific value has to be based on national standards, rather than local community standards.

The *Miller* test for obscenity did not pose much of a problem in the pre-internet era. Communities that exist in the real world simply had to adhere to the applicable laws within the state/society they reside in, which was fairly practical, particularly for print publication and material on a physical medium such as cassette or CD. The suitability of 'contemporary community standards' for intra-state services was at issue in the context of telephone services in *Sable v FCC*,[31] where the Supreme Court upheld an amendment to the Communications Act of 1934 which imposed a ban on obscene 'dial-a-porn' messages. This was in spite of the fact that the ban would subject operators to different community standards depending on where the service was accessed from, requiring them to adhere to the strictest community standard in the country. The new law would practically mean that an operator should comply with the state laws of all 50 states in the country if they wished to provide a nationwide service. The Supreme Court held that this alone did not render the statute unconstitutional and it was down to the distributors to implement a screening system which selectively served those areas of the country where they could legally provide the service.[32] The community standards test was therefore deemed to be appropriate and constitutional despite the notion of harshness it purported to give in this context. The court, however, invalidated a portion of the law that would have banned all dial-a-porn messages that were *indecent* as applied to minors, as the law, if permitted, would have the effect of unconstitutionally limiting lawful speech between adults.[33]

The advent of the internet renewed the debates on the suitability and practicality of a test for obscenity based on contemporary community standards. The internet is in many ways a unique medium compared to other traditional forms of media, where regulating content has a much more profound impact on freedom of speech compared to, for example, traditional telecommunication services. It is

29 Noah Hertz-Bunzl, 'A nation of one? Community standards in the internet era' (2011) 22 *Fordham Intellectual Property, Media and Entertainment Law Journal* 145.

30 481 US 497 (1987).

31 492 US 115 (1989).

32 Ibid, at 125–126.

33 Ibid, at 130–131. 'Indecency' is discussed in more detail later in this chapter.

therefore hardly surprising that the debate on the community standards criteria was reinvigorated following the rise of the internet as a popular medium of information and communication. The relevance of a community standards-based test was subsequently to be one of the key points to be decided in the legal challenges that followed the enactment of the Communications Decency Act 1996 and Child Online Protection Act 1998.

Early attempts to regulate internet pornography

The growing number of pornographic websites on the internet resulted in a 'moral panic' in the United States in the early 1990s. A particular concern was that children could access, deliberately or accidentally, and with relative ease, numerous pornographic web pages hosted on the internet from all over the world and there was the (rather overstated) fear that the internet was becoming almost synonymous with pornography. Whilst it was true that the internet facilitated an unprecedented level of access and distribution of adult content, concerns that the internet would be taken over by pornography turned out to be hugely exaggerated. For instance, in July 1995, TIME™ Magazine ran a cover story 'On a screen near you: Cyberporn', which claimed that 83.5 per cent of images on news groups were pornographic and that pornography was readily available to anyone with internet access, including children.[34] The article, however, was based on a now-discredited undergraduate research project at Carnegie Mellon University,[35] and failed to contextualise it with other relevant details.[36] Subsequent reports revealed that only 1 per cent of newsgroups were exclusively pornographic and in 1995 pornography accounted for less than 1 per cent of internet traffic.[37] It is also worth noting that the concerns stemming from children accessing inappropriate and unsuitable material existed long before the internet; as Boyd and Marwick (2009) suggest, technology perhaps merely 'inflects age-old issues in new ways'.[38]

Nonetheless, concerns that children had unfettered access to adult content online led to the US Government enacting legislation to regulate adult pornography. The first major attempt for this purpose was the introduction of the Communications Decency Act 1996 (CDA 1996) as Title V of the Telecommunications Act of 1996.

34 P. Elmer-Dewitt, 'Online erotica: On a screen near you', *TIME Magazine*, 3 July 1995.

35 Marty Rimm, 'Marketing Pornography on the Information Superhighway: A Survey of 917,410 Images, Descriptions, Short Stories, and Animations Downloaded 8.5 Million Times by Consumers in Over 2000 Cities in Forty Countries, Provinces and Territories' (1995) 83(5) *Georgetown Law Journal* 1849–1934.

36 See Anne Littlewood,'Cyberporn and Moral Panic: An Evaluation of Press Reactions to Pornography on the Internet' (Summer 2003) 27(86) *Library and Information Research* 8–18. Available at http://eprints.rclis.org/6070/1/article86a.pdf, accessed 23 July 2018.

37 Ibid.

38 danah boyd and Alice Marwick, A, 'The Conundrum of Visibility: Youth Safety and the Internet' (2009) 3 *Journal of Children and Media* 410–414.

Communications Decency Act 1996

The CDA 1996 was first introduced to the Senate Committee on Commerce, Science and Transportation on 1 February 1995,[39] and became law on 8 February 1996. The Act was Title V of the Telecommunications Act 1996, which amended Section 223 (47 U.S.C. 223) adding, inter alia, the following section:

> (d) Whoever–
>
> (1) in interstate or foreign communications knowingly–
>
> (A) uses an interactive computer service to send to a specific person or
>
> persons under 18 years of age, or
>
> (B) uses any interactive computer service to display in a manner
>
> available to a person under 18 years of age,
>
> any comment, request, suggestion, proposal, image, or other communication that, in context, depicts or describes, in terms patently offensive as measured by contemporary community standards, sexual or excretory activities or organs, regardless of whether the user of such service placed the call or initiated the communication; or
>
> (2) knowingly permits any telecommunications facility under such person's
>
> control to be used for an activity prohibited by paragraph (1) with the intent that it be used for such activity,
>
> shall be fined under title 18, United States Code, or imprisoned not more than two years, or both.

The breadth of the provisions was severely criticised by free speech activists and civil libertarian groups. Whilst the provisions were aimed at protecting children and young people from accessing pornographic content, which not many objected to in principle, the wording of the section was felt to be too broad to withstand constitutional scrutiny. In particular, the focus of the CDA 1996 on 'indecency' of the material, rather than obscenity, made it particularly problematic. As noted before, obscenity is not protected by the guarantee of free speech under the First Amendment, but the indecency standard advocated in the CDA 1996 was much broader than the traditional obscenity standard in *Miller v California*.[40]

In the US Supreme Court's First Amendment jurisprudence, 'indecency' is different from 'obscenity' and occupies a rather special place. Adults generally

39 It was introduced by Senators James Exon, a democrat from Nebraska and Slade Gorton, a Republican from Washington. In the same year, there was also a State level initiative in New York, with the introduction of § 235.21(3) to the New York State Penal Code.

40 413 US 15 (1973).

have a qualified right to engage in indecent speech.[41] The Supreme Court has held that Government can regulate indecency on radio and television or in a 'dial-a-porn' context, as long as the regulation does not operate as a complete ban.[42] In other words, regulation should not result in adults having *no* access to indecent speech which is their right. Regulation of indecent speech must also be justified by a compelling reason, and must be applied in the least restrictive manner. It is permissible for the Government to regulate the public use of indecent speech.[43] However, if the regulation is based purely on content, it will generally be subject to a strict scrutiny test, i.e., the Government should demonstrate that the regulation is necessary to serve a compelling governmental interest, and that it is narrowly drawn to achieve that interest.[44] Where the regulation is aimed at limiting the harmful secondary effects of speech,[45] or when the speech is broadcast,[46] the courts will generally apply a lower level test than strict scrutiny. A classic example of the application of the secondary effects doctrine can be found in *Renton v Playtime Theatres*,[47] which upheld a Government ordinance that required adult movie theatres to be confined to approximately 6 per cent of the city. The court found the restriction to be content-neutral and applied intermediate scrutiny, finding that preventing the secondary effects of adult movie theatres (crime, decreasing property values, etc.) was a substantial Government interest and by providing 6 per cent of the city as unrestricted land a reasonable alternative avenue of communication was deemed to be provided.[48]

Coming back to the CDA 1996, there were a number of campaigns organised by free speech activists right from the introduction of the Bill. Following its adoption by the US Congress on 2 February 1996, the Electronic Frontier Foundation (EFF)[49] led a protest which resulted in a number of websites turning black for a period of 48 hours. The EFF also launched its 'blue-ribbon' campaign on the internet which urged other websites to 'wear' a blue ribbon and link back to EFF's site to raise awareness, which received good support from a number of websites that participated in solidarity. As soon as the Bill was signed into law by President Clinton, the American Civil Liberties Union (ACLU), joined by a

41 *Sable Communications v FCC* 492 US 115 (1989) at 126; *FCC v Pacifica Foundation* 438 US 726, 747–748 (1978).

42 See for example, *Alliance for Community Media v FCC*, 56 F.3d 105, 116 S. Ct. 471 (1996); *Dial Information Serv. Corp. v Thornburgh*, 938 F.2d 1535 (2d Cir. 1991), 502 U.S. 1072 (1992); *Information Providers Coalition for Defense of the First Amendment v FCC*, 928 F.2d 866 (9th Cir. 1991).

43 *FCC v Pacifica Foundation* 438 U.S. 726, 744–751 (1978).

44 *Widmar v Vincent*, 454 U.S. 263, 270 (1981).

45 *City of Erie v Pap's A.M.*, 529 U.S. 277, 289–303 (2000).

46 *Pacifica*, 438 U.S. at 748.

47 *City of Renton v. Playtime Theatres, Inc.*, 475 U.S. 41, 51–52 (1986).

48 For a discussion on secondary effects doctrine see H.G. Ward, 'Indecency, Pornography and the Protection of Children' (2005) 6 *Georgetown Journal of Gender and the Law* 315, 2005.

49 See www.eff.org, accessed 24 July 2018.

number of civil liberties campaigners including the Electronic Frontier Foundation and Electronic Privacy Information Centre, filed a legal challenge against implementing the indecency provisions of the Communications Decency Act in the District Court of Pennsylvania. The grounds for the challenge were that the CDA 1996 was unconstitutional on its face as it criminalised speech protected by the First Amendment, its provisions were unconstitutionally broad and vague, and that it was not the most narrowly tailored means of achieving a governmental compelling interest.

The CDA was the first major attempt by the US Government to regulate adult pornography on the internet with a view to prevent children's exposure to it. The focus of the legislation was not illegal child pornography, but the regulation of adult pornography, which, whilst being legal for adults, may be harmful for children – an issue which was widely recognised as having a compelling interest for the Government. As the internet was still in its infancy and a relatively new form of technology, one of the issues the court had initially to consider was its specific characteristics. The District Court appointed a Finding of Facts Commission for this purpose. As these were still the 'early days' of the internet, there was naturally some confusion regarding the most appropriate regulatory regime to be applied to it. The primary means of accessing the internet at the time was by using a dial-up modem and a telephone line, rather than the modern-day high-speed fibre optic broadband. Analogies were drawn comparing the internet to other forms of existing media, including print, television, radio and telephone. As different forms of media have been subject to different levels of control and constitutional scrutiny, identifying the most accurate description for the internet for the purpose of applying appropriate regulatory precedent was highly pertinent. For instance, it is settled law that content which would be acceptable for publication in print might be restricted on broadcast, owing to the unique challenges of the broadcast medium (for example spectrum scarcity), and in particular the possibility that children might be easily exposed to the latter.[50] Cable television, although at first glance similar to broadcast, is subject to strict scrutiny following *United States v Playboy Entertainment Group*.[51] The ability to block channels on a household-by-household basis distinguished cable television from broadcast media, and applying strict scrutiny the court found that there were less restrictive alternatives than was proposed under section 505 of the Telecommunications Act of 1996, which was the subject of the legal challenge in *Playboy*.[52] The distinction relied primarily on the level of control the consumer was able to exert, and it appears that the higher the level of control or choice of

50 *FCC v Pacifica Foundation* 438 US 726, 748–749 (1978). The following were also provided for justifying stricter controls for broadcast In *Pacifica*: (1) communications are broadcast directly into the home, where privacy interests are at their highest, (2) inability to warn non-consenting adults who may tune into a station broadcasting indecent speech about the offensive content.

51 *United States v Playboy Entertainment Group Inc* 529 U.S. 803 (2000).

52 Ibid.

content for the end user, the higher the level of First Amendment protection available for content, even for indecent pornography.[53] Similarly, regulation of commercial indecent telephone communication was also held to be subject to strict scrutiny where a distinction was drawn with broadcast in *Sable Communications, Inc v FCC*.[54]

The Findings of Facts Commission reported to the District Court certain novel characteristics of the internet, during which analogies were drawn with other forms of obtaining and exchanging information.[55] The rather unique and novel characteristics of the internet were neatly summarised by Judge Dalzell as:

> 'First, the Internet presents very low barriers to entry. Second, these barriers to entry are identical for both speakers and listeners. Third, as a result of these low barriers, astoundingly diverse content is available on the Internet. Fourth, the Internet provides significant access to all who wish to speak in the medium, and even creates a relative parity among speakers.'[56]

It was further noted by the court that it takes several steps to enter cyberspace from having access to a computer connected to the internet, entering appropriate commands to find particular information, which on the World Wide Web normally involves using a search engine or entering an appropriate address. This means that communications over the internet 'do not invade an individual's home or appear on one's computer screen unbidden', nor do they 'encounter content by accident ... Almost all sexually explicit images are preceded by warning as to the content'.[57] It was also noted that the

> 'evidence adduced at the hearing showed significant differences between Internet communications and communications received by radio or television. Although content on the Internet is just a few clicks of a mouse away from the user, the receipt of information on the Internet requires a series of affirmative steps more deliberate and directed than merely turning a dial. A child requires some sophistication and some ability to read to retrieve material and thereby to use the Internet unattended'.[58]

Whilst many of these broad observations still hold true, technology has changed since these findings, rendering some of them outdated or no longer entirely accurate. For example, the finding in relation to 'affirmative steps' to retrieve content on the internet has proved to be misguided in some ways. Whilst it

53 See Ward (n 48).
54 *Sable Communications, Inc v FCC*, 492 U.S. 115 (1989).
55 *American Civil Liberties Union v Reno*, 929 F Supp 824 U.S. DC Penn (1996).
56 Ibid, 877.
57 Ibid, 843.
58 Ibid, 845.

remains true that internet access requires affirmative steps from the end user compared to 'turning a dial' for television or radio, there is evidence to suggest that children who have not deliberately sought out sexually explicit sites have been exposed to them at a significant level.[59] This could happen in a number of ways – through pop-up windows which appear unbidden on one's computer screen while one is looking for other information, mis-typing web addresses, misleading web addresses which resemble genuine websites but with minor differences that trick people into pages containing inappropriate content, or by clicking on links within emails.[60]

There were a number of defences available for the CDA's indecency provisions, including the use of credit card verification, adult age verification by password or adult identification number, and 'tagging'. It was reported by the Finding of Facts Commission at the time that verification of a credit card number over the internet was not technically possible.[61] Technology at the time was such that, although users could order products using their credit card over the internet, the seller would normally process the transaction with the credit card company offline using traditional phone lines. Technology has obviously changed since then, the possibility of which was acknowledged by expert witnesses during *ACLU v Reno*.[62] The fact that the fee charged by verification agencies to process a card will deter the use of the credit card regime by non-commercial entities and non-profit organisations was also highlighted as a drawback of the CDA 1996. The resulting delay in the retrieval of information, and the significant number of adults who do not have a credit card or the resources to obtain one, were also raised as potential issues with respect to this potential defence to the CDA 1996. Similarly, a number of factors that would impose an unreasonable burden on content providers as well as content users were raised in relation to the proposed age verification defence.[63]

59 Some studies point to the possibility of 'exposure' being more prevalent than deliberate 'access'. See Miranda A.H. Horvath, Llian Alys, Kristina Massey, Afroditi Pina, Mia Scally and Joanna R Adler *'Basically . . . porn is everywhere': A Rapid Evidence Assessment on the Effect that Access and Exposure to Pornography has on Children and Young People*, Office of the Children's Commissioner for England, London 2013. See also Janis Wolak, Kimberly Mitchell, David Finkelhor, 'Unwanted and Wanted Exposure to Online Pornography in a National Sample of Internet Users' (2007) 119(2) *Paediatrics.*

60 See Kimberly J. Mitchell, Lisa Jones, David Finkelhor and Janice Wolak, *Trends in Unwanted Exposure to Sexual Material: Findings from the Youth Internet Safety Studies*, Durham: Crimes Against Children Research Centre, University of New Hampshire 2014, available at http://unh.edu/ccrc/pdf/Unwanted%20Exposure%203%20of%204%20YISS%20Bulletins%20Feb%202014.pdf, accessed 24 July 2018. See also Chiara Sabina, Janis Wolak and David Finkelhor, 'The Nature and Dynamics of Internet Pornography Exposure for Youth' (2008) 11(6) *CyberPsychology & Behavior.*

61 929 F Supp 824 U.S. DC Penn (1996), 846.

62 Ibid.

63 Ibid, 847.

The Government's tagging proposal was also subject to criticism by the court as it would effectively 'require content providers to label all of their "indecent" or "patently offensive" material by imbedding a string of characters, such as "XXX", in either the URL or HTML'.[64] The court was also concerned that the tagging proposal would mean that all content providers that post potentially indecent material would be required to review all of their online content, which could be cumbersome for those who provided large amounts of material online unless they employed a large staff to review the material, which could be expensive and beyond the means of many.[65] It was recognised that, instead of reviewing each file individually, content providers could tag the entire site, but this had the downside that minors would be prevented from accessing a lot of material that was not 'indecent'.[66] The practical difficulties with tagging was summarised as:

> 'To be effective, a scheme such as the -L18 proposal would require a worldwide consensus among speakers to use the same tag to label "indecent" material. There is currently no such consensus, and no Internet speaker currently labels its speech with the -L18 code or with any other widely-recognized label.'[67]

Several years later, ICANN, the internet domain name governing body, approved the .xxx domain name in 2011 which effectively gives the internet its own 'red light district' exclusively for websites hosting adult content. The initiative was met with a lot of resistance from the adult entertainment industry, mainly due to the costs involved in having to repurchase domain names. There was also criticism that it will lead to the misuse of reputed names, for instance somebody registering the name Yale University under the .xxx domain name.[68] As domain name registration system still works largely on a first come first served basis, the only way to effectively avoid this possibility is for the university to purchase all likely combination of its .xxx names first (for example, www.yale.xxx, www.yaleuniversity.xxx, etc.).[69] ICANN, however, was hopeful that, despite the criticisms, it would protect minors from accessing sites hosting adult content and the likelihood of accidental exposure to pornography would be significantly reduced owing to the exclusive classification denoting sexually explicit content.

64 Ibid.

65 Ibid.

66 Ibid.

67 929 F Supp 824 U.S. DC Penn (1996), 848.

68 See for instance http://www.zdnet.com/blog/igeneration/brothel-owner-snaps-up-universitys-xxx-domain-name/13996, accessed 24 July 2018.

69 Some US universities had already purchased .xxx domain names worried about potential misuse of their names. For a short critique, see the article in TIME™, available at http://business.time.com/2012/01/13/icanns-new-top-level-domains-could-spell-trouble/, accessed 24 July 2018.

After considering the characteristics of the internet and the legal issues stemming from CDA 1996, the court reached the unanimous opinion that it was unconstitutionally vague and overbroad. The focus of the legislation on 'indecency', a term not defined in the CDA 1996, was particularly problematic and it was held that the Act was not narrowly tailored in the least restrictive manner as required by *Sable*.[70] There was no definition provided for what constitutes 'harmful to minors'. These, along with the cumbersome age verification requirement that the Act would undoubtedly impose, culminated in a unanimous decision that CDA 1996 was unconstitutional on its face and the District Court granted a preliminary injunction in favour of the plaintiffs. The court held that the CDA 1996 failed to withstand the strict scrutiny test as it was not the least restrictive alternative that 'is at least as effective in achieving the legitimate purpose that it was enacted to serve'.[71]

The Government appealed and eventually the US Supreme Court upheld the judgment, which brought an end to the litigation.[72] The Supreme Court took the view that the application of 'contemporary community standards' would mean that content would have to be judged according to the strictest, most conservative standard in the country. The community standard applied would therefore need to be that of the community most likely to be offended by the material, which would practically mean reducing the availability of material on the internet to what was fit for children. The Supreme Court held that CDA 1996 breached the rights granted under the First Amendment and by doing so essentially confirmed that the First Amendment applied to cyberspace.[73] This was a significant ruling and victory for the plaintiffs, as it reaffirmed that the US Constitution and First Amendment protection extended to the internet, dispelling any notion that cyberspace was beyond the protection of real world laws.

Child Online Protection Act 1998

Following the unsuccessful attempt to legislate with the Communications Decency Act 1996, the US Government responded with further legislation in the form of the Child Online Protection Act 1998 (COPA 1998). COPA 1998 was intended to address the deficiencies and criticisms of CDA 1996, and attempted to produce a 'more narrowly tailored' version of its predecessor. The remit of the Act was confined to communication for 'commercial purposes'. A definition was provided for 'harmful to minors' as:[74]

70 *Sable Communications v FCC*, 492 U.S. 115 (1989).

71 *Reno v ACLU*, 521 U.S. 844, 877 (1997). The Government must demonstrate that the regulation is: (1) necessary to serve a compelling governmental interest, and (2) narrowly drawn to achieve that interest. *Widmar v Vincent* 454 U.S. 263, 270 (1981).

72 *Reno v ACLU* 136 L Ed 2d 436 U.S. SC (1997).

73 See Andrew Murray, *Information Technology Law* (3rd edn, OUP 2016), 401.

74 47 USC § 231(e)(6).

> ... any communication, picture, image, graphic image file, article, recording, writing, or other matter of any kind that is obscene or that-
>
> (A) the average person, applying contemporary community standards, would find, taking the material as a whole and with respect to minors, is designed to appeal to, or is designed to pander to, the prurient interest;
> (B) Depicts, describes, or represents, in a manner patently offensive with respect to minors, an actual or simulated sexual act ...
> (C) Taken as a whole, lacks serious literary, artistic, political or scientific value for minors

Defences were available where the defendant could show that attempts were made in good faith for age verification using a digital certificate, credit card, debit account, adult access code, adult personal identification number, or any other reasonable measures feasible under available technology.[75]

In spite of this seemingly narrower approach, a legal challenge was brought against COPA 1998 as soon as it was enacted into law by the ACLU and others in the Eastern District Court of Pennsylvania. It was alleged that COPA 1998 was unconstitutional on the grounds that it imposed an impermissible burden on speech for adults, it violated the First Amendment rights of minors, and that it was unconstitutionally vague under the First and Fifth Amendments. The District Court granted a preliminary injunction holding that COPA 1998 infringed the right of adults to constitutionally protected freedom of speech and expression.[76] The court, whilst acknowledging that the state has a 'compelling interest' in the protection of children and that granting the injunction would delay 'once again the careful protection of our children', held that COPA 1998 would stifle the rights embodied in the Constitution.

Not surprisingly, the Government appealed, but the injunction was upheld by the US Court of Appeals for the Third Circuit.[77] The application of *Miller* test and contemporary community standards on the internet was again considered in relation to COPA 1998 by Circuit Judge Garth, who focused on the impossibility of determining a 'community standard' on the internet.[78] Noting that that the community standards in *Miller* 'are to be construed in a localized geographical context', the Circuit Court came to the conclusion that the application of contemporary community standards was not suitable for the internet. As the wording of COPA 1998 relied heavily on this concept, the court concluded that it made the Act overbroad. To cite the earlier example, applying *Miller* to the internet would mean that in order to avoid liability a publisher based in New

75 47 USC § 231(c).
76 *ACLU v Reno* 31 F Supp 2d 473.
77 *ACLU v Reno* 217 F 3d 162 US Ct App 3rd Cir. (2000).
78 Ibid.

York would need to be mindful of not just the norms and standards in the state of New York but also the more orthodox states such as Tennessee or Alabama. In fact, every publisher would need to conform to the strictest community standard anywhere in the country. The Circuit Court rejected *Miller* as a suitable test for the internet as it would impose an impermissible burden on the First Amendment right, but nevertheless it acknowledged that the test did remain 'a useful and viable tool in contexts other than the internet and the web'.

The Government appealed again to the Supreme Court, where the Court specifically considered the rejection of the contemporary community standards tests under *Miller*.[79] The Supreme Court, however, disagreed with the Circuit court's finding that it was inappropriate for the internet, noting that '[i]f a publisher wishes for its material to be judged only by the standards of particular communities, then it need only take the simple step of utilizing a medium that enables it to target the release of its materials to those communities'.[80] Justice Thomas went on to say, 'if a publisher chooses to send its material into a particular community, it is the publisher's responsibility to abide by that community's standards – the publisher's burden does not change simply because it decides to distribute its material to every community in the nation'.[81] The Supreme Court thus took the view that COPA's reliance on community standards to identify material harmful to minors did not by itself render the statute substantially overbroad for purposes of First Amendment. This change of stance from its own earlier finding in the CDA litigation was significant, as it effectively meant that 'contemporary community standards' and the broader *Miller* test was held to be workable in cyberspace. The Supreme Court in effect extended the law of the offline world to cyberspace, at least over that part of cyberspace where the US authorities could extend control. However, the Supreme Court's decision on community standards did not accord complete certainty to the law, as demonstrated by subsequent cases, discussed further below.

As the Supreme Court only considered one specific aspect of community standards, the case was remanded back to the Third Circuit for further evaluation. The Third Circuit considered whether COPA 1998 met the requirement of strict scrutiny[82] and whether it was constitutionally overbroad. The court found that although there was a compelling interest in protecting children, COPA 1998 was not the least restrictive way to achieve that end as the wording of the Act, for example the definitions 'harmful to minors' or 'commercial purposes' were not narrowly tailored and suggested that technological means such as filters might be less restrictive (and more effective) than COPA. The

79 *Ashcroft v ACLU* 535 US 564 U.S. SC (2002).

80 Justice Thomas, ibid, at 583.

81 Ibid.

82 Strict scrutiny would mean testing whether there was a compelling governmental interest, and whether the restriction was narrowly tailored in the least restrictive manner.

case arrived back at the Supreme Court in 2004, having not yet been the subject of a full trial.[83] It had been some time since the initial challenge to the COPA in 1998, during which technology had changed substantially, and the Supreme Court sent it back to the District Court for a full trial. The District Court ruled COPA 1998 unconstitutional and issued a permanent injunction, which was upheld by the Third Circuit. Hearing for a further appeal was denied by the Supreme Court, marking the end of what turned out to be one of the most protracted litigations in US history. The Government's legislative attempts to regulate adult pornography on the internet, for all practical purposes, failed.

The CDA and COPA litigation was watched by the world with keen interest. Whilst it was fundamentally a domestic matter for the United States, the fact that a substantial number of pornographic websites are hosted and originate from the United States meant that the ruling had a global impact. For most liberal democracies where the regulation of adult pornography has been focused on the points of supply and distribution rather than the recipient, it practically meant that internet pornography was left unregulated following the failure of COPA 1998. In the UK, people could freely access pornography hosted from the US, with the Government able to do very little to exert the level of control it traditionally held on physical imports of pornography into the country. Law enforcement authorities instead chose to prioritise other more extreme forms of pornography, such as child pornography, over adult pornography. This carried on for a long time until relatively recently, when renewed calls to do something about children accessing adult pornography resulted in the UK Government announcing measures to tackle this issue in 2013 – discussed later in the chapter.

*Internet community standards: post-*Ashcroft

The application of contemporary community standards on the internet has become a somewhat uncertain area of law in the United States following the COPA litigation. The decision in *Ashcroft v ACLU*[84] has been cited in a few subsequent cases in the context of federal obscenity laws, with some degree of uncertainty and confusion as to the application of 'local' and 'national' community standards on the internet.[85] It is sufficiently clear that the focus of COPA 1998 and the decision in *Ashcroft v ACLU*[86] was obscenity targeting *minors*. The view of the Court that the application of contemporary community standards did not in itself render COPA 1998 unconstitutional has had some interesting outcomes in subsequent cases relating to obscenity

83 *Ashcroft v ACLU*, 124 S Ct 2783, US Supreme Court (2004).
84 535 US 564 US SC (2002).
85 For a good discussion, see Hertz-Bunzl (n 29).
86 Ibid.

targeting *adults*.[87] A key question that came before the courts in some of these cases was whether *Ashcroft* has mandated the application of a 'national community standard' for Internet-based obscenity prosecutions, with different views expressed in *United States v Kilbride*,[88] *United States v Little*[89] and *United States v Stagliano*.[90] In *Kilbride*, Justice Fletcher of the Court of the Ninth Circuit, after considering the opinion of judges from *Ashcroft*, determined that the application of local community standards to federal obscenity statutes 18 U.S.C. §§ 1462 and 1465 'generate grave constitutional doubts'.[91] However, in *Little*,[92] the Court of the Eleventh Circuit rejected the argument of the appellants, who relied heavily on *Ashcroft* and *Kilbride*, that the use of local community standards of the Middle District of Florida infringed their First Amendment right. The court declined to follow *Kilbride* and held that the reference to a national community standard in *Ashcroft* was *dicta* and not the ruling of the court.[93] Essentially, what the court said here was that local community standards could be applied in determining an online obscenity case under federal statutes. Cases such as *Kilbride* and *Little* generated further scholarly debate in the United States on the relevance and suitability of community standards for obscenity on the Internet.[94]

Transposing traditional laws to cyberspace

As should be evident from the discussion so far, identifying the most appropriate community standard in cyberspace for the purpose of judging obscenity has proved to be problematic even within a national context. The traditional test for obscenity, whether it is in the United States or the UK, is intrinsically linked to community standards: whether content will be deemed 'obscene' or just 'acceptable pornography' will be measured against the prevailing norms and values of the relevant community. Transposing the traditional obscenity laws to the internet will require identifying an appropriate 'community' and a relevant standard against which to measure the content. It could be a national standard for

87 For example, see generally *United States v Extreme Associates, Inc* 352 F Supp 2d 578 (WD Pa. 2005), reversed on appeal in 431 F. 3d 150 (3rd Circuit 2005); *United States v Kilbride*, 584 F. 3d 1240 (9th Cir. 2009); *United States v Adams*, 337 F App'x 336, 340 (4th Cir. 2009); *United States v Little*, 365 F. App'x 159 (11th Cir. 2010).

88 *584* F.3d 1240 (9th Cir. 2009).

89 365 F. App'x *159*, 162–164 (11th Cir. 2010).

90 693 F.Supp.2d 25 (D.D.C., 2010).

91 Ibid at 1254. For a critique of the judgement see Hertz-Bunzl (n 29).

92 *United States v Little*, 365 F. App'x 159, 162–64 (11th Cir. 2010).

93 Ibid, at 164.

94 See Clay Calvert, 'The End of Forum Shopping in Internet Obscenity Cases? The Ramifications of the Ninth Circuit's Groundbreaking Understanding of Community Standards in Cyberspace' (2010) 89 Neb. L. Rev. 47, 80; Sarah Kagan, Note, 'Obscenity on the Internet: Nationalizing the Standard to Protect Individual Rights' (2010) 38 Hastings Const. L.Q. 233, 257.

the entire nation, but the complexities of this have already been discussed in the context of the United States. Even in a relatively small country such as the United Kingdom, it would be extremely difficult to identify a common national standard for obscenity. As cited in the example in Chapter 6, content that is acceptable in London may offend and be deemed to be obscene in more conservative parts of the country, for example the city of Lincoln in the East Midlands. The case of Simon Walsh,[95] discussed in Chapter 6, is a good example of how prosecutors misjudge (using their subjective minds) what the broader society might consider obscene, even within the same geographical area. So, what is the solution? Should a 'national standard' be accepted as a less than perfect compromise for the internet? This would obviously mean that publishers would need to conform to the strictest community standard within the entire nation with the implications noted in the COPA litigation. Or does this call for a fundamental reform of the obscenity laws, and revisiting the very application of community standards so that the law can be tailored to the requirements of cyberspace?

One option would be *sui generis* law for cyberspace, which is more prescriptive with a clearer and inflexible definition of 'obscenity' that is not reliant on a community standards test. It will, however, be fraught with difficulties. It would practically amount to a strict liability offence and is therefore not desirable. Defining obscenity, other than for specifically illegal content such as child pornography, will be far from straightforward. Courts have struggled to find a clear definition for pornography – in *Jacobellis v Ohio*[96]Justice Stewart famously referred to it, in the context of defining hard-core pornography, as 'I know it when I see it'. A *sui generis* law for internet obscenity that is too prescriptive and ignores community standards, the drafting of which will naturally reflect the moral perception of the lawmakers, will create conflict and tension with the broader society. No rigid legislation that seeks to be overly prescriptive about matters of obscenity can keep up with the pace of changing societal values. Norms and values in this context are dynamic and tend to constantly evolve with time, and this is particularly so in the context of cyberspace communities. Norms in cyberspace are shaped by participants and communities who come from different geographical locations and walks of life, and can change at a much faster pace than in the offline world. Communities being influenced by one another, resulting in changes in societal values, are not unique to the internet. As an example, globalisation, and in particular Westernisation of other cultures and communities, and the resultant changes in societal attitudes, demonstrate how communities and cultures influence one another in the physical world.[97] The internet has arguably

95 Unreported, Kingston Crown Court 2012.

96 378 US 184 378 US 184 (1964), 197.

97 There is plenty of literature on these topics. As an example, see Jeffrey Jensen Arnet, 'The Psychology of Globalisation' (2002) 57(10) *American Psychologist* 774–783. See also, on the 'westernisation' of broadcast content in Nigeria, Endong Floribert Patrick, 'Audience

accelerated this phenomenon owing to the multi-cultural, multi-national interactions that take place in cyberspace synchronously. A law that seeks to regulate content in a manner that is not respectful of the norms in cyberspace is unlikely to succeed, as persuasively argued by Reed.[98]

The interrelationship between law and norms has been very succinctly explained by Lessig.[99] He convincingly argues, inter alia, how law influences norms and others have developed his thesis further to demonstrate how norms, in turn, influence the law.[100] There are, of course, two other modalities of regulation that can shape behaviour – markets and architecture. Each of these modalities has served well to regulate *illegal* content on the internet: child pornography laws banning the production, distribution and possession of child abuse imagery offer a good example. Law has helped to shape people's behaviour in the context of child pornography: fear of prosecution and prison sentence, combined with the stigma attached to it, would stop many people from seeking child abuse images online. The deterrence value of child pornography laws also has a normative effect in that people will exercise diligence and caution about this kind of imagery. For example, if someone accidentally stumbles upon child abuse images on the internet there is a good chance that they will report it to a hotline rather than merely ignoring it. This could be due to two reasons: (1) a sense of 'doing the right thing' (the normative effect of the law), or (2) to avoid possible prosecution for viewing child pornography (this would be the case where the law mandates compulsory reporting, but even otherwise, whilst reporting is not a defence, if someone genuinely stumbled across it and reported it promptly it might help their case should prosecution be brought at a later date). 1 and 2 above stem from separate perspectives – 'doing the right thing' is out of respect for the law, whereas reporting illegal content is due to fear of the law. In both ways, compliance is ensured. The role of architecture (Code) in controlling child pornography is also pivotal – for example, when ISPs block illegal content upon receiving a notification from a hotline, the architecture of the internet is used to automatically block any access requests from its customers to the relevant URLs, as discussed in Chapter 5. Finally, the lack of demand in the market resulting from all of the above means that there would not be a large industry trading in child abuse images online, at least on the open Web.

Whilst this has worked well for combating child pornography on the internet, regulation becomes much more complicated when applied to adult pornography. People generally do not feel the same way about adult pornography as compared to child pornography. Whilst the latter is widely perceived as being illegal and

Westernisation as a Threat to the Indigenisation Model of Media Broadcast in Nigeria' (2014) 6(8) *Journal of Media and Communication Studies* 121–129.

98 Chris Reed, *Making Laws for Cyberspace* (OUP 2012).

99 Lawrence Lessig, *Code and Other Laws of Cyberspace* (Basic Books 1999).

100 Andrew Murray, *The Regulation of Cyberspace* (Routledge 2007).

unacceptable, it is fair to state that adult pornography enjoys a level of acceptance in cyber world. The sheer volume of pornographic content available on the internet is testament to this. In addition, whilst child pornography laws have a direct link to harm to children, the regulation of adult pornography is not necessarily premised on notions of harm (to the participants). The law has, of course, recognised the potential adverse effects of obscene material on its viewers, but this is different from the harm inherent in making the image, as is the case with child pornography. Adult pornography laws have traditionally focused on the indecency and obscenity of the image and its tendency to appeal to the prurient interest, or deprave and corrupt individuals, but both concepts of 'obscene' and 'indecent' are more complex to define in the cyberspace environment. Cyberspace users generally accept that adults have the right to access adult pornography. Therefore, if the state applies a law which severely restricts adult internet pornography on the basis of rather elusive notions of obscenity and indecency, it will be in direct contrast to the norms of the cyberspace community. The law will not have the same normative force to shape behaviour, unlike child pornography laws. As Reed has argued, the law ought to be 'respect worthy' to have normative effect to influence the behaviour of cyberspace users.[101] Law will fail to achieve its effect if its content is in conflict with an established cyberspace norm.[102] The cyberspace community will simply disregard the law and find new ways of bypassing the restrictions. A good example of this, when the law is in direct conflict with established norms in cyberspace and has failed to influence the normative behaviour of cyberspace users, is evident from the French experiment with copyright law through its HADOPI law (*Haute autorité pour la diffusion des oeuvres et la protection des droits d'auteur sur internet*). The HADOPI law resulted in fewer than 200 cases considered for prosecution, which brought in only €750 in fines. Considering the HADOPI authority employed 60 people at the cost of €12 million per year, who sent 1.6 million warning emails, it can be safely inferred that the law did little to deter individuals from committing acts of online copyright infringement.[103]

It should be clear from the discussion so far that transposing traditional obscenity laws to regulate adult pornography is simply not suitable for the internet. It is also a practical reality that as long as adult pornography remains unregulated in the US there is little chance for other countries to rely on traditional obscenity laws to exert any meaningful control to regulate its access within their local jurisdictions. Adult pornography regulation is a classic example of the problem identified by Reed in relation to transposing physical world laws into cyberspace without considering whether those laws clash with established

101 Chris Reed, *Making Laws for Cyberspace* (OUP 2012).

102 Ibid.

103 See Neil McAllister, 'France's 'three strikes' anti-piracy law shot down', *The Register*, 9 July 2013, available at https://www.theregister.co.uk/2013/07/09/france_three_strikes_piracy_law_shot_down/, accessed 24 July 2018.

cyberspace norms. For the law to be effective, therefore, it has to look towards other models that go beyond focusing on the obscenity of the image itself, and has to focus on establishing a framework that resonates with a generally accepted norm, not just in the offline world, but also in cyberspace.

In principle, preventing children's exposure to adult pornography has normative force and could well be the legitimising factor for such regulation. As noted below, there is an array of regulation in the offline world that restricts children's access to adult content in the offline world. Even the critics of CDA 1996 or COPA 1998 did not dispute that the state has a duty towards children in this context and in fact even the courts which struck down the indecency provisions of these Acts acknowledged the 'compelling interest' of the Government in protecting children from inappropriate content on the internet. In many ways, the only existing 'global community standard' in relation to adult pornography may be that it is inappropriate for children. In order to work in cyberspace the law should seek to achieve this sole objective – no more, and no less.

Regulating for child protection

The protection of children from exposure to adult content has offered a strong justification for controlling the publication and distribution of adult pornography in the offline world. As noted above there is little opposition, at least in theory, for the position that states have a compelling interest in protecting children from exposure to pornography and other age-inappropriate content. A cursory glance at the regulatory regime for pornography for traditional forms of media such as video and print suggests that child protection has provided a legitimate basis for the regulation of adult pornography, at least in liberal democracies. For example, cinemas in the UK and elsewhere use a classification regime, with appropriate age-based certification granted before public release.[104] In the UK, pornographic films rated as R18 can be shown only in licensed sex cinemas to which no one under 18 can be admitted; and R18 videos can be sold only to adults through licensed sex shops, and are not available for sale by mail order.[105] A child will not be allowed to go into a sex shop and buy pornographic material. Television broadcast is subject to a time-based restriction, whereby programmes that are unsuitable for children cannot be broadcast between 5.30 am and 9 pm, when most children are presumed to be awake and at risk of exposure to inappropriate content.[106] There is no strict restriction on selling a 'top-shelf' magazine with

104 In the UK, the British Board for Film Certification (BBFC) is the relevant body. See http://bbfc.co.uk/, accessed 24 July 2018.

105 See the BBFC Classification Guidelines, available at http://www.bbfc.co.uk/what-classification/r18, accessed 24 July 2018.. See also Video Recordings Act 1984, s 12.

106 For further details of the watershed, see OFCOM, http://ask.ofcom.org.uk/help/television/watershed, accessed 24 July 2018.

soft erotica to a child, but by convention most shopkeepers will refuse to sell to a minor out of their own discretion, or sense of moral duty. The net effect is that accessing pornography has not been an easy task for a child in the physical world, and in that sense adult pornography was arguably traditionally well regulated with respect to children. It is perhaps fair to state that protecting children from age-inappropriate content has been at the heart of the regulation of adult pornography in the offline world, notwithstanding the other justifications for regulation. It is illogical, therefore, that the law offers strong safeguards for children in the offline world and yet, in practice, no meaningful – let alone equivalent – regime exists in cyberspace. This is particularly problematic as children constitute a sizeable population of cyberspace users.

Children's use of the internet is increasing every year, and more and more young children are using the internet.[107] An OFCOM report in 2012 suggested that 87 per cent of 5–7-year-olds are known to use the internet in the UK.[108] In the Netherlands, 78 per cent of toddlers and pre-schoolers are already online according to one report (Brouwer et al); almost half of 3–6-year-olds use the internet on a regular basis in Austria (Jungwirth), and in Norway 58 per cent of 0–6-year-olds go online (Guðmundsdóttir and Hardersen).[109] A more recent study indicates that children form one-third of all global internet users.[110] By implication, it can be inferred that there is a credible risk of exposure of children to freely accessible adult content on the internet, which may occur both deliberately and inadvertently.

Exact figures are hard to obtain in relation to children's access and exposure to pornography, owing to the ethical issues involved in interviewing children as well as to various methodological and theoretical shortcomings.[111] In addition, the issue of what actually constitutes pornography is also problematic, as pornography

107 See Donnell Holloway, Leila Green and Sonia Livingstone, *Zero to Eight: Young Children and their Internet Use.* LSE, London: EU Kids Online 2013, available at http://eprints.lse.ac.uk/52630/, accessed 24 July 2018.

108 Ofcom, *Children and Parents: Media Use and Attitudes Report*, London 2012. Available at https://www.ofcom.org.uk/research-and-data/media-literacy-research/childrens/october-2012, accessed 24 July 2018.

109 Holloway et al (n 107), citing C. Brouwer, M. Duimel, S. Jansen, P. Nikken, J. Pardoen and R. Pijpers, *App Noot Muis. Peuters en kleuters op het Internet* (Buurtboek 2011); B. Jungwirth (2013) Safer Internet Day 2013: EU-Initiative Saferinternet.at unterstützt Eltern und Pädagogen bei der Interneterziehung. Wein: Österreichische Institut für angewandte Telekommunikation (ÖIAT), 2013; G.B. Guðmundsdóttir, and B. Hardersen, *Toddlers' Digital Universe: 0-6-year-olds access to and use of digital devices in your spare time*, 2011, available at https://iktsenteret.no/ressurser/smabarns-digitale-univers, accessed 24 July 2018.

110 Sonia Livingstone, John Carr and Jasmina Byrne, *One In Three: Internet Governance and Children's Rights*, Global Commission on Internet Governance, Paper Series: No 22, November 2015 (https://www.cigionline.org/sites/default/files/no22_2.pdf), accessed 24 July 2018.

111 For an analysis of empirical research published 1995–2015, see Jochen Peter and Patti M. Valkenburg, 'Adolescents and Pornography: A Review of 20 Years of Research' (2016) 53(4–5) *The Journal of Sex Research* 509–531.

is a bigger issue in some countries than in others and what is deemed to be obscene in one society may be 'culturally valuable' in another.[112] Nevertheless, children's exposure to internet pornography and its potential impact on children has been the subject of various studies and research in different countries over the past decades.[113] Pornography has featured as one of the prominent concerns identified by children themselves among other online risks.[114] It is estimated that about 28 per cent of children aged 9–16 reported seeing sexual images online or offline across Europe in the year 2013.[115] In the UK, the corresponding figure was 17 per cent for the same age group.[116] A more recent study commissioned by the NSPCC determined that by the age of 15, children were more likely than not to have seen online pornography with 65 per cent of 15–16-year-olds reported having seen pornography.[117] It was also noted in the study that young people are as likely to find it by accident as to find it deliberately.[118] It appears that more children now deliberately seek pornography, whilst accidental exposure has declined over time, as indicated by an older Australian study in 2003 which revealed that 84 per cent of boys and 60 per cent of girls in the age group 16–17 were exposed accidentally to sex sites on the internet, and 38 per cent of boys and 2 per cent of girls sought out pornography deliberately.[119]

112 See Antonis Rovolis and Liza Tsaliki, 'Pornography' in Sonia Livingstone, Leslie Haddon and Anke Görzig (eds), *Children, Risk and Safety Online: Research and Policy Challenges in Comparative Perspective* (Policy Press 2010).

113 See for example, Dick Thornburgh, Herbert S. Lin (eds) *Youth, Pornography and the Internet*, (National Academy Press 2002); NetRatings Australia, *Kidsonline@home: Internet use in Australian Homes*, Australian Broadcasting Authority and NetAlert Ltd, Sydney 2005; Alan McKee, Catharine Lumby, and Kath Albury, *Porn Report* (Melbourne University Press 2008); Sonia Livingstone, Leslie Haddon, Anke Görzig, and Kjartan Ólafsson, *EU Kids Online: Final Report*, EU Kids Online, London School of Economics & Political Science, London, 2011.

114 Livingstone, Haddon, Görzig and Ólafsson (2011) ibid. See also Sonia Livingstone, Lucyna Kirwil, Christina Ponte and Elisabeth Staksrud, *In Their Own Words: What Bothers Children Online? with The EU Kids Online Network*, EU Kids Online, London School of Economics and Political Science, 2013, available at http://eprints.lse.ac.uk/48357/1/In%20their%20own%20words%20%28lsero%29.pdf, accessed 24 July 2018.

115 Sonia Livingstone, Leslie Haddon, Jane Vincent, Giovanna Mascheroni and Kjartan Olafsson, *Net Children Go Mobile: The UK Report* London School of Economics and Political Science 2014, available at http://eprints.lse.ac.uk/57598/, accessed 24 July 2018.

116 Ibid. See also Horvath et al (n 59).

117 Elena Martellozzo, Andy Monaghan, Joanna R. Adler, Julia Davidson, Rodolfo Leyva and Miranda A.H. Horvath, *'I wasn't sure it was normal to watch it…' A Quantitative and Qualitative Examination of the Impact of Online Pornography on the Values, Attitudes, Beliefs and Behaviours of Children and Young People*, London: Middlesex University 2017, available at https://www.nspcc.org.uk/globalassets/documents/research-reports/mdx-nspcc-occ-pornography-report.pdf, accessed 24 July 2018.

118 Ibid, 23.

119 Michael Flood and Clive Hamilton, *Youth and Pornography in Australia: Evidence on the Extent of Exposure and Likely Effects*, Discussion paper no 52, The Australia Institute, Canberra 2003. Available at https://eprints.qut.edu.au/103421/, accessed 24 July 2018.

In the early days of the internet, children, like everyone else, accessed the internet through the home PC or at school. As technology advanced, the internet became accessible through other devices, including internet-enabled mobile phones. Young children are a large user group for accessing the internet through mobile devices.[120] Unlike traditional home personal computers, the level of supervision parents can exercise over children's use of such devices is comparatively limited, further raising a range of safety and privacy issues, resulting in calls for stricter regulation.[121]

It is also worth noting that the internet is not the only source for children to access pornography. In some cases, children accessed pornography through offline media more than through the internet, although this is attributed to older studies. For instance, in Australia, a 2003 study reported that 73 per cent of 16–17-year-old boys had watched an X-rated video, whereas only 38 per cent admitted to have searched the internet for sex sites (a much larger proportion reported having been accidentally exposed to pornographic sites on the internet).[122] The prevalence of the internet and mobile phones among children has since grown, and therefore a similar study carried out today may present a different picture.

Concerns that children are facing unprecedented danger and harm owing to the widespread availability of internet pornography eventually resulted in the Government responding to the issue. David Cameron, then Prime Minister, described it as the 'corroding of childhood', while in July 2013 announcing his plans to introduce stricter measures to prevent children from accessing pornography.[123] It should be noted that there is often some hype in the media coverage which conflates entirely different issues in this context. For instance, when the Prime Minister announced his plans to introduce mandatory filters to prevent children from accessing adult pornography *and* to introduce further measures to curb child pornography including requiring search engines such as Google to block certain search terms, a lot of discussion and coverage in the media ignored the fact that these are two distinctly different issues, giving the impression to the public that letting adults watch adult pornography results in children being sexually abused.[124] Such misinformation carries the risk of

120 Tablets and mobile phones are now the most popular devices for children for going online. See Ofcom, *Children and Parents: Media Use and Attitudes Report*, London 2016, available at https://www.ofcom.org.uk/__data/assets/pdf_file/0034/93976/Children-Parents-Media-Use-Attitudes-Report-2016.pdf, accessed 24 July 2018. See also Sonia Livingstone et al, *Net Children Go Mobile: The UK Report* n 115.

121 For a discussion from a legal perspective see Abhilash Nair, 'Mobile Phones and the Internet: Legal Issues in the Protection of Children' (2006) 20 (2 & 3) *International Review of Law, Computers and Technology*. See also Maria de Miguel Molina, 'Self-Regulation of Mobile Marketing Aimed at Children: An Overview of the Spanish Case' (2007) 2(2) *Journal of Theoretical and Applied Electronic Commerce Research* 80–93.

122 Flood and Hamilton (n 119).

123 See http://www.bbc.co.uk/news/uk-23401076, accessed 24 July 2018.

124 As noted in Chapter 3, there is however some research that points to evidence that individuals who start watching adult pornography at a younger age are more likely to progress to engage

potentially undermining the legitimacy and respect-worthiness of not just child pornography laws, but also the genuine efforts to regulate children's exposure to adult content online.

Clearly, media hype or moral panic stemming from distorted views about adult pornography should not form the basis of regulation. The precise nature of any harm that adult pornography might cause to children is difficult to ascertain. The 'harm' attributed to pornography and its effect on children is one which is presumed (by adults), rather than based on conclusive evidence of causal link. For instance, Helsper argues that there is no evidence of causal link between impairment of mental, physical or moral development in minors and exposure to adult material.[125] There seems to be, however, some consistent findings suggesting that consumption of adult pornography can lead to the development of unrealistic sexual values and beliefs and also linking consumption of violent pornography with sexually aggressive behaviour.[126] As research in this area does not provide conclusive evidence, a more reliable and convincing parameter for the purpose of regulation seems to be the likelihood, or *risk of harm* rather than inevitable harm.[127] It is pertinent to note that age-based restrictions on pornography in the traditional forms of media were not necessarily based on any proven evidence of harm to children caused by pornography.[128] The law has, however, for a long time recognised a *risk of harm* that obscene material might cause to children and young people – the tendency to 'deprave and corrupt' test found in the Obscene Publications Act 1959 is a good example of this.[129] Policy

in deviant pornography including child pornography and bestiality, compared to those with a later 'age of onset'. See Kathryn C. Seigfried-Spellar and Marcus Rogers, 'Does Deviant Pornography Use Follow a Guttman-like Progression?' (2013) 29(5) *Computers in Human Behaviour* 1997–2003.

125 Ellen Helsper, *R18 Material: Its Potential Impact on People Under 18. An Overview of Available Literature*, Ofcom, London 2005, available at https://www.ofcom.org.uk/__data/assets/pdf_file/0022/19345/r18.pdf, accessed 24 July 2018.

126 See Eric W Owens, Richard J. Behun, Jill C. Manning and Roy C. Reid, 'The Impact of Internet Pornography on Adolescents: A Review of the Research' (2012) 19 *Sexual Addiction and Compulsivity* 99–122.

127 See Andrea Millwood Hargrave and Sonia Livingstone, *Harm and Offence in Media Content: A Review of the Evidence* (2nd edn, Intellect 2009).

128 For example, an Ofcom report, which inquired into the potential impact of R18 rated pornography on children following a public consultation on the Broadcasting Code, concluded that there is "no empirical research that proves beyond doubt that exposure to R18 material seriously impairs the *mental or physical development* of minors". The report however acknowledged the existence of research that "indicates that sexual material influences the *moral development* of young people under the age of 18". See Ellen Helsper (n 125).

129 Section 1 of the Obscene Publications Act 1959 defines obscene articles as material that has a tendency to 'deprave and corrupt' those who are likely to come across it. This could mean that content that is lawful for adults may be deemed obscene if targeted at children. The law simply recognises the potential harm that pornography *may* cause to children or other vulnerable audience. It is not something measured on a case by case basis with the assistance of proven evidence, for example clinical trials, or expert evidence – content is simply judged against the ordinary standards of propriety by the jury.

decisions to restrict children's access have also been made on the basis of a 'precautionary approach'.[130]

The internet presents a *risk* of harm on a scale much bigger than other forms of media in the offline world. It would be illogical for the law to provide safeguards in the physical world, and at the same time let children have unfettered access to adult content on the internet. The fundamental premise of regulation in this respect ought to be that what is illegal offline should remain illegal in the online world. If children were entitled to a degree of protection with respect to pornography in the offline world, at least the same level of protection, if not more, should be available on the internet. Failure to provide this has the effect that it will practically render offline laws meaningless, as children can easily access pornography on the internet without having to attempt to obtain it through other traditional (well-regulated) media.

Relying on obscenity-focused laws, however, will not achieve that objective: we have already noted how previous legislative attempts such as CDA 1996 and COPA 1998, despite their intention to prevent children's exposure to adult content, failed to succeed in cyberspace. So, what alternatives are available? In the section below, by setting out recent developments in the UK, I argue that the current image-based, 'content-focused' regulation should give way to an 'access-focused' approach, and this is the only way the regulation of adult pornography can succeed on the internet.

New regulatory models

In the UK, calls for protecting children from exposure to pornography on the internet have gathered momentum over the last few years. The Government commissioned an inquiry, the Bailey Review, to examine the 'commercialisation and sexualisation of childhood', which recommended that the internet industry should develop and introduce effective parental controls to enable them to block adult and age-restricted material from the internet.[131] The recommendation was embraced by the UK Council for Child Internet Safety (UKCCIS), an influential body comprising members from Government, industry, academia, and charity

130 In its report in relation to regulating video-on-demand service in the UK following the Audio Visual Media Services Directive, the Ofcom justified policy making on the basis of a 'precautionary approach' on the basis of a 'risk of harm' to children. See *Sexually Explicit Material and Video on Demand Services: A Report to DCMS by Ofcom*, Ofcom, August 2011, London. Available at https://lx.iriss.org.uk/content/sexually-explicit-material-and-video-demand-services-report-dcms, accessed 3 August 2018.

131 Reg Bailey, *Letting Children be Children: Report of an Independent Review of the Commercialisation and Sexualisation of Childhood*, Department for Education, The Stationery Office, London 2011. Available at https://www.gov.uk/government/uploads/system/uploads/attachment_data/file/175418/Bailey_Review.pdf, accessed 3 August 2018.

sectors.[132] Four big ISPs (BT, Sky, Talk Talk and Virgin Media) agreed a voluntary Code of Practice in October 2011, to provide all *new* customers with an active choice on parental controls within a year, to enable them to filter adult content if they wish to do so in their home network. This meant that parents were given an unavoidable choice in setting up adult content filters, which was set up in such a manner that the filters were left in a default 'on' rather than 'off' mode (i.e., it required a mandatory 'opt-in' to enable adult content). Mobile operators had already published a voluntary code of practice in 2004 which undertook, among other things, to restrict children's access to adult content by providing default filters which could be turned off following appropriate age verification.[133]

In the summer of 2013, the Prime Minister proposed a number of reforms ranging from calls for ISPs to provide mandatory filters for *all* customers, to prohibiting pornography in public Wi-Fi spaces. Whilst parents could exercise a certain degree of control over their children's use of the internet at home, it is obviously difficult to exercise parental control over content accessed through publicly available free Wi-Fi spots such as shopping malls, public transport or cafes. A number of major public Wi-Fi providers subsequently introduced filtered services that blocked adult content in public spaces.

The Prime Minister's speech also called for search engines such as Google to block certain search terms, which was primarily aimed at tackling child pornography rather than at children accessing adult pornography.[134] Google and Microsoft accordingly reached an agreement to block 100,000 search terms that might lead to retrieving child abuse images through their search engines.[135]

The proposals for the use of internet filters and blocking were subject to some criticism.[136] In particular, there were concerns raised that filters could block legitimate web content and blocking search terms could block genuine search terms. For instance, websites hosting sexual health information (which could actually benefit young people) could inadvertently be blocked by the filters. Similarly, 'teenage sex' could both be a genuine search term for a researcher looking for scientific material for a legitimate purpose, and for a paedophile

132 https://www.gov.uk/government/groups/uk-council-for-child-internet-safety-ukccis, accessed 24 July 2018.

133 For an updated version of the Code, see http://www.mobileuk.org/codes-of-practice.html, accessed 24 July 2018.

134 The transcript of the speech is available at https://www.gov.uk/government/speeches/the-internet-and-pornography-prime-minister-calls-for-action, accessed 24 July 2018.

135 See Belinda Goldsmith, *Google, Microsoft tighten online searches to combat online porn*, Reuters, 18 November 2013, available at https://www.reuters.com/article/net-us-britain-internet-porn/google-microsoft-tighten-online-searches-to-combat-child-porn-idUSBRE9AH0HF20131118, accessed 24 July 2018.

136 See for example Joanna Impey, 'UK criticised over plans to block Internet porn', *DW*, 24 July 2013, available at http://www.dw.com/en/uk-criticized-over-plans-to-block-internet-porn/a-16974180, accessed 24 July 2018.

looking for illegal content. As happens with technology based restrictions, filters are not fool proof and might block genuine scientific or educational material in the process. This possibility raises free speech issues for adults as well as children, as children obviously have the right to seek information beneficial to them. However, it may be possible for search engines to develop smarter algorithms to minimise this as technology advances further. In addition, as child protection activists point out, whilst technological solutions will not be perfect, they will nevertheless make it harder and more difficult for children to be exposed to age-inappropriate content.[137]

These initiatives, involving a multi-stakeholder self-regulatory approach, broadly mirror the self-regulatory model traditionally advocated for adult pornography by European regulators.[138] The UK largely followed it, albeit with the threat of possible legislation if the parties involved did not achieve the intended outcomes. It is perhaps ironic that it was actually an EU Directive that eventually paved the way for the UK legislating specifically to address adult pornography on the internet, as discussed below.

Video-on-demand

The convergence of technology with the growth of internet TV, pay TV and on-demand services resulted in the distribution models for audio visual content undergoing significant changes over the past decade. Television content was increasingly becoming available online, and other 'TV-like' online services referred to as on-demand services (which also include adult content) was growing in popularity, but this sector was largely unregulated. In light of these technological changes, the European Commission proposed a regulatory framework which culminated in a new Directive, the Audio Visual Media Services (AVMS) Directive.[139] The AVMS Directive extended the scope of existing regulation to on-demand services. The Directive drew a distinction between 'linear' and 'non-linear' services – the former being mainly television in its original form, and the latter broadly encompassing on-demand services defined as audio-visual services 'provided by a media service provider for the viewing of programmes at the moment chosen by the user and at his individual request on the basis of a catalogue of programmes selected by the media service provider'.[140] The UK amended the Communications Act 2003, which brought under its remit services

137 Ibid, citing John Carr, Secretary, Children's Charities' Coalition on Internet Safety.

138 For a succinct analysis see Brian O'Neill, 'Internet Policies: Online Child Protection and Empowerment in a Global Context' in D. Lemish (Ed.), *The Routledge Handbook of Children, Adolescents and Media* (Routledge 2013).

139 Directive 2010/13/EU on the coordination of certain provisions laid down by law, regulation or administrative action in Member States concerning the provision of audio visual media services (Audio Visual Media Services Directive). The Directive was originally adopted in 2007 amending the Television Without Frontiers Directive 1989 and renaming it to the AVMS Directive. The 2010 AVMS Directive is a codified version of these two instruments.

140 Audio Visual Media Services Directive 2007, Art 1(1)(g).

that provide programmes the form and content of which are comparable to those normally included in television programme services.[141]

Whilst the new Directive meant that previously unregulated on-demand content was subject to regulation, uncertainties remained as to what exactly constituted 'TV-like' services rather than 'normal' internet content.[142] As for adult content, the Directive envisaged two tiers of regulation for linear and non-linear services. Linear TV services were subject to a stricter regime of control whereby programmes that might 'seriously impair the physical, mental or moral development of minors' were prohibited.[143] On-demand services had a lower threshold of regulation with the stipulation being that the same materials 'are only made available in such a way as to ensure that minors will not normally hear or see such on-demand audio visual media services'.[144] The AVMS Directive was incorporated into UK law through the Audiovisual Media Services Regulations 2009,[145] which introduced a new Part 4A into the Communications Act 2003. The provisions on harmful material were found in section 368E(2) of the amended Communications Act 2003.[146] In March 2010 Ofcom designated the Authority for Television on Demand (AVTOD) as a co-regulator for on-demand services. Ofcom and AVTOD recommended to the Government that legislation should be introduced that would require on-demand service providers to use access controls for content that would be classified by the BBFC at R18 had it been distributed on video.[147] This resulted in new legislation: the Audiovisual Media Services Regulations 2014 amended the Communications Act 2003 to require video-on-demand (VOD) services to adhere to the British Board of Film Classification (BBFC) guidelines that already applied to 'video works' under the Video Recordings Act 1984.[148] This now means that Ofcom has the power to regulate and require access control for content distributed through on-demand services which has been rated as R18 by the BBFC, or if it would be equivalent to R18 had it been classified.[149] This would also mean a complete prohibition of content that

141 Communications Act 2003, s 368A(1).

142 For an excellent analysis of the regulatory issues pertaining to video on demand services, see Daithi MacSithigh, *Medium Law*, (Routledge 2017) Ch 6.

143 AVMS Directive, Art 27.

144 Ibid, Art 12.

145 SI 2009/2979.

146 Communications Act 2003, s 368E(2). It is titled 'Harmful Material' and reads, 'If an on-demand programme service contains material which might seriously impair the physical, mental or moral development of persons under the age of eighteen, the material must be made available in a manner which secures that such persons will not normally see or hear it'.

147 See for a detailed and critical account of the history of the new regulations, Julian Petley, 'The Regulation of Pornography on Video-on-Demand in the United Kingdom' (2014) 1(3) *Porn Studies* 260–284.

148 The BBFC Classification Guidelines is available at http://www.bbfc.co.uk/sites/default/files/attachments/BBFC%20Classification%20Guidelines%202014_0.pdf, accessed 24 July 2018.

149 ATVOD's role in relation to video on demand ended in December 2015 with the Ofcom taking over as the sole regulator from 1 January 2016.

has been refused classification, or would be refused classification had it been considered by the BBFC. The new regulatory regime for on-demand content was criticised as going way beyond the requirements of the AVMS Directive and therefore only enforceable against UK-based providers.[150]

These new regulatory measures had a peculiar effect in that they brought adult content providers based in the UK into a strict regulatory regime, but at the same time providers based abroad were left unregulated and could freely stream content to the UK without any obligation of mandatory age verification checks. In addition, the reference to R18 rating by the BBFC had another consequence. The nature of permissible content that UK-based providers were allowed to distribute was seriously constrained compared to their foreign counterparts, owing to the BBFC's relatively strict classification policies.[151] This led to some criticism that the Government was interfering with sexual freedoms and that the rules amounted to moral policing of individuals.[152] It was anything but a level playing field for UK-based providers compared with content providers based elsewhere, and consumers in the UK continued to access similar services hosted abroad without any hindrance. It was only a matter of time before access control requirements would be made mandatory for all websites, and not just for UK-based providers already regulated under the AVMS Regulations 2014: this would become part of the new Digital Economy Act 2017.

Digital Economy Act 2017: mandatory access control

Whilst the new video-on-demand regulations ensured that UK-based providers of pornography were subject to mandatory age verification of customers, it did very little to control access to the vast amounts of pornography hosted on websites abroad. The number of UK-based adult content providers was small in any case, in comparison to global commercial pornography providers. The regulations prompted some of these providers to move their services abroad, and some companies had to shut down. In this sense the effect of the law was felt more by a handful of companies, than causing any real impact to protect children from internet pornography.

Recognising the limitations of the existing law, the Government proposed new legislation that would require all commercial providers of pornography on the internet to establish age verification checks, rather than just UK-based providers. The Government launched a Public Consultation in early 2016[153] and draft legislation was subsequently introduced on 5 July 2016 under Part 3 of the

150 See Petley (n 147). See also MacSithigh (n 142).

151 BBFC Classification Guidelines (n 105).

152 See for example Abhilash Nair, 'Policing porn and the new enforcement of moral standards that don't exist', *The Conversation*, 10 December 2014, available at https://theconversation.com/policing-porn-and-the-new-enforcement-of-moral-standards-that-dont-exist-35133, accessed 24 July 2018.

153 Department for Culture, Media and Sport, *Child Safety Online: Age Verification for Pornography* February 2016. The consultation document and summary of responses can be

Digital Economy Bill 2016 – 20 years after the failed Communications Decency Act was enacted in the US. The Digital Economy Act 2017 (DEA 2017) received Royal Assent on 27 April 2017 and requires commercial providers of online pornography to employ age verification controls to ensure so that it is not accessible to those under the age of 18:

> A person contravenes this subsection if the person makes pornographic material available on the internet to persons in the United Kingdom on a commercial basis other than in a way that secures that, at any given time, the material is not normally accessible by persons under the age of 18.' [154]

The new law in some ways drew inspiration from German initiatives regarding mandatory age verification for online pornography. Since 2003, Germany has had legislation requiring mandatory access controls for online pornography (and other harmful content for minors) directed at German users,[155] and as a result commercial pornography providers have age verification controls in place on websites with .de domain names. Whilst international companies that provide content on websites with .de domain names are subject to age verification controls, those who do not have a German presence and are wholly based abroad were not within the reach of the law. As for individual consumers, people could still access pornography hosted abroad on, for example, .com domain names. Nevertheless, a number of international providers complied with German law and introduced age verification for websites targeted at German users (i.e., websites with .de domain names). The UK Government saw this as a positive sign in that domestic law could achieve compliance by international companies, and decided to build on this success and to go ahead with its own age verification regulation.[156]

As most commercial pornographers are based outside the UK and therefore not strictly subject to domestic laws, the biggest challenge for the success of DEA 2017 would be in relation to the enforcement of its age verification provisions. There are a number of ways in which DEA 2017 seeks to ensure compliance. It provides for the establishment of one or more 'age-verification regulator' who will have wide-ranging powers to oversee and ensure compliance with the law.[157] The regulator can require ISPs, or anyone who makes pornography available on a commercial basis targeting the UK, to provide it with information to assists the regulator to exercise its functions (section 18). It can

accessed on https://www.gov.uk/government/consultations/child-safety-online-age-verifi cation-for-pornography, accessed 24 July 2018.

154 Digital Economy Act 2017, s 14(1).

155 The rules are set out in the 'Jugendmedienschutzstaatsvertrag', available at http://www.kjm-online.de/recht/gesetze-undstaatsvertraege/jugendmedienschutz-staatsvertrag-jmstv.html, accessed 24 July 2018.

156 See DCMS Consultation, (n 153) 35.

157 Digital Economy Act 2017, ss 16–23

issue financial penalties to non-compliant websites up to £250,000 (section 20). In addition, the regulator can serve notice to payment-service providers (for example, credit card companies) and ancillary service providers of non-compliant websites (for example, those who advertise on the offending websites) and request them to withdraw their services to those websites (section 21). The idea behind this provision is to 'follow the money' in such a manner that it undermines the revenue flow to the offending websites, thereby forcing them to comply with the law. In addition, and perhaps unsurprisingly controversially, the regulator has also been conferred with the power under section 23 of the Act to require ISPs to block access to non-compliant websites in terms of age-verification obligations under section 14(1), as well as blocking websites that contain extreme pornographic material as defined in section 63(7) or 63(7)A of the Criminal Justice and Immigration Act 2008.[158] The British Board of Film Classification (BBFC) was officially nominated as the age verification regulator on 21 February 2018.

It is too early to predict exactly how the new law will operate in practice. The age verification check was originally intended to come into effect from April 2018, but it has been delayed and it is likely that it will not take effect until the end of 2018. The main criticism raised against the new law so far relates to its implications for individual privacy and data protection. The overall practicality of determining what exactly constitutes 'pornography' under the Act, and its implications for freedom of expression and the right to access information, also remain a concern. Whilst the law envisages certain measures to enforce compliance, as noted above, it remains to be seen how effective these will be in practice and critics worry that the blocking measures may amount to censorship. It is worth examining some of these issues in further detail.

In terms of the definition of 'pornography', DEA 2017 is broader than the scope of the video-on-demand regulations, in that it will not be just R18 content that will be under the purview of the law, but any material 'if it is reasonable to assume from its nature that it was produced solely or principally for the purposes of sexual arousal, and that any classification certificate issued in respect of a video work including it would be an 18 certificate'.[159] Content that is rated '18' is much wider than 'R18', and includes simulated material whose primary purpose is sexual arousal or stimulation.[160] In the offline world, 18-rated materials cannot be made available to children, either in video format or by means of admittance

158 The latter category refers to the material which was the subject of discussion in Chapter 6 on extreme pornography.

159 Section 15(1)(f). An '18 certificate' is the equivalent of a classification certificate under section 7(2)(b) of the Video Recordings Act 1984, i.e. that the video work is suitable for viewing only by persons who have attained the age of 18 and that no video recording containing that work is to be supplied to any person who has not attained that age.

160 See the BBFC Guidelines for age ratings, at p 23, available at http://www.bbfc.co.uk/sites/default/files/attachments/BBFC%20Classification%20Guidelines%202014_0.pdf, accessed 24 July 2018.

to the cinema. The new law in this sense seeks to achieve parity with offline laws, but unlike the physical world (with relatively limited amount of content) where age ratings are formally decided by the BBFC, the internet contains vast volumes of pornography. It is impractical to know for certain whether 'borderline' material would fall above or below the threshold for 18 rating unless, of course, the material is actually submitted to the BBFC for formal classification. Whilst content providers can refer to the publicly available BBFC Classification Guidelines for guidance, the inherent subjectivity of such assessments would render it an ongoing and onerous task for the regulator to monitor content that would inevitably slip the net both deliberately (from non-compliant sites) and accidentally (providers who made the content available in good faith assuming it did not come under 18 classification).

Privacy and related concerns surrounding age verification in the context of online pornography is not new and dates back to CDA 1996 and COPA 1998 initiatives in the US. The criticisms back then focused on concerns that a mandatory age verification requirement might cause website owners to lose visitors owing to concerns about privacy and security, which in turn has economic implications for website owners. In addition, it was felt that the cost of age verification tools might make it more difficult for smaller commercial providers to remain in business.[161] This is due to the financial implications for websites both from the direct cost associated with age-verifying customers as well as the indirect cost stemming from loss of visitors. Whilst the broad concerns regarding privacy and security of personal information are still relevant 20 years on, it is also the case that technology has since made advances which has rendered online age verification processes more resilient and trustworthy. As Nash et al point out, 'age verification has come a long way since the Internet Safety Technical Taskforce Report of 2008'.[162] In addition, age verification has been successfully implemented in other sectors in the UK, for example, age verification has been a legal requirement under the Gambling Act 2005.

The UK already has a strong data protection framework, which has been strengthened with the new General Data Protection Regulation (GDPR).[163] Age verification services and commercial pornography providers will no doubt

161 See Heather L. Miller, 'Strike two: An Analysis of the Child Online Protection Act's Constitutional Failures' (1999) 52(1) *Federal Communications Law Journal* article 7, available at https://www.repository.law.indiana.edu/cgi/viewcontent.cgi?article=1220&context=fclj, accessed 24 July 2018.

162 Victoria Nash, Rachel O'Connell, Bendert Zevenbergen and Allison Mishkin, *Effective Age Verification Techniques: Lessons to be Learnt from the Online Gambling Industry: Final Report, December 2012–December 2013* University of Oxford, available at https://www.oii.ox.ac.uk/archive/downloads/publications/Effective-Age-Verification-Techniques.pdf, accessed 24 July 2018.

163 Regulation (EU) 2016/679 of the European Parliament and of the Council of 27 April 2016 on the protection of natural persons with regard to the processing of personal data and on the free movement of such data, and repealing Directive 95/46/EC.

need to comply with data protection laws in the UK. The GDPR, which came into effect in May 2018, imposes additional safeguards on data controllers including principles of data minimisation,[164] data protection and data security by design and default,[165] and the right of erasure.[166] The BBFC's Draft Guidance on Age Verification published as a public consultative document on 26 March 2018 suggests that the BBFC will work closely with the Information Commissioner's Office (ICO) in order to ensure that data protection laws are adhered to by age verification services and pornography providers.[167]

In practice, it is likely that age verification services will be dominated by one or two large players, for example AgeID services offered by MindGeek, which is one of the largest online pornography providers in the world.[168] Privacy activists raise concerns that it could lead to a monopoly of age verification and too much personal data being compiled by a handful of major players.[169] As legitimate age verification service providers would be relatively more open to scrutiny, the biggest risk comes from the potential for cybercriminals deliberately obtaining personal data for nefarious purposes. This could take the form of, for example, fly-by-night websites that are set up with the sole objective of obtaining personal information of unsuspecting users.

The BBFC has clarified that age verification will not necessarily mean identification checks and all that would be required to be established is proof of age, rather than proof of identification.[170] Whilst such reassurances can help to mitigate the concerns of internet users, the potential impact of the law on individual privacy is a legitimate concern. There are numerous precedents of personal data breaches generally, and in particular incidents such as the *Ashley Madison* hack, where user data from a 'dating' website describing itself as enabling 'affairs', was hacked and leaked, would naturally make users wary of sharing their personal information for viewing online pornography.[171] Mandatory age verification might effectively create

164 General Data Protection Regulation, Art 5(1)(c).

165 GDPR, Art 25.

166 Ibid, Art 17.

167 This will be inevitable given that the BBFC does not have statutory authority on matters relating to data protection. Section 25(1) DEA 2017 requires the BBFC to publish guidance about the types of arrangements that it will treat as complying with the provisions of the Act, which must be submitted to the Secretary of State and approved by Parliament. The Draft Guidance was published as part of a public consultation on 26 March 2018. See http://www.bbfc.co.uk/sites/default/files/attachments/BBFC_Draft_Guidance_on_Age-verification_Arrangements_March_2018.pdf, accessed 24 July 2018.

168 MindGeek owns the so called 'tube sites' including PornHub, Redtube and YouPorn.

169 See for example Damien Gayle, 'UK website age checks could create Facebook of porn, critics warn', *The Guardian*, 27 March 2018, available at https://www.theguardian.com/technology/2018/mar/27/uk-website-age-checks-create-facebook-porn-critics-warn, accessed 24 July 2018.

170 This could be achieved, for example, through trusted third parties, which would mean that the identity of the user will not be available to the pornographic website provider.

171 See Steve Mansfield-Devine, 'The Ashley Madison Affair' (2015) 2015(9) *Network Security* 8–16.

a 'blacklist' of people who have chosen to access adult content by complying with the law, which leaves the potential for the list to be misused and may lead to discontent among cyberspace users. It would therefore be in the interest of everyone, and for the success of the law in particular, that appropriate safeguards for protecting the privacy and security of personal information be in place for age verification.

The regulatory framework envisaged in DEA 2017 which actively involves payment service providers and 'ancillary service providers' is novel in many ways. There are many websites that provide content free of charge from the perspective of end users, but nevertheless operate profitable business models on the basis of advertising revenue and premium subscription (for higher quality content). A closer look at the business models of the 'free' tube sites would reveal that there is no such thing as 'free porn'. The idea behind targeting payment service providers is to disrupt the revenue stream in a way that adversely impacts the non-compliant website. The BBFC Draft Guidance on Ancillary Service Providers published on 26 March 2018 contains a 'non-exhaustive list of classes of ancillary service provider' that the regulator will consider notifying pursuant to section 21 of the Act. The list includes online platforms, including social media, on which the non-compliant site has a presence, search engines, IT service providers, third parties who provide advertising space to the non-compliant party as well as those who provide advertising space on a website, app or other service belonging to a non-compliant party, and third parties advertising on or through any internet site operated by a non-compliant party. A notice issued under section 21 will contain a request that the relevant ancillary service providers should withdraw their services to non-compliant persons.

It is clear from the diverse category of services found in the non-exhaustive list above that a number of stakeholders have been brought into the framework for the regulation of adult pornography. If the stakeholders cooperate with the regulator it will no doubt have a significant impact on the visibility, business model and profitability of non-compliant commercial pornography providers, which should force them to comply with the law. In most cases, payment providers can legitimately withdraw their services. For example, the terms and conditions of major providers such as Visa and MasterCard require parties to comply with national law and therefore receipt of a notice from the BBFC should offer sufficient ground to withdraw their services. A similar logic applies to ancillary service providers. For example, advertisers in the UK are subject to a voluntary code of practice, which requires that marketing communications comply with the law. Offering an advertising space for a non-compliant website in spite of a BBFC notice is likely to be seen as a breach of the Code.[172] Search engines are more

172 The UK Code of Non-broadcast Advertising and Direct & Promotional Marketing (CAP Code). See https://www.asa.org.uk/codes-and-rulings/advertising-codes/non-broadcast-code.html, accessed 24 July 2018.

likely to comply than not, given their previous history of self-regulatory initiatives at the request of the Government, as noted earlier.

Regulation envisaged under DEA 2017 has parallels to the existing framework for the regulation of child pornography, albeit in slightly different ways. The role of the regulator is analogous to that of the IWF, in that it is an independent body in the regulatory framework, although the BBFC's role is more proactive in nature as it is not intended to serve as a reporting hotline. The IWF makes assessments as to the illegality of images based on laws that govern child pornography. The DEA 2017 empowers the BBFC to block access to websites containing extreme pornography, which means that they will also have a content assessment role for all practical purposes. This carries an element of risk in that the regulator is required not just to monitor compliance of websites with the age verification requirement, but will need to judge pornography in terms of its legality as per the extreme pornography law. However, there are some safeguards put in place for the age verification regulator's activities. First, it has statutory authority under DEA 2017 to perform its duties, including its content assessment role (unlike the IWF). Second, the regulator has to inform the Secretary of State of its decision to give notice to an ISP before doing so, as well as to the non-compliant website.[173] The notice must state the reasons why the regulator considers the offending material to be extreme pornography, and should provide information about arrangements for appeals. Third, it is a requirement that the age verification regulator maintain arrangements for appeals and that the appellate body must be sufficiently independent of the age verification regulator.[174] The age verification regulator, therefore, in all likelihood will be considered as a 'public authority' for the purposes of the ECHR rights. This imposes a duty on it to be consistent with the right to freedom of expression under Article 10 in its decisions, which offers additional safeguards for the aggrieved parties in terms of appeals and judicial review.

Staying focused on access control

Nevertheless, the content assessment role of the regulator could be problematic. Readers should be persuaded by now that traditional image-based laws that focus on notions of obscenity have not worked in cyberspace. The new law presents a golden opportunity as an alternative to traditional content-focused regulation. It would perhaps be better if the role of the regulator were more narrowly confined to ensure that adult content, with all its ambiguities, is not freely accessible to children. No more, and no less. Anything more than that renders the role of the regulator that of a content assessor, and by implication a censoring body, rather than as an enforcer of access control laws to protect children from exposure to adult content.

173 Section 23(10) Digital Economy Act 2017.
174 Section 16(5).

This is not to suggest that content that is illegal should be freely available – after all, it would be odd for the regulator to 'green light' content that is illegal to publish and distribute under the law. Extreme pornography, therefore, should be subject to some form of regulation. As noted in Chapter 6, the current law imposes criminal liability on the end user for the possession of extreme pornography, the problems of which I have set out in some detail in that chapter and therefore a possession offence is not desirable. DEA 2017 presents an opportunity for an alternative and more purposive and meaningful regulation of extreme pornography by returning the focus of the law to controlling its publication and distribution, which is more proportionate and less intrusive on individual freedoms than a possession offence. The BBFC undoubtedly has a lot of experience in content classification, and is therefore well placed to identify *potentially* criminally obscene content. I have stressed 'potentially' because that is where the remit of the regulator should end. It can be problematic if the authority to judge what is essentially adult pornography, even in its more 'extreme' forms, is left to the age verification regulator. We have seen the challenges of the application of extreme pornography law in practice in Chapter 6 – the failed prosecutions in the *Walsh* trial and also the earlier *Peacock* trial (re obscenity) demonstrate how subjective and inconsistent the concept of 'obscene' can be, even in the context of criminal trials.[175] These cases are not to be dismissed as one-off incidents; instead, they highlight the importance of recognising that societal values, and notions of indecency and obscenity, are not set in stone and continue to evolve with time. It is a risky business, therefore, for the age verification regulator to take on the role of content assessor due to the inherent subjectivity of what constitutes 'extreme pornography', even with its wealth of experience in terms of content classification.[176]

The final assessment as to whether the material is 'extreme' and subsequent issuance of a blocking order should therefore ideally be delegated to the judiciary, rather than the BBFC doing it themselves albeit with the 'approval' of the Secretary of State. This will render the new regulatory framework for adult pornography more legitimate and fit for purpose. As noted before, cyberspace users are likely to reject measures that would be seen as imposing a moral code in terms of content. The limit of the law in this sense should really be child protection – the age verification regulator should only be required to ensure compliance in terms of commercial websites providing robust age verification mechanisms prior to making adult content accessible. This narrower remit of the regulator is likely to have more acceptance among

175 See Chapter 6, 141–142.

176 This would be less of an issue for certain categories of 'extreme pornography', for example images that depict bestiality, where a relatively straightforward assessment can be made, but images that depict 'serious injury', which is not defined in the Criminal Justice and Immigration Act 2008, are more problematic to assess. See Chapter 6.

cyberspace users, and thus command more respect for age verification law as a whole, rendering it more likely to succeed.

The new regulatory framework envisaged under DEA 2017 is poised to be a step change in the regulation of adult pornography on the internet. Attempts to transpose traditional laws that focus on the obscenity and indecency of the material to cyberspace have failed, and there is no reason to believe that this will change in the future. The new regulatory framework has the potential to mark a step change in the way adult pornography is regulated on the internet with old content-focused laws giving way to access-focused regulation. The law will have normative force in cyberspace as long as its purpose remains the protection of children from exposure to adult content, and the regulator's remit is not stretched beyond those strict confines. The new approach is much more likely to succeed if robust measures are put in place to protect the privacy and security of personal data of individuals. It will only be a matter of time before other countries adopt this model of access-focused regulation which might just offer the solution, if not a perfect one, to the complex issue of regulating online adult pornography.

It is also worth noting that age verification law, or as a matter of fact any regulation, will not guarantee that every child will be protected from exposure to adult content. Protecting children from inappropriate material and generally looking after the best interest of the child is primarily a parental responsibility. Schools and educators have a crucial role to play in this context too. It is not in anybody's interest, and definitely not in children's interest, if people assume that child protection is purely the responsibility of the state. Regulation carries the risk that it is likely to create that sense of false security whereby parents become complacent and trust the state and technology to protect their children from internet pornography. This is a risk which regulators need to be conscious of, and educating children and creating awareness about not just the biology of sex, but also about healthy relationships and sex are equally important in this context.

'Revenge pornography' and other issues

This monograph is about the regulation of internet pornography, and therefore I was initially keen to include a discussion on 'revenge pornography'. As I examined the issues in more depth, however, it became apparent that 'revenge pornography' depicting adults is not really appropriate for inclusion in this study.[177] This is because, contrary to popular belief, 'revenge pornography' is not really pornography. 'Revenge pornography' is in many ways a misnomer, as the images and videos are not usually produced for pornographic purposes.[178] The term 'revenge pornography' refers to the disclosure and publication of private images without the consent of

177 The issues stemming from redistribution of self-generated images of children are nevertheless pertinent and raise challenges for the law, as discussed in Chapter 3.

178 See Mary Anne Franks, '"Revenge porn" Reform: A View from the Frontlines' (2017) 69 *Florida Law Review* 1251.

the subject of the image, which typically occurs after a relationship breaks down. In fact, both the terms 'revenge' and 'pornography' are problematic. I will address the latter term first.

In cases of 'revenge pornography', the image or video is typically originally created with the consent of the person depicted within the safety of a relationship, either taken by the partner or self-generated by the subject of the image and sent to the partner. The purpose for which the private images or video are exchanged could vary from just fun, or as a virtual extension of intimate sexual activity, to simply an act of affirmation of trust in the other partner by sharing a very private image. The images are not intended to be pornographic in the traditional sense of the word – at best it is an intimate private photograph, the non-consensual publication of which does not render it 'pornography'. The intention behind the publication and redistribution of such private images is primarily to cause distress or harassment to the victim. It is not intended as material created primarily for the purpose of sexual arousal.[179] In this sense, the offence is one of causing annoyance, distress and harassment to the victim by means of malicious communication. It could also be breach of confidence, invasion of privacy or copyright infringement. This category of content therefore only sits in the periphery of the scope of this study, which seeks to examine pornography laws in the context of the internet. The subject nevertheless merits consideration as it is certainly an area that raises challenges for the law, and whilst the images were originally not created as pornography, they often end up on pornographic sites, including on dedicated sites.[180]

By conceptualising it as an act of revenge we fail to appreciate that revenge is not the sole, and in many cases not at all the motivation for the non-consensual disclosure of private images. For example, a study carried out in the United States reveals that among all perpetrators interviewed, only 12 per cent stated that that the motivation was to upset the victim and/or to harm them.[181] In fact, the most commonly chosen reason for distribution was to 'share with friends without the intention to hurt the person'. Whilst the sample used in this study is relatively small and more research needs to be done, it nevertheless offers valuable insights into offender motivations for the so-called revenge pornography.

179 Readers will remember that 'material produced primarily for the purpose of sexual arousal' aligns with the definition of 'pornographic', as defined in the Criminal Justice and Immigration Act 2008 (s 63(3)), and the Digital Economy Act 2017 (s 15).

180 It is estimated that there are over 3000 online sites perpetrating revenge pornography. See W. De Keseredy, M.D. Schwartz, 'Thinking Sociologically about Image-based Sexual Abuse: The Contribution of Male Peer Support Theory', 2(4) *Sexualisation, Media and Society* (October–December 2016) 1–8. A more recent study shows that 'revenge pornography' is featured in around 10,000 websites – see Mary Anne Franks (n 178).

181 Asia A. Eaton, Holly Jacobs and Yanet Ruvalcaba, *Nationwide Online Study of Nonconsensual Porn Victimisation and Perpetration: A Summary Report*, Cyber Civil Rights Initiative, June 2017, available at https://www.cybercivilrights.org/wp-content/uploads/2017/06/CCRI-2017-Research-Report.pdf, accessed 25 July 2018.

Whilst 'revenge pornography' is not the creation of the internet, it has certainly made the publication and accessing of private images a lot easier without any geographical constraints. There are dedicated websites that host images of 'revenge pornography', where people can post and access materials that were never intended to be publicised when first created.[182] Until not too long ago the legal and police response to incidents of 'revenge pornography' was weak and often clouded with confusion. The experience of Holly Jacobs and the campaign that she started which resulted in a number of states in the US enacting legislation to counter revenge pornography offers a good example.[183] The law eventually caught up with the issue of non-consensual disclosure of private images, and at the time of writing 34 states and DC in the United States have enacted laws against revenge pornography. In the UK, revenge pornography has been criminalised by the Criminal Justice and Courts Act 2015.[184] A national 'Revenge Porn Helpline' offers confidential advice and support to victims.[185] The offence is found in section 33 of the Act, which criminalises disclosing private sexual photographs or films without the consent of an individual who appears in them and with intent to cause that individual distress.

There have already been some criticisms of the scope and efficacy of the offence. For example, causing distress is an essential ingredient of the offence, and therefore if someone distributes the image because they thought it was funny they will not be committing the offence. Further, there is a defence available under the Act which excludes images that are altered or created by combining two or more images (pseudo images) using software or digital technology. This has been criticised as a potential lacuna in the legislation as an image created by morphing the face of someone with the body of another person to artificially create a 'sexual' image would cause distress to the subject, but is not covered under the offence.[186] The law rightly focuses on consent, i.e., whether appropriate consent obtained from the subject for disclosure of the images. Further questions can be raised – what degree of consent would be required? Context is an important factor here – consent cannot be limited consent; instead it should be full and informed for the breadth and full extent of the disclosure made. For example, A takes a photograph of B performing a sexual act on A with B's consent: if B agrees for A to distribute the image within a closed network of a members-only community, for example a virtual swingers club, could consent be

182 See Franks (n 178).

183 Dr Holly Jacobs, who was a victim of 'revenge pornography' herself, began the 'End Revenge Porn' campaign in the United States which was later incorporated into the Cyber Civil Rights Initiative (CCRI) which have assisted a number of states to legislate to criminalise non-consensual pornography. See https://www.cybercivilrights.org/, accessed 25 July 2018.

184 In Scotland, the corresponding (and slightly broader) offence can be found in s 2 of the Abusive Behaviour and Sexual Harm (Scotland) Act 2016.

185 See https://revengepornhelpline.org.uk/, accessed 25 July 2018.

186 See Alisdair A. Gillespie, '"Trust me, it's Only for Me": "Revenge Porn" and the Criminal Law' [2015] 11 *Criminal Law Review* 866–880.

implied to extend to disclosure in any other parts of the internet? The answer should be no, but again there may be instances where it is difficult to ascertain the degree of consent, which could put victims at a disadvantage. There were more than 200 prosecutions in the first year after the law came into force in England and Wales. However, a recent study in the UK urges the need for training across police forces in the country, suggesting that the police have a limited understanding of revenge pornography legislation and lack confidence in responding to victims and investigating cases.[187] These are just a few examples of how a narrowly tailored law that specifically addresses 'revenge pornography' may fail to protect victims.

There are divergent views regarding the best way to regulate 'revenge pornography'. Whilst Citron and Franks argue for criminalisation,[188] commentators such as Lilian Edwards argue that a more effective way of dealing with so-called revenge pornography is by approaching it through the prism of data protection laws.[189] The rationale here is, that what victims of revenge porn primarily need as a remedy is the removal of the images from the internet (or at least from search results to minimise the chances of locating them) rather than prosecuting the perpetrators. Of course, the latter is important, but merely punishing the offender does not in itself remedy the situation and a prison sentence for the perpetrator does very little to actually remove the material from the internet.

The real issue, however, is a broader one which prompts further questions as to the very approach of the law from the narrow prism of 'revenge pornography' to protect victims of non-consensual disclosure and publication of sexually explicit private images. 'Revenge pornography' is only part of the wider problem of what McGlynn and Rackley refer to as 'image based sexual abuse'.[190] There is a range of other situations where private images of a sexual nature can be created and distributed online without the subject's consent, with different motivations. For example, the act of photographing underneath a woman's dress or skirt by voyeurs using mobile phone cameras in public places such as in escalators, referred to as 'up-skirting', and distributing it can be equally distressing for

187 Emma Bond and Katie Tyrell, 'Understanding Revenge Pornography: A National Survey of Police Officers and Staff in England and Wales' (2018) *Journal of Interpersonal Violence* 1–16.

188 Danielle Keats Citron and Mary Anne Franks, 'Criminalising Revenge Porn' (2014) 49(2) *Wake Forest Law Review* 345–391.

189 See Lilian Edwards, 'Revenge porn: Why the right to be forgotten is the right remedy', *The Guardian*, 29 July 2014, https://www.theguardian.com/technology/2014/jul/29/revenge-porn-right-to-be-forgotten-house-of-lords, accessed 25 July 2018.. Also see her written submission to the Justice Committee of the Scottish Parliament, http://www.parliament.scot/S4_JusticeCommittee/Inquiries/ABSH19._Lilian_Edwards.pdf, accessed 25 July 2018.

190 Clare McGlynn and Erika Rackley, 'Image-based Sexual Abuse' (2017) 37(3) *Oxford Journal of Legal Studies* 534–561. Also see Clare McGlynn, Erika Rackley and Ruth Houghton, 'Beyond "Revenge porn": The Continuum of Image-based Sexual Abuse' (2017) 25(1) *Feminist Legal Studies* 25–46.

victims. The motivation might be voyeurism, perversion, or just humour albeit in unacceptably bad taste, but if the image is made public on the internet in a manner in which the victim is identifiable it can cause distress and harassment regardless of the offender's motivation. Morphing photographs, for instance by superimposing the face of someone onto the nude body of a porn actress to convey the overall impression that the image is of the person whose face is depicted will not in many cases raise challenges for the law. In fact, technology has advanced so much that not just still images but artificial intelligence video tools are now available to create fake videos called 'deepfake videos', by superimposing someone's face on another person's (typically a pornographic actor) body.[191] 'Sextortion' is another form of image-based sexual abuse where perpetrators blackmail victims with sharing their private images or sexually explicit videos. The material is produced either by luring unsuspecting victims online by befriending them, or by coercing them into carrying out sexual acts.

It is the breadth of such activities that render it a problematic area to regulate, and one that calls for more robust and holistic legal responses. Pornography laws generally can only assist where the images are obscene in nature, which is a high threshold to meet and we have already noted the difficulties in applying traditional laws to the internet. Age verification laws will prevent children's access to these materials, but they will remain accessible to adults. Revenge pornography laws will not be capable of dealing with many of these situations, and only address a specific form of image-based sexual abuse. McGlynn et al call for a broader conceptual recognition of 'image based sexual abuse' that is perpetrated mostly against women, and which the law is currently incapable of addressing.[192] They call 'image-based sexual abuse' a form of sexual assault and argue that the dichotomy between online abuse and physical contact abuse is no longer tenable owing to the impact that online image-based sexual abuse has on victims. It is not an argument that has been won among legislators and policy-makers yet, as legislators tend to not perceive abuse perpetrated on the internet as a form of sexual offence owing to the absence of physical contact.

Whilst some of these issues overlap with pornography, and images that are obscene will still be subject to obscenity laws (or in cases where children are depicted, child pornography laws), treating these categories as content offences diminishes the gravity of the underlying criminal acts. As with the way child pornography laws have evolved, by recognising the inherent harm in the making of the material, in order to respond robustly to image-based abuse the law should recognise the harm caused to the victims. It is beyond the scope of this discussion to ascertain whether the appropriate response lies within the reach of the criminal or civil law, or whether entirely new regulatory strategies will need to evolve, but

191 See Kevin Roose, 'Here comes the fake videos, too', *The New York Times*, 4 March 2018, https://www.nytimes.com/2018/03/04/technology/fake-videos-deepfakes.html, accessed 25 July 2018.

192 McGlynn et al (n 190).

I am confident that obscenity and pornography laws are simply inappropriate and inadequate to deal with image-based sexual abuse. I am in no doubt that, with more awareness of the issues and further research into the scale of the problem, there will be a shift in attitudes and the current position will change – after all, the law has to reflect societal realities.

Concluding remarks

It should be clear from this discussion that attempting to transpose traditional laws that centre on the obscenity and indecency of images are simply inappropriate for the internet. Concepts of what is obscene and indecent are measured against the prevailing standards of a society at any given point in time. Norms and values of societies continue to evolve with time, particularly so in a culturally diverse cyberspace. Laws that rely on moralistic notions of obscenity and indecency of images will not command the obedience or respect of cyberspace communities. As demonstrated by the failed legislative attempts to regulate online adult pornography in the United States, laws that purport to delineate adult pornography on the basis of indecent and obscene speech – even in relation to minors – have failed to meet the high threshold of First Amendment scrutiny.

States have a compelling interest in controlling the unfettered access of children to freely available adult pornography on the internet. Adult pornography will not remain unregulated forever on the internet: alternative regulatory models will continue to evolve, as evident from the Government-inspired self-regulatory initiatives as well as the recent legislation in the UK. As the UK is experimenting with the new regulatory model envisaged in DEA 2017, lessons from the past should be applied wisely to increase the likelihood of success.

Law must have normative force to be successful in cyberspace. The sole legitimising factor which might lend normative force to the law is the prevention of children's access to adult content – no more and no less. Any regulatory framework that has content controls premised on notions of obscenity and indecency, that interferes with the right of adults to consume content, will not succeed in cyberspace. The primary purpose of the law should be to ensure that children do not access adult content, without hindering the rights of adults to access lawful pornography. It is a delicate balance that the law has failed to strike for over two decades in cyberspace. This balance can be achieved only by access-focused regulation, rather than content-focused regulation.

The recent legislation in the UK marks a fundamental shift in the regulation of adult pornography on the internet. As the law has grappled with the ineffectiveness of regulation focusing on the publication of obscene material, a new regulatory model is evolving that seeks to prevent children's access to adult content on the internet. Relatively new stakeholders, perhaps better described for our purpose as 'indirect intermediaries', such as payment providers and advertising and other ancillary service providers, are becoming part of the regulatory framework. Direct intermediaries such as ISPs will form a crucial part of the regulatory framework with the requirement to block non-compliant websites.

The Digital Economy Act 2017 presents a golden opportunity for a potentially workable regulatory model to change this, provided that the law aligns itself to accepted norms in cyberspace. It is likely that other states will adopt the new regulatory model in the future. As technology evolves further, newer regulatory models will also evolve. States have a natural tendency to retain control over pornographic content available within their geographical boundaries, and it is only logical to conclude that adult pornography will never cease to be a target of regulation for governments.

8 Conclusion

Regulating internet pornography

The main objective of this book has been to demonstrate how the internet has necessitated a change in the regulation of pornography. As I hope I have by now persuaded readers, the regulation of pornography has undergone a significant, and in many ways irreversible change as a result of the internet and digital technologies. The specific nature of these changes is, of course, dependent on the nature of the pornography in question, which I broadly categorised into three classes for the purpose of the analysis – child pornography, extreme pornography, and adult pornography. Each of these categories raises its own distinct issues and challenges for the law, but one common theme that has emerged from the study is that transposing traditional laws to cyberspace to regulate pornography has not been, and will never be, successful. In order to respond to the unique challenges presented by the internet, specific laws have had to be introduced, and existing laws needed to be amended.

There are two step changes that can be identified from the study. One is in the nature of the substantive law itself, and the second relates to its enforcement model. From a substantive law perspective, it can be seen that the overall focus of the law has changed: the law is no longer concerned merely with controlling the publication and distribution of obscene pornography, and is now increasingly focused on regulating private conduct, i.e. the consumption of content. This is evidenced by the imposition of criminal liability on end users, for instance through the introduction of simple possession offences across a broader spectrum of pornography. In a common law context, the post-internet age has also witnessed some innovative interpretations of the law by the judiciary in order to adapt the law to the changing requirements and challenges posed by technology, which has resulted in the imposition of greater liability on end-users. As for the enforcement of the law, there has been a progressively increasing level of involvement of non-state actors and intermediaries in the broader regulatory framework. This was initially confined to 'independent' organisations such as the Internet Watch Foundation (IWF) and ISPs specifically for the purpose of combating child pornography, as seen in Chapter 5, but was later extended to extreme pornography. More recently, other stakeholders such as payment providers, search engines, and advertising providers have been brought into the regulatory framework to regulate adult pornography. It can be seen that, although these non-state actors mostly participate 'voluntarily', a closer examination reveals that their participation stems from factors that are tantamount to *de facto* liability for non-compliance. Whilst intermediaries have largely retained their *legal* immunity in terms of content, soft-law approaches and threats of possible legislation that might hinder existing immunity have, in effect, resulted in intermediaries assuming more liability in terms of distribution and access to pornography. There are two driving forces that have led to these changes – first, the desire of states to address genuine criminal activities such as the sexual abuse and exploitation of children online, and second, in relation to non-child pornographic content, the inherent tendency of states to regain control over content disseminated within their virtual borders.

One thing that has become abundantly clear to me through writing this book is that the notions of obscenity or indecency on their own will no longer provide a sufficient basis for regulating pornography on the internet. The reason child pornography laws are relatively successful on the internet is that they seek to prevent the harm inherent in the material, or at the very least address a credible risk of harm to children. There is consensus among states and cyberspace users that child pornography harms children, which lends normative force to the law, at least as far as images that depict real children are concerned.

The law had in fact recognised the harm inherent in producing child pornography long before the internet became popular – the criminalisation of the production and distribution of child pornography in the UK, through the Protection of Children Act 1978, offers a good example. The rise of the internet meant that the nature of criminal activity also steadily evolved. For child pornography, it meant that the ways in which content is produced, shared and accessed significantly changed. Perpetrators had access to newer methods of creating child pornography without the need to physically abuse a child, as seen with pseudo and virtual child pornography, which could then be easily shared on the internet. The law responded to this challenge by criminalising pseudo-pornography and treating it on a par with existing child pornography laws, and later also extended the simple possession offence to virtual pornography, but these raised a further set of new legal issues. The lack of physical harm caused to children during the production of such material became a contentious issue in terms of justifying its criminalisation, and drawing criticism not only from some legal commentators but also from the courts, as we saw in *Ashcroft v Free Speech Coalition*.[1] The rationale for criminalising the possession of child pornography was analysed in Chapter 3. Whilst no physical harm is usually caused to a child in the production of pseudo images, it has been noted that there is still a degree of direct harm, or at the very least a real *risk* of direct harm, caused to the subject of the image. As I pointed out in the discussion, 'harm' is not to be narrowly interpreted as mere physical abuse, but should extend to any psychological harm suffered by the child: prevention of harm to children is ultimately the central

1 535 U.S. 234 (2002).

objective of child pornography laws. The internet carries a real risk of permanence: in spite of the advances in technology such as PhotoDNA, the potential for the image to remain on the internet and be seen or downloaded by someone at some point leaves a lasting and distressing legacy for the child. Criminalising the possession of child pornography will deter consumption and contributes to minimising the secondary victimisation of the child, and is therefore well justified for child pornography that depicts real and identifiable children, regardless of whether there was physical abuse involved in its production. In addition, as argued in Chapter 3, the indirect harm that possession could cause to other children also offers a strong basis for criminalising the possession of pseudo imagery featuring young adults on the basis of a reasoned risk of harm if the overall impression conveyed by the image is that of a child.

As for material that is entirely computer generated, which does not depict any real or identifiable children, it is more difficult to justify criminalisation on the basis of direct harm. The potential for such images being used in the grooming process, or to normalise behaviour not just for children but also for paedophiles, could arguably justify criminalisation, but, as noted in Chapter 4, there are also strong opposing arguments in this regard. The ruling in *Ashcroft* neatly summarises the criticism against criminalisation, i.e., that the harm is not directly linked to the content itself (as opposed to real child pornography), but stems from the conduct (such as grooming) for which the images *may* potentially be been used as an aiding tool. Whilst conclusive evidence of harm is hard to obtain, what can safely be inferred is a reasoned risk of harm to children from the possession of such images. Whilst there are strong arguments that support and oppose the criminalisation of possession of virtual pornography, on balance criminalisation appears to be a reasonable and proportionate response. A further point to note in relation to criminalising virtual child pornography is that the law may, in this way, (unintentionally) serve to be futuristic. There are two challenges that are pertinent in this context: first, as technology becomes more sophisticated, it will be possible to create a virtual representation of a child which is so realistic that it would be difficult to differentiate it from a real child. Second, with advances in 3D printing technology, it will someday be possible to create a three-dimensional child sex doll from a two-dimensional virtual representation of a child. The act of 3D printing itself will be difficult to police if not connected to the internet, and consequently it will be difficult to track down offenders. In comparison, a two-dimensional image stored in a computer is easier to track and regulating this may perhaps be more efficient, and serve to protect children.

A further challenge raised by digital technologies is the growth of self-generated sexual images of children. The laws that address child pornography generally predate the extensive use of internet-enabled, camera-embedded mobile phones, and practices such as 'sexting' are now prevalent among older children to the point that they have become almost commonplace. Child pornography laws were originally enacted to address the issue of adults exploiting children, and at the time those laws were drafted it could not have been envisaged that the images would be created by children themselves. This now has the unintended consequence of children being victimised in a different way – the very laws that were enacted to protect them could be used against them. Changes in technology can influence norms and practices in cyberspace, and the law cannot be blind to the prevailing norms in cyberspace communities. As pointed out in Chapter 3, the current conflict between the law and norms in relation to self-generated images will not last and, as evidenced by reforms in some states of the United States and Australia, the law will eventually adapt to societal norms.

Whilst child pornography laws have evolved substantially over the last four decades, the internet also presented challenges for regulating the more obscene forms of adult pornography, which was the second broad category of pornography considered in the book, discussed in Chapter 6. The legal response to extreme pornography followed the regulatory model for child pornography in that it carried a possession offence combined with an identification and blocking strategy, which was delegated to the IWF's remit of illegal content until not too long ago. Criminalising the simple possession of 'extreme pornography' marked a fundamental shift for the regulation of adult content with the focus of the law moving away from the point of supply to the point of consumption. Criminalising the possession of what is essentially adult pornography, even in its more extreme forms, is fundamentally different from child pornography and therefore it is problematic to adopt the same regulatory model. The possession offence for extreme pornography is a good example of bad law-making in cyberspace, and serves only to confirm the fears of the critics of 'mission-creep' of legitimate child pornography laws. This is not just dangerous for extreme pornography law; it risks undermining the very legitimacy of child pornography. I have analysed at some length how the lack of conclusive evidence of harm linked to the possession of extreme pornography poses problems for criminalisation, unlike child pornography featuring (and representing) minors. Law-making should not equate to the imposition of an elusive and puritan moral code on those who are bound by the law: it should, instead, respect contemporary attitudes on permissible content generally, and harmless sexual practices of the minority within the privacy of their homes. In relation to extreme pornography, criminalising conduct that is essentially carried out in private on the basis of what appears to be purely moralistic considerations can be problematic and amounts to legal moralism. The jurisprudence of the European Court of Human Rights would seem to suggest that the 'protection of morals' would fall within the margin of appreciation afforded to Member States (*Handyside v UK*),[2] and therefore the law criminalising extreme pornography is unlikely to be found to be in breach of Article 10 of the ECHR. Whilst criminalising private conduct on the basis of moralistic considerations may still stand the test of legality from an ECtHR perspective, whether this amounts to the law overstepping the mark in terms of individual freedoms nevertheless remains a pertinent question. It is not my contention that extreme pornography should be encouraged or supported, but I am convinced that targeting the end

2 (1976) 1 EHRR 737.

user is fundamentally flawed. As I have argued, the law should seek to regulate its publication and distribution rather than focusing on the end-user individual. The new regulatory initiative involving mandatory age verification under the Digital Economy Act 2017 offers a golden opportunity to reinstate the focus of the law back to the point of supply, if implemented in a manner that safeguards constitutional rights and freedoms. The regulator could play a vital role in identifying potential extreme pornographic content, and could reduce the availability of such material in the country. Establishing a system whereby the supply of extreme pornography can be controlled renders a possession offence all the more indefensible.

In the third and final part of the book, I examined the regulation of other forms of adult pornography that is not specifically deemed illegal. Adult pornography on the internet has perhaps presented the biggest challenge for the law. As early legislative initiatives failed in the United States, adult pornography has largely remained unregulated on the internet – not just for America, but also for the rest of the world. The regulation of adult pornography on the internet offers a classic example of the difficulties in transposing offline laws to cyberspace. It is clear that laws that rely on notions of obscenity and indecency cannot be transposed to the internet without infringing the rights of adult members of the cyberspace community, and will therefore never work. In my view, preventing access of children to adult pornography online will provide the sole basis for successful regulation. There needs to be a fundamental shift in the focus of regulation. The current image-based, content-focused regulation should give way to a new access-focused regulatory model. Adult pornography regulation may well be at the point of a step change, as such a model is being experimented in the UK which requires all commercial pornography providers to age-verify their customers before making content available. The law, in order to succeed, should seek to design a framework for age verification that is independent of, and separate from, any assessment of content for obscenity or indecency. The sole objective should be the protection of children, no more and no less. As I argued in Chapter 7, this is the only way the law will have normative force in cyberspace. Whilst it is too early to predict how the law will work in practice (and there are legitimate concerns regarding the safety and security of personal data and privacy concerns stemming from age verification) it has the potential to mark the beginning of a new regulatory model for adult pornography which, if successful, will be adopted by other states.

As technology advances further, other changes will no doubt be necessary for the regulation of internet pornography. I have cited some examples of related future challenges in Chapter 7, some of which go beyond traditional conceptual framework of 'pornography', for example 'revenge pornography' and sextortion. These should be recognised as a direct form of abuse, meriting a robust regulatory response, going beyond those for content offences – perhaps calling for another book.

As states will continue to attempt to retain control over pornographic content accessed from within their territories, it is clear to me that regulation based purely on notions of morality is unlikely to succeed in cyberspace. Law-making will instead be premised on considerations that either address harm, as with the case of child pornography, or prevent the access of vulnerable groups such as children to adult content. In this process, the liability of intermediaries will increase further, and the definition of 'intermediaries' itself will broaden with new stakeholders being brought to the regulatory framework. The values and norms of cyberspace are not dictated by governments, nor are they linked to particular geographical locations. The global intercultural interactions that take place between members of cyberspace community are what influence and shape norms on the internet. At the same time, 'cyberspace communities' are not separate from the real world: as the internet is increasingly becoming an integral part of our lives, and to a great extent an extension of our persona, it would be naïve to treat cyberspace communities as separate from physical communities. Law as an instrument of control still has a crucial role in shaping the behaviour of those who are subject to the law, and pornography is no exception. For the regulation of pornography to succeed on the internet, lawmakers need to respect those very norms of cyberspace which are, in fact, reflective of real world norms.

Index

Page numbers followed by 'n' refer to notes.

www.ingramcontent.com/pod-product-compliance
Ingram Content Group UK Ltd.
Pitfield, Milton Keynes, MK11 3LW, UK
UKHW021302190926
475701UK00009B/588
* 9 7 8 0 3 6 7 5 8 3 4 9 1 *